The Compassionate-Mind Guide to Building Social Confidence

Using Compassion-Focused Therapy to Overcome Shyness & Social Anxiety

Lynne Henderson, PhD

Copyright Page from the Original Book

Publisher's Note

This publication is designed to provide accurate and authoritative information in regard to the subject matter covered. It is sold with the understanding that the publisher is not engaged in rendering psychological, financial, legal, or other professional services. If expert assistance or counseling is needed, the services of a competent professional should be sought.

Distributed in Canada by Raincoast Books

New Harbinger Publications, Inc.
5674 Shattuck Avenue
Oakland, CA 94609
www.newharbinger.com

Printed in the United States of America

Acquired by Tesilya Hanauer; Cover design by Amy Shoup; Edited by Nelda Street

Library of Congress Cataloging-in-Publication Data on file with the publisher

13 12 11 10 9 8 7 6 5 4 3 2 1 First printing

TABLE OF CONTENTS

TABLE OF CONTENTS

Preface

Let's start with a brief account of my history with shyness. What is now the Palo Alto Shyness Clinic developed from the Stanford Shyness Clinic, which was set up in 1977 and opened to the public shortly before I became director in 1982. The Stanford Shyness Clinic, in turn, had grown out of a famous study by Philip Zimbardo in 1971, in which normal college students were randomly assigned the role of prisoner or guard in a simulated prison in the basement of the psychology building. The study was supposed to run for two weeks, but the prisoners became so anxious and the guards so cruel that it had to be stopped after six days. Phil and his students formed a seminar to try to understand what had happened. During their discussions, one of his students said that shyness was like being both a prisoner and a guard toward the self. The prisoner self wanted to come out but was afraid, and the guard self was hostile and kept the prisoner trapped. Inspired by this insight, Phil and his students established the shyness clinic and started to gather data that culminated in Zimbardo's book, *Shyness.*

From the time I became director of the Shyness Clinic, Phil Zimbardo served as a consultant, research supervisor, and collaborator. Through my work with groups of shy people over the following years, I began to realize that the vast majority of extremely shy and socially anxious people did not lack social skills when they felt accepted and respected. In fact, they demonstrated considerable social skills when they were not in the spotlight. I also noticed that they were conscientious and collaborative, and considerate of other group members. They were enormously relieved to be with other people they liked and respected who also considered themselves shy. Each usually held the self-perception of being the most shy and inadequate in the group. I became struck more by their strengths than their weaknesses—but I also saw how much they struggled with shame and self-blame, and how great their suffering could be. And yet in spite of that, we usually managed to have a good time in the groups, with humor and laughter at ourselves playing a big role.

These shy people were so hard on themselves and felt so much shame that I realized they felt stigmatized for their shyness and considered it a disease that needed a cure. That seemed to me absolutely the wrong way to look at the problem, because it led them to feel powerless to change their own situation. So I decided that treatment needed to be based on an approach where people were treated with respect as colleagues, learning alongside me and my fellow practitioners what it might take for all of us to be socially fit. So, at the clinic, we gently refused their invitations to be dominated and instead requested their input on role-plays, asked them to offer criticism and comments on the book we used for social skills training, and invited them to give us feedback on whether or how much particular exercises in the groups helped and how they felt toward us. When they began to confront me, the groups became very lively, and soon the participants were beginning to take leadership roles in the group. From there we moved on to work on developing trust, verbal and nonverbal self-expression, listening skills, nonverbal communication, handling conflict, and self-assertion.

In this new phase of the work, we addressed negative automatic thoughts, such as *When people see my discomfort, they feel superior; People do not identify with me when I am uncomfortable; People will be rejecting and hurtful if I let them close to me.* Listening to what clients said in groups and comparing this to what students (both shy and non-shy) said on the same points, we discovered that our clients in the shyness clinic had more of these negative automatic thoughts about others than either shy or nonshy students. These findings suggested that chronically shy people and those with social anxiety disorder (discussed in chapter 1) also had difficulty trusting others, in that they viewed others as critical, condescending, and hurtful. We also found that although, through group work in the clinic, our clients were able to reduce self-blame and shame, negative thoughts about others, resentment, shyness, and depression, once the group work was over, they still seemed to have trouble managing their emotions. I wanted to find ways to help clients hold on to what they had gained in treatment, and to find out what would help them cultivate compassion for themselves in the long term and manage their emotions. With these aims in mind, I explored mindfulness techniques with the intention of incorporating them in treatment at the clinic.

That is when I met Paul Gilbert. I had heard about his work in compassionate mind training, was fascinated and impressed, and wanted to learn more. I attended a workshop in England and realized I needed to learn a lot more about the compassion-focused therapy he was developing, which seemed to me to have enormous potential for treating chronic shyness and social anxiety disorder.

When Professor Gilbert invited me to write a book on a compassionate approach to shyness, I welcomed the chance. I am deeply grateful to him for the opportunity, and for helping me write and revise several chapters. He is a kind and patient man, for which I respect him as much as for his expertise and competence in combining his understanding in several fields to help us all lead more compassionate lives.

This book is the result.

Lynne Henderson

Acknowledgments

Many thanks go to Philip Zimbardo, mentor, colleague, friend and codirector of the Shyness Institute, our nonprofit research and public education organization. From his passionate lecture about the famous Stanford prison study and his seminal research, which drew me into the treatment of chronic and painful shyness as director of the Shyness Clinic; through his original shyness treatment, which I developed in the following years; to our research collaborations at Stanford University, his support and mentorship have been the foundation of my work with shyness. He both gave me the freedom to develop independently and supported me when I got stuck, whether intellectually or emotionally. I am deeply grateful for his faith and trust in me, and for this being one of the most exciting people with whom to brainstorm and explore ideas about shyness. Thanks also to Paul Gilbert, who trusted me to write this book applying his compassion-focused approach to chronic shyness, and who let me combine it with my social fitness training model. Thanks to Sally Reese, whose clinical expertise, friendship, and writing skill contributed greatly to early drafts of this manuscript; to Fritha Saunders, my editor at Constable & Robinson, who helped me develop a more accessible writing style; and to Gillian Somerscales, my copy editor. Thank you to my children, Kimberly, Mark, and Brooke, who anchor me in terms of what is important in life, and whose humor, love, and candid feedback provide laughter and grounding; and to my husband, Austin, best friend, love, and research partner, for whom I am grateful every moment, whose life is built around his curiosity and his dedication to making computers serve their users. With him I share the belief that the people for whom we design are equal partners in the design. Finally, thanks to my shy clients, whose expertise and wisdom have guided and continue to guide me. They are my most powerful research colleagues.

Introductory Note

This book falls into two main parts. Chapters 1 through 3 discuss what shyness is, how our understanding of it has developed, and how compassion can be developed as the basis of a helpful approach to overcoming the problems associated with it. Chapters 4 through 8 then describe in detail, with the aid of practical exercises, how we can develop the compassion that is innate in all of us to benefit both our own shy selves and those of others. Chapter 9 draws the book to a close with some suggestions for continuing work using the principles described throughout the book.

Foreword

In our hearts and in our spiritual traditions, we have always understood that compassion is very important for our well-being. However, there has been a recent revolution in our scientific studies relating to com passion and kindness—indeed, to such an extent that we now understand how compassionate qualities of the mind (of understanding, kindness, and helpfulness) really do influence our brains, bodies, and social relationships, as well as our health and well-being. Yet despite this knowledge and wisdom, we live in a modern age of seeking the competitive edge, driving ourselves to achieve and want more and more, comparing ourselves to others and being dissatisfied and critical if we don't match up. Evidence tells us that such environments actually make us unhappier and that mental illness is on the increase, especially in younger people. Learning how to pursue the best in ourselves, but with a slower, kinder orientation, can help rebalance our overstressed and shy minds in this fast-paced world.

Compassion is sometimes viewed as being a bit soft or weak, and people can feel that they are letting their guard down. However, research has shown us that compassion can also be difficult because it requires us to be open to, and tolerate, our own and others' suffering and difficulties. Compassion is not a turning away from suffering or an attempt to get rid of it but, rather, is an openness to suffering, with a commitment to do what we can to alleviate or cope with it. Compassion requires us to be honest about the sources of our suffering and to act against our anxieties.

It is helpful to stand back from our personal feelings about things and recognize that the disposition to suffer and to feel anxiety, including shyness, is built deep into the fabric of our being. We are a species that has arrived from a long and continuing evolutionary journey. Within our minds is a whole set of abilities to feel anger, anxiety, disgust, joy, various lusts and desires, and affection and care—many of which we share with other animals. So when they are activated within us, when we are flushed with anger, anxiety, or shyness, we are experiencing the activation of brain systems that were built *for* us, and these systems exist in all humans and many animals too.

The origins of our emotions lie deep within our evolved brains, and along with our unique genetic profile and our own personal histories, they can give rise to shyness. So in one way, when we experience those flushes of anxiety or shyness, this is absolutely not our fault—because they are part of our makeup. Once we acknowledge this, and that there is nothing wrong with feeling these powerful emotions, we open up to a truly compassionate approach that enables us to face up to emotions, and to take responsibility for how they operate within us. For instance, we may decide that although we feel anxious, we won't act on that and run away from the situation but will stay and work through it; although we feel angry, we don't want to hurt anyone, so we are careful how we act with others; and although we feel shy, we want to learn how to behave in a more confident way.

If we can pay attention to how our minds work and become mindful and observant, we can learn to have compassion for, and work with, difficult feelings. Rather than fighting with ourselves, being self-critical, or engaging in unhelpful avoidance, we learn how to deal with these emotions as a skilled surfer would tackle a wave. Key to our ability to recognize the nature of our suffering is to recognize self-blaming (which often makes us feel worse) and begin a move toward self-compassion. In fact, although anger, anxiety, and shyness can be part of our basic human nature, we also have the innate ability to be kind, supportive, understanding, and compassionate. Our capacities for compassion are also key parts of our nature. So it can come down to what we choose to focus on within ourselves, what we choose to pay attention to and develop. Do we focus and ruminate on things that upset us or we're critical about? Or do we choose to focus on things that are helpful, kind, and supportive? Compassionate mind training is specifically designed to help train those parts of our mind that provide feelings of support, encouragement, kindness, and compassion and that enable us to call on these parts more automatically and with greater wisdom.

Given the choice, all of us would prefer to live in kind, supportive, and understanding places rather than those that are critical, harsh, and rejecting. So we can do our best to try to create kindness for others, in the knowledge that this is good for their well-being and health. But it is also the same for ourselves, in how we think and treat ourselves. If our relationship with ourselves is critical and harsh, then our inner worlds are also not comfortable places to be in. Indeed, this can make our anxieties much worse. Self-compassion is a way of being with our suffering without being self-condemning but being supportive and encouraging. Research shows that the more *self*-compassionate we are, the happier we are, the more resilient when faced with difficult life events, the better able to reach out to others for help, and the more compassionate with other people. This is because self-compassion is also a source of wisdom that teaches us the value of understanding and encouraging, in contrast to criticizing. We all recognize that we all just found ourselves living here on this planet with this strange and tricky brain, with its orchestra of pleasant and difficult emotions, doing the best we can.

In this book Lynne Henderson brings together her many years of considerable experience in working with shy people at the Shyness Institute. Here she developed the Social Fitness Program to Shyness, derived from cognitive behavior therapy and modern research on the way people think, ruminate, imagine, and behave. In addition, Lynne has drawn extensively from Buddhist and other spiritual traditions, as well as the approaches developed within compassion-focused therapy. She outlines a compassionate way of thinking about shyness and provides a number of steps and exercises that will enable you to develop a compassionate approach and a compassionate mind toward your shyness. You will learn about the nature of compassion and how to develop compassionate attention, compassionate thinking, compassionate feelings, com passionate behavior, and compassionate images. Compassionate images that are either visual or aural (such as imagining a compassionate voice speaking to you when you need it) can be especially useful, because they can enable you to get in touch with your internal compassionate feelings and systems. If you practice the guidance Lynne offers here, you may well find that it has a very beneficial effect on you. These helpful steps are merged with the important development of your inner compassion: developing an inner voice that conveys a sense of understanding, encouragement, and warmth for you. If, by the end of this book, you have learned how to speak to yourself kindly, you will have gained a valuable skill.

Many people suffer silently and secretly with their shyness, some ashamed of or angry with it, others sometimes fearful of it. Opening your heart to being compassionate toward your shyness can be the first step to dealing with it in a new way. Our compassionate wishes go with you on your journey.

Paul Gilbert

March 2010

CHAPTER 1

Understanding Shyness

Nearly all of us have experienced periods of shyness, social awkwardness, uncertainty, and anxiety. Think back in your life to the times when you felt shy and socially apprehensive. What was happening around you? Who was there, and what kind of situation were you in? Many of us have feelings of shyness and self-consciousness when we meet new people, go on a first date, have a job interview, speak to people in authority, or talk in and to small groups of people. We may also feel anxious and worry about being criticized if we think other people are judging us. That sense of being observed and assessed can be quite painful, not only when we think we are being judged negatively; we can also feel acutely self-conscious when people are praising us and putting us in the limelight for positive reasons.

If you recall those times when you felt shy or self-conscious, you may also recall physical sensations that accompanied the feelings of anxiety, such as a dry mouth, butterflies in the stomach, or a voice that sounded shaky and trembling or that perhaps went gravelly and croaky with repeated throat clearing. When we feel that people are watching us, we may sense blushing as our faces turn red. We may also find our minds going blank, so that only afterward, perhaps hours later, we think to ourselves, *What happened? Why didn't I say this or that?*

It's important to recognize that these are common feelings and reactions. In fact, over 98 percent of U.S. college students have these shy and anxious experiences. Nearly 60 percent now say they are shy and that shyness is sometimes a problem. In fact, it is challenging to imagine someone who *never* feels shy, because shyness is considered a basic human emotion; it is a blend of fear and interest.

The degree to which we experience shyness depends on a variety of things, some internal (inside us) and some external (outside us). For example, when we're approaching a situation that is very important to us, such as a job interview, we worry more and can become very anxious. On the other hand, if we're among people who seem friendly and relaxed rather than stern and critical, we are likely to be less anxious. We also react to situations in our own individual ways, and while for some of us shyness and social anxiety are just occasional mild irritants, for others they can appear very easily and be felt very intensely, significantly affecting the quality of life. So, while nearly all of us share these experiences to some degree, we vary as to how intense and intrusive they are and how much they interfere in our lives.

In this book we are going to explore the phenomena of shyness and social anxiety; gain valuable insights into our shy feelings, thoughts and behaviors; and look at the many ways to cope with them. One of the most important lessons we'll learn is how to develop understanding and compassion toward our anxiety rather than trying to ignore it, avoid it, or even hate it. After all, as we will see, anxiety has developed as our brain has evolved, because it is useful: there are good reasons why humans, like all animals, are capable of anxiety and social wariness. As we explore this idea, we will learn that difficulties connected with shyness and anxiety are not our fault, but arise from how our brains are designed. We will explore what helps us deal with shyness and what can make it worse. We will look at how shyness makes us vulnerable, but also at the strengths that go with being shy, including the values associated with it. We'll investigate how normal shyness can become a problem for us and how to work with it when it does. We will also explore ways we can resist the negative stereotypes of shyness that have developed over the last few decades. These unhelpful stereotypes are a result of misguided ideas in society, encouraged by media hype, about extroversion and individualism. Stereotypes can undermine your self-confidence and the acceptance of your valuable temperament if you don't understand where they come from and how they work.

ORDINARY SHYNESS AND PROBLEM SHYNESS

Before we go on, it is important to distinguish between ordinary shyness, which nearly all people feel from time to time, and more problematic, chronic, or extreme shyness. It is helpful to realize that only 1.3 percent of U.S. college students deny ever having been shy, and that 36 percent of the 57.7 percent who say they are shy don't see it as a problem. For those of you who do struggle with shyness from time to time, which is probably why you are reading this book, I hope that the exercises set out in later chapters of the book will be helpful to you when you do feel shy.

For some of you, probably as a result of painful experiences and events in your life, shyness has become a barrier in the way of what you want to do in life. You label yourself as shy and see it as a problem. Others may label you as shy because you are quiet, maybe a bit more introverted than extroverted, and perhaps not overtly assertive. Some others of you are aware of feeling painfully shy inside sometimes, yet people around you see you as outgoing and socially skilled, not shy at all. If this is you, you may be concerned that if people get to know you, they will be disappointed and see you as inadequate. This in turn may mean that you're more afraid of becoming intimate with people than of meeting new people.

Some of you may get help with problematic aspects of your shyness from time to time. Some of you may be coping and learning on your own: perhaps you have at least one friend, maybe more, and are gradually reducing aspects of your shyness that interfere with what you want to do socially and in your work life. You may be like the people who have called in when I've been on talk shows, who told me how they've overcome their shyness through reading self-help books and trying out new ways of coping on their own.

Some of you are painfully and chronically shy, and so afraid of being judged that you avoid social situations altogether or just endure them without enjoyment, in fact with considerable discomfort. There may be one particular kind of situation, or more than one, that makes you intensely and consistently uncomfortable: perhaps public speaking, meeting new people, asking someone for a date, talking or going out in a small group, dealing with managers or teachers, sexual encounters or other intimate situations. You may have become isolated and mildly depressed; you may be aggressive to compensate for your shyness; you are probably very lonely. These are the experiences of people who come to my shyness clinic. If they are your experiences, too, the exercises in this book will help you. You may also want to find a therapist to guide you through them; you will be able to decide whether that would help you as you try out the exercises and see how they go for you.

SHYNESS AND SOCIAL ANXIETY DISORDER

I have set out in box 1.1 the signs and symptoms of social anxiety disorder, a condition where social anxiety has become very severe and requires treatment. There is a good deal of overlap between shyness and social anxiety disorder, but shyness covers a wider range of feelings, varying from ordinary shyness, a personality trait that may not be a problem, to more debilitating shyness, where many of these symptoms apply.

In 2009 social anxiety disorder affected about 15 million American adults, making it the second most common psychiatric disorder, behind depression in first position and ahead of substance abuse and addiction in third. While many people with social anxiety disorder realize that their fears about being with people are excessive or unreasonable, they feel unable to overcome them.

Various studies have calculated that around 7 to 9 percent of people suffer from social anxiety disorder, while as we have already seen, 50 to 60 percent of people say they are shy. The discrepancy between these figures may suggest that only a small proportion of the population suffering from chronic, even debilitating, shyness are seeking treatment. Another possible explanation is that shyness itself is not debilitating and that many people cope with their shyness, capitalize on its strengths, and lead rewarding lives. I have been on talk shows where people in their fifties or sixties have called in and talked about how they didn't let their shyness interfere with what they wanted to do. They set goals and pursued them in spite of setbacks. They also capitalized on the strengths of shyness, such as being thoughtful and reflective, sensitive to others, and often collaborative and supportive in their actions. In fact, many people overcome shyness by being active participants in causes they care about and in service to others. Interestingly, most of the talk show callers had used the same techniques to overcome problematic shyness that we use at the shyness clinic.

Box 1.1 Signs and Symptoms of Social Anxiety Disorder/Social Phobia

- You feel extremely uncomfortable in social situations, consistently avoid them, or both, or you find ways to be safe, such as looking down or avoiding eye contact.
- You are excessively self-conscious and think everyone is watching you.
- You are always scrutinizing your own behavior, worrying about what you do or say.
- You have an intense, chronic fear of being watched and negatively evaluated by others, and worry about doing something embarrassing.
- Your anxiety or worry may begin weeks before a dreaded situation.
- Your anxiety and worry are severe enough to interfere with work, school, social activities, and relationships, making it hard to engage in satisfying and lasting friendships.
- You may feel frustrated and angry with yourself or others.

• You may experience physiological symptoms, including muscle tension, aches and pains, blushing, profuse sweating, trembling, nausea, and difficulty talking.

NEGATIVE STEREOTYPING

It is often negative social stereotyping that makes people self-conscious and shy; in the extreme, negative stereotyping may cause chronically and painfully self-focused shyness. For example, I had an African American student from an upper-middle-class family in a shyness class at Stanford who never realized that the reason she did not speak up in class was that she felt that maybe she wasn't as smart as the other students. After we studied Claude Steele's research on stereotype threat (more about that later) she realized that she had felt stereotyped and had stereotyped herself because she was African American. She'd gone to good schools all her life, and it hadn't occurred to her. Having become aware of this, she started to speak more in class, and two years later she entered law school, confident that she could speak up even if she felt nervous.

This student had never realized that feeling different and experiencing others' responses to that difference may have led to her shyness in the first place. Anything that makes a child distinctive, whether it's wearing glasses, being overweight or underweight, or being shorter or taller than others, makes that person self-conscious and can lead to shyness if the person thinks others think negatively about it. We work actively together at the clinic to identify and resist these subtle negative stereotypes, developing ways to counteract them through determined behavior or helping people to think differently, for example, by saying, "Isn't it sad that our society is still so scared and undeveloped that these stereotypes exist? Maybe we can help counteract those stereotypes and think of ways to do it." Of course, now that we understand that shyness is itself negatively stereotyped, we work together with clients to help detect and resist that stereotype as well, and to educate themselves and others about all these unhelpful attitudes.

POSITIVE ASPECTS OF SHYNESS

Those who are shy are *not* particularly motivated to have the upper hand, to be forceful with others, to be seen as number one and control others; they are more concerned with connecting with others, getting along, and doing a good job. People who report being shy use what researchers have called the "pause to check" approach. That is, they sort of "case the joint" before they participate. People with this temperament may be considered every bit as well adjusted as those with a bold temperament who charge in, participating immediately. Those who are very bold may not be as sensitive to the thoughts and feelings of others. The only time shyness becomes a problem and may be painful, even debilitating, is when bad experiences and events in your life (for example, frequent moves, the loss of a parent, or constant criticism at home or school), deprivation, or frequent rejection make normal shyness and sensitivity a hardship.

Shy children tend to be sensitive to the thoughts and feelings of others. They are likely to be helpful to classmates, behaving in cooperative and altruistic ways, and to show sympathy to children in distress. We also know that children who behave in this way—using what psychologists call *prosocial behavior*—are likely to behave in similar ways as young adults. And indeed, shy adolescents are also likely to be sympathetic to others, unless they are in severe personal distress and their focus is directed inward on their anxiety and unhappiness. If you're feeling that bad, it's hard to see what others are feeling and needing.

Shy children are physically healthier than nonshy children when their parents and teachers are warm, benign, and supportive, but if they aren't supported and are under stress, they may suffer more from allergies than nonshy children. When children or adults who are particularly aware of and sensitive to others are put in a highly competitive, nonaccepting, callous environment, they begin to withdraw and avoid other people. At this point it may be in their best interests to get out of that environment and look for one that is more collaborative and supportive. In the case of shy children, this is a judgment call that parents need to make—but not by overprotecting a child, for example, keeping the child home from school or another child's party because of shyness. These are normal life experiences that give children the opportunity to reduce shyness with experience and practice.

I think of shy people as canaries in our social coal mines; just as the birds were the first to notice the presence of toxic gas that endangered the miners, so shy people may be the first to notice when a social environment changes from supportive and inclusive to competitive and cliquey. People who are thicker skinned may not notice these changes until later, by which time it may be too late to change the prevailing milieu without considerable effort. Listening to the perceptions of shy people can help us all deliberately "niche pick" as we determine which situations are compassionate environments.

We all need people to support us, love us, listen to us. These universal needs can play to the strengths of our shy emotions and to those of us with shy temperaments, who tend to be good listeners, supportive, loyal, and constant. These are compassionate qualities. When we are compassionate to others, they tend to respond to us with compassion. In fact, research on interpersonal relationships reveals that one of the basic tendencies of human beings is the reciprocity of friendliness: when we smile and are friendly, people are friendly back. Interestingly, people tend to be complementary in terms of dominance. When we are submissive, others will lead, and when we are assertive, others will defer to our lead. For shy people, the trick is to smile and extend friendliness to evoke a friendly response, and to learn to be more assertive in cases where others tend to be consistently dominant or have difficulty following. People in shyness groups are often surprised to find that others will follow them when they suggest activities, put forward ideas, and behave more assertively.

Another interesting thing about the way shy people behave is that it often involves cooperation and maintaining trusting relationships, rather than dominating and defeating others. I have a videotape of clients at my shyness clinic role-playing in an exercise involving choosing several people who will escape the demise of the earth in a spaceship. With their permission, I showed it at a conference. In the video, these clients were polite and good at taking turns and listening, and they gave their own opinions and efficiently solved the problem. The audience was suitably impressed.

FAMOUS SHY PEOPLE

More examples of the strengths of shyness can be found in famous people, both historical figures and our contemporaries. The list of the shy and famous is a very long one. What are they like?

The historical figures include Abraham Lincoln, which was no surprise to me, as I have read biographies of him, including *A Team of Rivals* by Doris Kearns Goodwin. He was shy with women, particularly women to whom he was attracted—a very common experience, because it involves the most important evolutionary goal, to reproduce, and it's only natural to feel a bit shy or nervous in situations where the outcome is important to you. But as he got older he learned to approach women and, once married, also began to share more of his thoughts and feelings with his wife. Lincoln's sensitivity, collaborative nature, ability to reflect on and analyze issues, empathy, strong moral sense, and courage also enabled him, as president, to include men in his cabinet who were more prominent, wealthy, and experienced in national politics than he was. During his campaign for election, he refused to criticize his rivals, preferring to deal with the issues and to speak from his heart and intellect to the American people. In turn, his political rivals respected him enough to serve in his cabinet, arguing with him about the issues but remaining loyal and dedicated to him and to the country.

Lincoln is a prime example of a shy leader and an example of the kind of shy leaders we desperately need today. Barack Obama, the current U.S. president, largely modeled his campaign on Lincoln's, taking advantage of modern technology to extend it to the Internet, a vastly wider forum for his ideas that includes most of the world. He seems to have many of the traits characteristic of shy leaders like Lincoln.

Other famous shy people of the past include Harriet Beecher Stowe, author of *Uncle Tom's Cabin,* whose writing promoted debate that led to the American Civil War, and Clara Barton, who founded the Red Cross and cared for the wounded on the battlefields in that war; Thomas Jefferson, who wrote the American Declaration of Independence but spoke in public only at his inauguration; Henry Cavendish from Derbyshire, England, one of the world's greatest scientists, who felt there was a gulf between him and all others and experienced it as an infirmity; and George VI, who, after the scandal surrounding his brother Edward's abdication, was thrust on to the throne and surprised the world by becoming one of the best loved and most competent of modern monarchs. Thomas Edison gave up on being a Shakespearean actor and invented the light-bulb; Eleanor Roosevelt, shy as a child and young adult, became one of the foremost female leaders in America; and Theodore Roosevelt, also shy in childhood, with asthma and a slight build, became president of the United States.

Moving into the present, Queen Elizabeth II and Prince Charles are both considered shy. Diana, Princess of Wales, was shy and was greatly loved by the British people. Soccer star David Beckham; Brandon Flowers, lead singer of the Killers; and Daniel Radcliffe, hero of the *Harry Potter* films, are all shy yet have huge followings.

Another compelling example is the widely esteemed actor, writer, and broadcaster Stephen Fry, whose shyness has sometimes cost him dearly. He walked out of a play at one point with stage fright, an experience that made him contemplate suicide. He acknowledges having bipolar disorder, and he is a good example of how shyness, like anxiety more generally, can be triggered by other conditions and may also be a symptom of mental illness. We all feel shy when we feel different from our peers, when our experience feels different from that of others. Fry is gay, which could have made him feel not only different from others, but also at risk of being stigmatized if people knew. He has shown great courage in being open about his life and his emotions.

Yet another famous shy person who is particularly fascinating to me is the actor Sidney Poitier. The son of a tomato farmer in the Bahamas, he was one of Hollywood's first black leading men, "almost single-handedly reversing the passive Stepin Fetchit image of African American characters that Hollywood had popularized onscreen.... He walked with the knowing caution of a man who's nobody's fool." He made movies about tough moral choices and was the first African American to win the Academy Award for Best Actor. He describes himself as a shy outsider, saying, "There is nothing I can or wish to do about it." I have always felt that he showed great courage, in the years of the civil rights movement, in the roles he chose, and the way he acted them.

The list goes on: Albert Einstein, Garrison Keillor, Johnny Carson, Diane Sawyer, Sigourney Weaver, Henry Fonda, Ingrid Bergman, Harrison Ford, Kevin Costner, Robert de Niro, Richard Gere, Neil Armstrong, Nicole Kidman, Julia Roberts, David Letterman, Bob Dylan, Brad Pitt ... If you are interested in the lives of famous shy people, a trip to Renée Gilbert's website for fascinating details about the lives of famous shy people is worth the time: www.shakey ourshyness.com/shypeople.htm.

Looking at all these people you can see why I believe that shyness is an unsung trait of great value in our current world, one that lends itself well to the development of new focus on compassion and to service in the world. You can also see that if you are shy, you are up there with the greats! I hope those of you who are shy will understand this and remember it. It is not your fault that we live in a world where some of humanity's best traits are out of fashion because they might get in the way of what corporations want from workers; that is, to compete with their fellow men and women to the point of being unable to see them or care for them. Despite what some governments and businesses think, high-stress competition is not a good way to encourage better performance, either in the business as a whole or in the people who work there. It is also very bad for our mental and physical health, as a good deal of current research makes clear. In fact, in contrast to the rather narcissistic, "me first" attitude characteristic of modern Western societies, it is sensitivity, conscientiousness, and a willingness to put others' needs first that keep people emotionally connected and functioning well—at work as well as in their personal lives. There is good evidence now in the business research literature that collaborative, cooperative working groups are higher not only in well-being, but also in productivity.

HOW SHY PEOPLE THINK

Researchers have made a distinction between two equally normal strategies in people's behavior. One (the shy approach) they call *prevention focused,* and the other (the extrovert approach) they call *promotion focused.* Either is perfectly appropriate, so long as it's not pursued rigidly or carried to extremes. According to Walter Mischel, a well-known personality researcher, prevention-focused people want to make sure that things don't go wrong and they don't like to make mistakes. Imagine that you are due to have brain surgery. Wouldn't you be glad to know that your neurosurgeon had this personality trait? People with this temperament are sensitive to cues that unwelcome things may be about to happen, so they are careful and considerate, automatically avoiding behavior that may lead to such outcomes.

Extroverted, sociable, promotion-focused people can be more impulsive generally; often they are focused on having fun, but they can be equally focused on pursuing their goals, and many are hardworking and ambitious. They tend to focus on all the great opportunities in a situation rather than the risks it might hold. They, too, can be good surgeons because they are strongly focused on doing well. They are sensitive to cues related to impending rewards. Imagine that you've just made it to the end of an incredibly stressful workweek and want to turn off your brain for a while. Which friend would you like to party with?

Of course, the distinction isn't absolute: some people are strongly prevention focused or promotion focused, but many combine elements of both. And shyness is not the same as introversion, although they often go together. Introverts simply prefer solitary to social activities, but are not afraid of social encounters. Extroverts prefer social to solitary activities. Although the majority of shy people have introverted traits, there are many shy extroverts who are shy in private even though they are outgoing in public. These shy extroverts are able to be sociable in highly structured, predictable situations, but may still feel anxious and believe that if others really got to know them, they would not accept them. Shy extroverts may find it difficult to be intimate with others because they fear revealing any vulnerabilities or qualities that others might see as less than ideal. The truth is that we all have our vulnerable points, and normally, as we get to know each other, we tell each other what we really think and feel, including sharing what we see as our shortcomings. Imagine having a best friend or a partner with whom you never felt comfortable enough to reveal your fears, sadness, feelings of uncertainty, or concerns about being adequate; it's a lonely prospect.

Shy extroverts may also struggle in situations where control must be shared or is irrelevant, or social expectations aren't clear. For example, they may be torn about leading in a situation where they are capable of doing a competent job. They may fear that if they do take a lead, others will be jealous or competitive and put them down or withdraw. Where taking turns is casual and talk is relaxed and a little offbeat, shy extroverts may become self-conscious and have difficulty being spontaneous, so they may avoid doing things like making a joke or laughing at themselves, even though they are fully capable of doing so.

SHYNESS, COMPETITIVENESS, AND BULLYING

Western society focuses so much on competitiveness, encouraging us to prove ourselves tough, fearless, decisive, and confident, that it's easy to overlook the fact that individuals who are prone to shyness and may not present themselves in this way have very valuable and important positive traits. For example, people who say they are shy like to work collaboratively—a huge plus in a global economy where cooperation with others is increasingly important. Shy people can work independently and are usually good students, careful and conscientious. They tend to be well represented in graduate-level education. Shy people may also be very successful in technical or information-oriented jobs, where reflection and attentiveness are important.

In fact Jerome Kagan, a leading researcher in the biological bases of shyness, says that he looks for shy graduate students to help with his research because he trusts them with projects that require attention to detail and careful reflection on the meaning of results. They are sensitive to the feelings of others, tend to put others' needs first, and are motivated to avoid anger and social humiliation, and to feel connected with others. These are the personality traits that foster negotiation and deeper understanding in collaborative environments.

In our competitive, materialistic societies, star status tends to be attached to an overidealized, dominant, cavalier, "alpha male" image of fearlessness and toughness. Just as women compare themselves to hyper-skinny computer-enhanced models, believe that they fall short, and then feel down and inferior, so shy males may compare themselves to media images of dominant or extroverted, aggressive males, see those as the norm and feel inferior—and reinforced in their anxiety and feelings of being judged by others.

Consequently, I believe men can have a particularly difficult time, not because being shy is necessarily a problem (although it can be if it interferes with what you want to do in life) but because American society, and other highly competitive societies, don't value men who appear to be less than highly dominant and overtly confident. A society isn't in good shape when its media spread and encourage negative social stereotyping of a particular temperament. Ours is hostile to vulnerability, sensitivity, or embarrassment, especially in men. In Western, competitive societies, males are trained not to show vulnerability but to defend themselves and their positive image at almost all costs. This can lead to overdefensiveness and, at times, aggressiveness in responding to any kind of challenge or conflict.

Societies emphasize their preferred stereotypes, encouraging people to copy them and to aspire to be like the models portrayed. So our media, including the Internet, are full of images of dominant, extroverted, overly confident, and socially cavalier, even bullish or aggressive men; shy, sensitive men are notably absent. Asserting your dominance without regard for the impact on others can often end up as bullying, and children learn and copy what they see. A report in 2001 revealed that nearly 30 percent of American school pupils in grades 6 through 10 (aged 11 to 16) reported moderate or frequent involvement in bullying, as either the bully or the bullied, or both. And bullying isn't confined to the school playground. A report on bullying in Britain revealed that 75 percent of respondents may have been bullied at some point in their lives, and workplace bullying in both Britain and the United States is common. Obviously, some children and adults are learning to overdevelop their assertive and extroverted traits, and although when these turn into bullying, they have a significant impact on everyone around the bully, they perhaps have a disproportionately great effect on the more sensitive and shy children and adults.

So we need to acknowledge that our competitive society, reflected in the media, affects how we act toward each other, how comfortable we feel in our relationships with others, and how secure and accepting we are of our own personality traits. These environments, which undermine our confidence and increase social anxiety, are quite clearly not our fault. They are external factors particular to the current social structure and culture. Fifty years ago shyness was considered an ordinary—indeed, a valued—personality trait; now it has come to be stereotyped as a weakness to be overcome or derided. It may, therefore, take quite a lot of effort to maintain a compassionate focus and stance toward yourself and others in today's highly competitive Western societies.

WHEN SHYNESS BECOMES A PROBLEM

Some children are born less bold than others because of variations in their nervous systems that lead them to be more cautious and wary. As infants, they react more strongly to loud sounds and new experiences, and as they grow older they take more time to feel confident in social situations. These children are sometimes referred to by psychologists as "behaviorally inhibited," along the lines of the "pause to check" approach mentioned earlier in this chapter. They are also likely to have relatives who say they are shy.

If these children feel loved and are offered a secure environment, with many opportunities for being with others and firm guidance to socialize, then they become bolder, their tendency to be anxious subsides, and they become able to cope with mild shyness and anxiety. Anxious children with anxious parents, however, have more problems. In trying to prevent their child from feeling anxious or shy, they encourage the child to avoid those feelings and so avoid learning how to cope with them. A parent might say, for example, "I know you are anxious about going to Sally's party. You don't have to go. You can stay here with me." If parents are overprotective in this way, and don't help their shy child get involved in age-appropriate social situations, such as socializing with other children and participating in school activities, the child's shyness may increase and become a problem. So a lot of treatment with shy children involves helping parents to give their children the chance to learn how to cope with their feelings, rather than avoid them and the situations that trigger them.

Shy children tend to be sympathetic and sensitive to others' feelings, so if they experience loss through, for example, death or divorce in the family, they may struggle in a number of ways, perhaps more than other children. Parents' pain, anger, and sadness may be especially hard for them to bear, in addition to their own pain and grief. They also like stability, so they can find frequent family moves very challenging, because they must reach out to new friends again and again. I have heard painfully shy patients recount heartrending stories of loneliness related to losses and frequent moves. Others say that, even though it was very hard, they learned to reach out for friendship, often to one person at a time, and often remained in touch with these friends even after another move.

Given the importance of experiences in early childhood, researchers acknowledge that it is impossible to predict whether any particular infant will become shy as an adult. Genes are certainly not the sole basis for shyness. Children with bolder temperaments who grow up in a difficult or traumatic environment, such as a chaotic or physically or verbally abusive home, can become painfully shy.

While anxious and loving parents may overprotect children, preventing them from learning how to deal with their feelings, some shy children have the opposite problem, living with lack of protection or even under threat. Any child will suffer if parents, siblings, or teachers are harsh or critical, or do not accept the child's temperament; if bullying is allowed at school; or if parents try to motivate them by humiliating them when they don't perform as expected, but the impact on shy children, who may be less likely to defend themselves or get help, can be particularly severe.

"It Must Be My Fault": Shyness and Self-Blame

Children who are criticized, bullied, abused, neglected, or rejected may turn to criticizing themselves and trying to be perfect to avoid criticism or harsh treatment from others. This often takes the form of monitoring everything they do or say *(Am I doing this right? Did I make a mistake there?)* and blaming themselves for anything that goes wrong. For example, if someone is unpleasant to such a child, rather than think the problem might be in the other person, the child will focus on what she might have done to provoke the unpleasantness. So these children will blame themselves for things that are absolutely not their fault. A research study showed this process in action. The researchers asked a group of students, some of whom were socially anxious and some of whom weren't, to engage in a conversation with a lecturer while being videotaped. The lecturer was (unbeknown to the students) instructed to break conversational rules, such as butting in when someone else was speaking and changing the subject, and even being quite rude. When the students were shown the videotape later and were asked about these interruptions by the lecturer, the socially anxious ones blamed themselves for the problems in the conversation, saying that the lecturer had reacted in this way because they were boring him. The students who were not socially anxious blamed the lecturer.

My own research has also shown that shy college students who are also fearful tend to blame themselves and feel ashamed after social situations that they think did not go well, especially if they are aware of their inner thoughts and feelings—which makes sense, because if we are privately self-aware, we know what we are feeling. Also, whereas when we are in an ordinary calm emotional state, we may have a pretty good sense about how others are reacting, but when we are upset or anxious, the balance between awareness of our own feelings and others' may shift; focused on ourselves, we may feel very threatened and may think people are judging us and fail to notice if they are feeling shy, self-conscious, or awkward too.

When we studied three separate groups of shy high-school students, we found that those who tended to blame themselves if things went wrong were more likely to be socially anxious and avoid social interaction. Interestingly, however, the students who were shy but didn't blame themselves were no more socially anxious than the nonshy. All these students were well above average in mental ability and had obvious advantages in terms of academic and social opportunities. However, it was very noticeable that those who were willing to try again after a disappointing encounter—for example, to approach someone, begin a conversation, or to ask someone over—felt less anxious and distressed overall.

Although shyness is associated with many positive traits, enabling us to be socially sensitive, cautious, and careful, as well as considerate and thoughtful, it can also cause problems. If our shyness is too easily triggered, is too intense, lasts for too long, or is too frequent, and if it starts to control our lives so that we avoid things we really want to do and blame ourselves for everything that doesn't go quite right, then it becomes very unhelpful. We can become too concerned that we might be criticized or rejected and stop participating in life, becoming sad and lonely. We can even become less physically healthy. Feelings of shyness can lead us to avoid telling our doctors about our physical or mental problems. To give an extreme example, some people who are shy will avoid seeing doctors and, when they do, will avoid telling them about their symptoms; this can mean that signs of dangerous illnesses like cancer, which can spread quickly, may go unnoticed because sufferers are too embarrassed or too worried about “wasting” the doctor’s time to discuss these issues with their doctor.

The chronic loneliness and stress that severe shyness and isolation can cause are not only emotionally painful, but are also physically bad for us. Psychological stress can cause or exacerbate pain, heart disease, sleep and digestive problems, obesity, skin conditions, depression, and autoimmune diseases. Someone whose anxiety about social situations becomes so extreme that it leads to almost unendurably painful emotions may develop social anxiety disorder (see box 1.1 earlier in the chapter for a reminder of what this involves). If that happens, help is available from therapists trained in particular strategies that are known to reduce shyness and increase participation. Our main focus in this book is on techniques to help ourselves develop a compassionate approach to the emotions involved in shyness, which have evolved to help us, but can sometimes interfere with our living lives to the fullest.

THE THREE CYCLES OF SHYNESS

Putting together the themes we just discussed, we can outline three important linked processes that form three vicious cycles of our shyness experience. The key feeling in the middle process is shame, and it's worth pausing here to say a little more about this feeling, which is perhaps less familiar to us than fear and avoidance.

I began to study shame around 1990 because I observed it in shyness clinic clients. When they felt ashamed, they found it hard to tell people about themselves or tell us what they needed, and they avoided getting help when they needed it. They often avoided eye contact with us. Shame has been defined as the gap between your ideal self and your actual self. It often involves feeling inadequate or flawed, and wanting to hide or sink through the floor. It is called a *self-conscious emotion* because it is an emotion about the self. Professor Paul Gilbert, the originator of the "compassionate mind" approach on which compassion-focused therapy is based, makes a distinction between external and internal shame. External shame is related to our sense of how we exist in others' minds, that is, what we think others think about us. Internal shame refers to judgments about ourselves, and can be seen in thoughts like *I am useless, I am no good, I am a failure, I am a bad person.* Both kinds of shame can trigger emotions of anxiety, anger, disgust, and self-contempt. All of us, if we feel excluded by those around us, will feel threatened, so we feel anxiety, shame, and anger in defense, to protect ourselves. Shame is now understood to be one of the most powerful activators of stress responses in social interactions, raising the heart rate and stimulating production of stress hormones such as cortisol.

The three vicious cycles of shyness are:

- fear/flight
- self-blame/shame
- resentment/other-blame

Figure 1.1 shows how these cycles are linked.

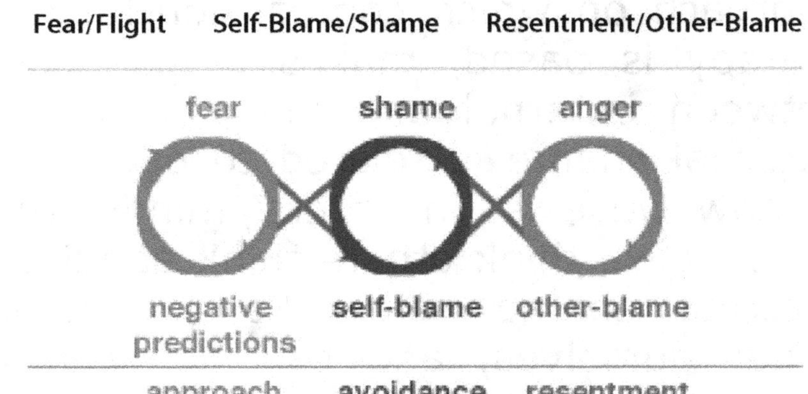

Figure 1.1: The three vicious cycles of shyness. Reprinted with kind permission from the Shyness Institute.

This is how the three linked cycles work. When we enter a social situation that is challenging and seems threatening, we have thoughts that anticipate things going wrong, such as *I won't be able to think of anything to say; this will be a disaster.* That is the first vicious cycle, which we can call the *approach/fear/negative predictions cycle.* If we do think of something to say, or at least don't go screaming from the room, we can challenge these thoughts in the situation; but if we are chronically shy, desperately wanting to avoid attracting criticism, we tend to be perfectionistic, so we are seldom satisfied with our social behavior even when it is perfectly adequate.

We may leave the situation early, leading to the second vicious cycle, called the *shame/self-blame cycle.* When we leave, our fear is reduced, but in its place comes shame: *I don't have to do this—I'm out of here! But oh, I'm* so *inadequate...'* What is more, leaving a difficult situation not only brings on feelings of shame but also actually reinforces social anxiety, because it makes us more likely to leave a challenging situation early next time, or avoid it altogether. At the shyness clinic we used to call it going to our rooms and sucking our thumbs or licking our wounds. We were using some dark humor here, because shame is a very painful state, and self-blaming and shaming thoughts can be debilitating. We may feel relieved because we don't have to "go out there" right now, but we are sad; feel ashamed; and think we are not good enough, never have been good enough, never will be adequate to meet the expectations of our daily social lives. Thoughts like this do not give us much motivation to get up and go back out there. When we are in this state, we are not kind and warm to ourselves, nor are we understanding.

This brings us to the third vicious cycle. After we have sat there and felt terrible about ourselves for a while, blaming ourselves, thinking of all the things we should have done differently and how much more comfortable and competent everyone else was (a stretch if 50 to 60 percent of people are shy), we then start to have other thoughts, like these: *Well, Michael or Allison could have come over and talked to me. They are supposed to be my friends. I know them from classes/work/clubs. People certainly didn't put themselves out to be friendly. They probably don't, or wouldn't, care how I feel anyway.* This is called the *resentment/other-blame* cycle. These thoughts may temporarily reduce our shame because they stir up our resentment, even sometimes anger, so that we feel more powerful. On the other hand, we don't really know what other people's reactions were, and now we're feeling alienated not only from ourselves, but from everyone else as well. As we'll see in the next chapter, these thoughts tend to arise automatically, prompted by processes that have developed through evolution, so they are not our fault; and rather than beat ourselves up for them, we'll learn how to work with them.

It's all too easy to slip back and forth between these vicious cycles, driving ourselves into more difficulties each time—a process we call passing through *infinite loops,* because if we're constantly blaming ourselves, we build up negative ideas about ourselves that are reinforced again and again and thus become hard to change. The good news is that all those negative feelings of fear, self-blame, shame, and resentment toward others that go with problematic shyness can be markedly reduced when we work to change them. Clients in our shyness groups tell us that their negative beliefs about themselves have changed after rehearsing a particular situation through role-playing in group sessions and then putting themselves in similar challenging (but not overwhelming) situations between sessions, or even simply when they had spent time consistently practicing standing back in a social situation and trying to generate alternative thoughts that were more balanced and less driven by anxiety. These techniques enabled them to replace negative beliefs about themselves with more accepting and supportive beliefs. This in turn enabled them to reappraise situations they would previously have thought overwhelmingly daunting as challenges that might not always be easy to face but that could be handled with effort and practice.

BLAME, SHAME, AND FEAR

To help us understand why shy people get drawn into these vicious cycles, it is useful to take a look here at some research on how many nonshy people deal with failure and disappointment, the kinds of experience that so easily send shy people sliding into shame, self-blame, resentment or anger, and back into fear. Earlier researchers investigating how people assign responsibility for what happens found that many assign responsibility for failure to *external, specific, unstable,* and *controllable* factors. In other words, if something goes wrong, either it is not our fault but is due to something outside ourselves *(external),* or if we did cause something to go wrong or fail, our blunder is confined to this situation and not likely to happen in other situations *(specific);* it is not likely to be repeated *(unstable),* and we can fix it *(controllable).* This way of thinking is more common in Western than in Eastern cultures, and more common in men than in women—and you can see how useful it is in the competitive Western environment. After all, we need to maintain our motivation in the face of failure and be prepared to pick ourselves up and try again, because in the complexity of modern culture, frequent failure is only to be expected. However, it can be carried too far: current research confirms—as our own intuition tells us—that people who are always shuffling off responsibility for what happens aren't necessarily the most popular or valued and may harm relationships.

Shy people, on the other hand, tend to assign responsibility in just the opposite way in social situations (though not necessarily in nonsocial situations) and to attribute failure to *internal, global, stable,* and *uncontrollable* factors. When we are shy, we see things like disappointing conversations, dates, or work meetings as the result of something we did or said *(internal);* and we think that it will happen in other situations *(global),* that we'll repeat whatever we did or didn't do *(stable),* and that we can't fix it or change things *(uncontrollable).* My research has shown that we also tend to blame ourselves as well.

When we blame ourselves, we often take a skewed view of our behavior and ourselves. We start organizing all the information we have about ourselves around very detailed negative beliefs that become more and more entrenched as we rehash in our minds again and again whatever failure (as we see it) we are dwelling on. We are less and less likely to notice and take account of information that doesn't match up with these beliefs; in fact, we frequently ignore it altogether. If we get unfavorable feedback, on the other hand, we're more likely to think it accurate than people who are not shy; we discount positive feedback and even feel uncomfortable when we get it. All this means that we don't have the positive information about ourselves that is necessary for us to develop and maintain self-esteem and motivation.

As human beings we are all vulnerable to this kind of thinking. It is just the way we're built. We are particularly vulnerable if we don't have consistent sources of genuine acknowledgment and constructive feedback, and if we have a hard time stepping back from our emotions. Think of the last time you forgot someone's name when you were introducing the person to a friend. Maybe you were a little nervous. Now imagine each of these scenarios. The person you were introducing laughs and says, "No worries, I have a terrible time remembering names. Hi, I'm Jane (or Andrew)," or "I forgot my best friend's name at a party last week." Now imagine that the person looks a bit blank and doesn't volunteer his name. Maybe the person is feeling a little nervous, too. Perhaps at this point your friend bails you out by smiling and saying, "Hi, I'm Louise (or Jerry)." Maybe the person extend her hand. Anyway, you get the point about being there for each other and helping each other out.

When we don't get this kind of help—and, thank goodness, we mostly do—it makes us vulnerable to thoughts like *Oh, I looked like such an idiot; he'd only just told me his name. I'm never going to remember names!* If we feel shy most of the time, it can get worse: *I want to be friends with this person. She probably thinks I'm a loser and won't want to be friends. Other people don't get this nervous.* It can be hard to step back and remember that everyone does this from time to time and nobody thinks much of it. Frequently using words like "idiot" and "loser" about ourselves suggests that we have some fairly entrenched negative beliefs about ourselves. One of the reasons why it's so important to try to catch problematic shyness in childhood or adolescence is to prevent young people from getting into the habit of being ashamed of themselves to the point of believing that they are personally inadequate.

Once these negative beliefs about ourselves have taken root, it takes time and practice to change them. Thinking about ourselves at all becomes strongly associated with these negative thoughts and beliefs, and if we're in a sad mood, they come to mind even more readily, which just makes things worse.

We found that shy students thought in this way about others' perceptions of them to a greater degree than nonshy students did. The shy students might think things like *When people see my discomfort they feel superior, People do not identify with me when I am uncomfortable,* and *People will be rejecting and hurtful if I let them close to me.* And our clients at the shyness clinic are even more likely to think such things than shy students. It seems that chronically shy people and those with social anxiety disorder also have more difficulty trusting others, and tend to see other people as critical and condescending. You might want to take a look at the scale in appendix 1, which sets out some of the thoughts our clients had about other people, to see if you have those thoughts as well.

Much of the fear and shame suffered by shy people is linked to the fact that they are acutely aware of how they may exist in the minds of others, and of what other people may be thinking of them. People who feel shy easily believe they are creating poor images and impressions; they believe people can see their anxiety or notice their blushes and view them as lacking in confidence. It is not unusual for people who are chronically shy to be fearful of positive attention, of being praised or even viewed as attractive, feeling that it puts further demands on them and fearing that once people know them better, they will be disappointed. They may also fear that the observer can see that they lack confidence and are not at ease being the center of attention. And if other people show that they have noticed outward signs of anxiety, such as a shaky voice or a blush, they feel even worse about themselves, and occasionally feel quite angry. They can also feel envious of colleagues who appear not to be shy. In our groups at the shyness clinic, we work on all these feelings and reactions in learning how to interrupt the vicious cycles of shyness.

STEPS TO HELPING OURSELVES: SOCIAL FITNESS TRAINING AND A FOCUS ON COMPASSION

I hope that by now you have come to understand how it is that problem shyness and social anxiety can develop and become entrenched. The good news is that we can learn to tackle the tendency to blame ourselves for every less-than-perfect outcome; we can learn how to treat ourselves in a more balanced way, with compassion, focusing on how to improve rather than labeling ourselves and berating ourselves for past events. This book will show you how it is possible to reduce the distress caused by extreme shyness by learning how to encourage yourself and how to trust yourself to try again.

Why Do We Need to Train in Social Fitness?

The capacity to pick yourself up when things don't go as you had hoped and try again is a part of what I call *social fitness training.*

Just as a physically fit person is in good physical shape, a person who is socially fit is in good physiological, behavioral, emotional, and mental shape; that is, the person functions well and has a sense of well-being. The person is capable of having satisfying interpersonal relationships, can handle his emotions, is able to pursue his personal and professional goals, and can think in balanced ways. The idea of social fitness addresses our human needs for both emotional connection and a sense of influence or control over our lives and events around us. And just as someone who wants to stay physically fit plays a sport, works out in the gym, or does exercises, a socially fit person takes frequent "social exercise" by meeting new people, and maintaining and cultivating close relationships.

It's important to remember that social fitness is not about perfection, any more than physical fitness is. Even the tennis pro doesn't consistently have a flawless serve or an unreturnable backhand. An Olympic runner can drop the baton—and we've all seen top soccer players accidentally score a goal for the other team! But they learn to encourage themselves to go back and try again. In the same way, we can reduce the distress of shyness by learning to soothe and support ourselves. We can learn to be like good parents and mentors to ourselves, to distinguish between anxious or frustrated self-criticism, and understanding and supportive self-correction.

In social fitness training we work toward:

- noticing, monitoring, and recognizing how our thoughts can make us more anxious—paying particular attention to the assumptions we might be

making about other people or our negative self-critical thoughts
- learning to develop thoughts, focus of attention, and feelings that will support us
- focusing on what our goals are and what steps we can take to achieve them
- practicing in each of these three areas regularly in the spirit of self-acceptance and with a genuine desire to help ourselves with shyness (in contrast to getting angry or feeling ashamed by our shyness)

Why is it called social fitness training? We all have a temperament to manage, whether we are more or less talkative, outgoing, reserved, energetic, and so on. And we all face social challenges in our environments, such as making friends, earning a meaningful living, finding a mate, and caring for children. Social fitness training aims to make us fit to meet these challenges, to equip us with the behavior, thoughts, and emotions that will help us to survive and thrive. Like physical fitness, social fitness requires that we work out regularly, preferably every day. We can’t work out once a month and be physically fit, and we can’t work out socially once a month and be socially fit. And, as social athletes, we have many situations in which to practice and many social sports to take part in. Both a tennis player and a golfer may be physically fit, but they use very different skills and moves as they play; the same applies with social fitness. Developing and maintaining social fitness involve meeting new people, belonging to groups and communities, cultivating and maintaining friendships, and developing intimacy with a partner—each of which draws on different skills.

The social fitness perspective is useful in overcoming shyness because it doesn’t ask us to think of shyness as a “disease” that needs “a cure,” but rather to think of it as a personality style, like any other, that has both strengths and vulnerabilities. Training our minds to be kind and supportive in the contexts where we feel shy can help us to develop the skills and confidence that some of us find more challenging than others.

Why Do We Need Compassion?

In my work with shy people, I've found it interesting that some of them, even when they've worked really hard at learning to be kinder to themselves, struggle to really *feel* their self-supportive statements. Learning new thoughts to replace the familiar self-critical ones, they say things like, "I understand the logic of the new thoughts I'm practicing, and I know I'm not to blame, but I still *feel* to blame." A related difficulty concerns the tone of voice people use on themselves: even when they're trying to be reassuring rather than critical, sometimes the alternative thought comes out in a cold or even aggressive manner. For example, imagine that you feel shy and try to reassure yourself by saying, "It's only natural to feel shy because this is a new situation. I expect other people feel shy too. I have felt these feelings many times before and I know I will cope with them and do okay." It sounds sort of reassuring, doesn't it? Now, imagine that you say that in your mind in a rather cold, logical way, or even in a slightly irritable way (because you are irritated at feeling shy again—remember the vicious circles mentioned earlier). It's as if you're trying to *make* yourself feel better, even *bully* yourself into feeling different. What effect would that have on you? Just imagine that for a moment. But now, suppose you hear these thoughts in your mind in a very understanding, kind, and supportive way, so that you can feel the real understanding and desire to be helpful with shyness. How will that affect you?

So, it's not just what we say to ourselves that's important; it's how we say it as well. Recognizing this, the approach that we're going to take in this book is to work on developing compassionate and caring feelings *while* focusing on thoughts and behavior using the idea of social fitness. Woven together, these two strands form a strong combination that can genuinely help with problematic shyness.

By using these two key ideas, a focus on compassion and training for social fitness, you can become more aware of your real motives and values, and come to understand better what it is that has been leading you to avoid socializing and becoming closer to people. Armed with these insights, you can build up your capacity to enjoy social contact at whatever level you choose, from casual social encounters to intimate personal relationships.

KEY POINTS

- Shyness can vary from ordinary shyness that is not a problem to extreme shyness that is painful and even debilitating.
- Shyness has many strengths, which can contribute greatly to relationships, to the workplace, and to society. Indeed, there have been many outstanding shy leaders throughout history, and many media personalities are shy.
- There are three vicious cycles of shyness: fear/flight, self-blame/shame, resentment/other-blame. Fear, shame, self-blame, anger, and other-blame

can all be significantly reduced by social fitness training.

• A compassionate approach to shyness can be immensely helpful in working to overcome problem shyness and the painful emotions that go with it.

CHAPTER 2

The Way We Are: Shyness and How We've Evolved

We now know that the human brain has been evolving over many hundreds of millions of years. In fact, the origins of brain structure date back much farther, to times before any humans existed, when reptiles and other creatures dominated the earth. What this means is that within our brains we have many basic emotional and behavioral systems that we share with other animals. So, like them, we can become anxious or angry. Like them, we have impulses to form sexual relationships, friendships, and attachments to our offspring; to fight for status; and to belong to "tribes." We like to be part of a group; we feel secure if we know we're accepted and wanted, less secure if we're uncertain of this. Many of our basic passions, emotions, and motives for social behavior are the product of evolution. As Paul Gilbert points out in his book *The Compassionate Mind,* this has enormous implications for us. It means that much of what goes on in our minds, including many of our desires and emotions, is there because evolution designed us in that way; our own experiences in life go on to shape them further, but don't produce them in the first place. We are set up to feel certain things, for example, to be anxious or afraid of this or that; these feelings are built into us. Think about this carefully, because it's really important. What it means for us in understanding shyness is that problems related to shyness are *not your fault.* This realization is the foundation of the compassionate approach that forms the keystone of this book and its program for overcoming chronic and distressing shyness. When we give up feeling inferior and blaming ourselves for our problem shyness and social anxiety and the situations in which we find ourselves, we become freer to dedicate ourselves to working with this difficulty in compassionate ways.

TAKING RESPONSIBILITY

It is important to understand that our brains have been designed to experience anxiety in certain contexts, and that some of us feel uncomfortably shy or socially anxious more readily than others. However, that is not a reason to do nothing about shyness if it is interfering with something you want to do in life—quite the contrary, in fact. Recognizing that we might have a brain that is sensitive to certain situations is a call to action. This is true, of course, for many of our individual sensitivities. If you have a body that gains weight easily, that is not your fault; but to stay healthy, it will help you if you're careful about your diet and get plenty of exercise. It is not your fault that you love those cream cakes and that your metabolism is a bit slow, but it *is* your responsibility to regulate your eating as best you can and to stay active. It's challenging, I know, but this is the nature of life: understanding the way we are made and bringing out the best in ourselves. Applying this principle to problematic shyness means that while we recognize it's not our fault that we are sensitive and vulnerable to painful experiences, we can make a commitment to work with whatever is problematic or painful in our shyness, in compassionate ways, so that our social anxiety doesn't rule our lives.

This doesn't mean that a sensitive or shy temperament needs to be changed to a bold temperament, or that you need to become extroverted if you are introverted or become the life of the party if you are happier out of the limelight. We've all had the experience of trying to make conversation with the life of the party and finding that jokes are the only way the person communicates. Sharing anything less than perfect about themselves or even sharing ordinary reactions and emotions is out of the question. This isn't an ideal to emulate. What we're aiming at is reducing social anxiety and painful shyness in situations where you are so concerned that other people will judge you that you don't reach out for friendship and social support, don't apply for the job you really want, or don't try to get into the college you'd really like to attend. The aim is to get you to the point where you feel able to do what you really want to do and care about.

My experience in working with chronically shy people over many years has taught me that when shy people commit themselves to working with problematic shyness, with practice they are able to reduce it so that they feel better about themselves, are more engaged in their lives, and feel more effective in social situations. So, once we take responsibility for ourselves, we can work to bring out the best in our brains; but taking responsibility does *not* mean blaming ourselves for the anxieties that hinder us. Quite the opposite—it's at the moment when we give up blaming ourselves that we set ourselves free to face our difficulties and challenges with greater ease. Having said that, habits of self-blame are easy to acquire and can take time to change, but that certainly doesn't mean you can't make progress with problem shyness in the meantime. In fact, many shy people I have worked with have shown great courage in doing things they were scared of even while they were still blaming themselves.

ANXIETY AND SOCIAL RANK: DO WE NEED HIERARCHIES?

Social anxiety and shyness are by no means exclusive to humans; they are very common in other animals too. It makes good evolutionary sense for animals to live in groups so that they are not all fighting one another all the time over resources, and these groups tend to be organized around hierarchies, where the strong and dominant wander about in a confident manner and those less powerful are more wary. It is often the social anxiety of the less powerful, in fact, that maintains the social order; if the less dominant don't challenge the more dominant, conflict is kept to a minimum. These less powerful individuals have specific ways of showing their anxiety, which we call submissive behavior. Typical instances of submissive behavior are avoiding eye contact, making the body look smaller rather than larger, staying on the edge of things, and not drawing attention to yourself.

Humans are just like this, if you think about it. Indeed, some believe that shyness and social anxiety are linked to sensitivity to social rank. The idea is that, as in animal groups, social anxiety helps to maintain the social order by limiting the amount of aggression around so that groups can settle down and live peacefully. On this view, mild forms of shyness and social anxiety usefully keep us a little wary so that we don't take things for granted; we pay attention to what other people are doing and thinking, and take trouble not to upset them too much. This is arguably—up to a point, at least—good for social harmony.

This idea, called *social rank theory,* seems particularly relevant both in traditional societies with strong social hierarchies and in highly competitive individualistic cultures such as our own. This is not to say, however, that it describes the way things have to be, or will always be, in human society. Indeed, in some societies a different principle is gaining hold as the notion of "tend and befriend"—that is, make friends and give and receive social support—and replacing the principle of "fight or flight" that previously dominated politics, business, and academia. People are realizing that making friends, and seeking and giving social support are just as effective ways of protecting ourselves as fighting or fleeing. This alternative principle has a lot to offer even for those who seemed to have most to gain from the fight-or-flight setup, for even the most dominant individuals become vulnerable as soon as their hold on power slips: among our close relatives the baboons, the most aggressive males at some point lose power, and when this happens other aggressive males tend to torment and bully them.

Many shy people incline toward this different—more peaceable and more collaborative—way of being in the world, perhaps more similar to our other close relatives, the peaceful bonobos, than to the combative and competitive baboons. Yet this alternative way of being is still widely viewed as inferior in Western culture. For shy people living in a competitive world, compassion can be a great help—both in understanding this evolving world, and in working out how to live within it and how to help it evolve into something better.

Another way to think about this is that a shy temperament and the sensitivity and emotions that go with it are like being blond. If the rest of the world thinks blonds are stupid, you may have to cope with that. If you are fairskinned, you may have to pay more attention to how much sun you get than your olive- and brown-skinned friends do, even if they think you are a bit of a sissy.

HOW HUMANS THINK: THE SENSE OF SELF AND NEEDING TO BE LIKED

Humans don't just react to social situations, for example, being shy in the face of uncertainty: we also think about them, imagine them, and fantasize about them, put meaning on them and running through possible past and future scenarios in our heads. If we're going on a new date, we will imagine what the other person will be like, and how we imagine the person—as kind and interested or cold and indifferent—will affect our feelings. In this we are *not* like other animals. People who study how our minds have evolved point out that about two million years ago, we humans began to evolve a new type of brain that could think and ruminate, and have a sense of self and self-awareness. Importantly, this is probably why we now have a brain that is very concerned about the impressions we make in the minds of others. Chimpanzees, another species of great ape who are our cousins, clearly show social anxiety and wariness around powerful or dominant others who could hurt them, but they don't sit around worrying about how they look, the fact that they've put on weight, and how others will respond to their spare tire or lopsided nose. Humans do—and we do it a lot of the time. Why do we all get up in the morning and put on clean clothes and maybe makeup to face the day? This is all about how we want to exist in the minds of others.

Most of the fears of nonhuman animals are related to physical threats. For humans, highly sensitive to how others view us, the primary anxieties are different. We are far more concerned with social and psychological threats, such as being rejected or ignored, teased or criticized. What really bothers humans in our concern about how we exist in the minds of others is *not wanting to be seen as inferior.* So we humans are still very concerned with rank and social position—but more in terms of our attractiveness, our likability, our being seen as competent and being wanted by other people. When I talk to problematically shy and socially anxious people, they're very rarely worried that people might be violent or aggressive to them, and much more concerned that others will see them as unattractive, undesirable, boring, incompetent, or silly in some way. In consequence, they feel vulnerable to being ignored, passed over, or left behind; rejected, criticized, or picked on.

But while our fears may be different from other animals' fears, when those fears are activated we may well react in exactly the same way—with submissive behavior. Even though our fears are not (usually) about physical aggression, if we feel *devalued* in the minds of other people, our social fear can set off all those ways of behaving we noted in submissive animals—avoiding eye contact, trying to make our bodies smaller, not drawing attention to ourselves, slipping to the edge of things—along with various physical and emotional sensations. It is as if there is a part of us that starts holding us back to protect us.

Now, while submissive behavior has traditionally been valued in women, and as many shy women marry (and at the same ages) as nonshy women, boys and men who behave submissively may suffer, particularly in highly competitive environments with traditional ideas about manhood, that is, where the masculine ideal involves being insensitive and tough and not showing emotion. However, the more educated, or the more psychologically aware, women are, the more they tend to prefer men with a mixture of what are considered feminine and masculine traits, and the less tolerant they are of traditional models of masculinity where men are supposed to be tough and insensitive. At the clinic we often say to shy men who are worried that they are not dominant enough and are too sensitive to find girlfriends or mates: "We have good news for you! Ask a woman to go out for coffee or dinner, tell her you feel a little shy, and see how she reacts." This exercise tends to go very well. It doesn't *always* go well, of course; there are indeed women who prefer very dominant, even tough, men. Sometimes these are women who have been badly hurt or abused and who are looking for strong protectors; unfortunately, those they choose may not always be the best partners for them.

When we think about shyness, it's clear that our shy emotions relate to our sensitivity to how we exist for the other person; it's all about our thoughts and feelings about what other people are thinking and feeling about us. So why have we, as a species, become so sensitive to what people think about us? Well, once again we can turn to evolution.

Humans are a very cooperative species. We need the support and help of others from the day we are born to the day we die. However, outside our immediate families, we also know that getting this support and help requires us to be appealing to other people. So we want to create good impressions in the minds of others, because we want them to like us and so choose to help us. When we first go to school, we are aware that some children seem more popular than others, that some children are better at sports than others and get chosen to play in informal sports games, and that some children seem more confident than others. We also become aware that some children receive more attention than others. Children who become very socially anxious may be particularly aware of these differences, especially if they have picked up at home that their parents are very concerned about "what the neighbors think" and what other people are thinking about them, and believe that you need to do just the right thing socially to be accepted.

It's worth mentioning here, too, that if your family is part of a minority in the neighborhood where you live, or makes much less money than most people in the area, these anxieties might be compounded by the fear of being stereotyped. Ironically—because stereotyping is much reduced when people get to know each other personally—this might make it even harder for you to let people get to know you. The encouraging news for the more introverted or quiet among us is that when people first meet, they tend to judge each other on what they say, but very soon, within weeks, they start to judge others by what they do. Humans are very discerning: recent studies show that college students can see in one meeting which people will be giving and cooperative, and which will exploit them. So, as long as you are not so anxious and withdrawn that it is hard for people to see who you really are, unless the other person is exploitative and hurtful you are likely to do well.

When people get to know you a bit, then, you can capitalize on the strengths of shyness. But the fact remains that to be valued and accepted, we have to engage with other people, show them what kind of person we are and what we can do, and we have to cope with some level of anxiety in the process. After all, how are people going to choose us as friends, or ask us to play on their team or join in a group after school, if they don't know anything about us? We must also compete with others sometimes for attention, support, or resources, and recognize when others are competing with us; sometimes, when you feel socially anxious and insecure, it doesn't occur to you that others are competing with you or see you as threatening.

Also, in the normal course of things, we can get into conflicts with others. When we begin to show ourselves, our preferences and our values, we discover differences. You suggest playing football or basketball, but somebody else wants to play baseball. You want to go to the movies, but someone else wants to play computer games or stay home watching TV. You want to do your homework together, but your friend wants to go to a party.

All these situations involving the self and others—showing something of who you are, letting people get to know you, offering suggestions, and sharing your values, but also being able to cope with the odd conflict or two—may bring on anxiety. Socially anxious or problematically shy children can struggle in all of these situations and, as a result, stay more in the background, waiting to be chosen.

In some ways, then, it is important to be liked. If people like you, they are going to help you in your hour of need, choose to be with you, share things with you, support your goals, and so on. Think how valuable that was over the hundreds of thousands of years of human evolution. Being liked, accepted, and valued could have been the difference between life and death. To be disliked and rejected would certainly have been bad news for our ancestors tens of thousands of years ago. Today, whether people like us or not is usually not a life-or-death issue, but it still matters a great deal for our quality of life. On the other hand, learning to tolerate being disliked and rejected in order to stand up for something you believe in is also important, as is choosing friends you genuinely respect rather than choosing out of the need for everyone to like you. If you are introverted, you may never need more than a few friends—some people are perfectly happy with just one or two deep and lasting friendships—but even so, to find those few good friends, you have to participate and reach out to people—and you may have to kiss a few frogs before you find your prince or princess!

It's clear from even the most casual social contact that we all want to be liked. When we meet new people, we would like them to say, "It was nice meeting you," rather than "It was pleasant meeting you, but it was nothing special." If you invite a friend to your house for dinner, you would like that person to say, "That was a lovely meal," not "That was an average meal."

As therapists we like our patients to say how much they enjoyed working with us, rather than, "You're an average sort of therapist, not quite what I had hoped." Behind so much of what we do is a desire to be accepted, valued, approved of, and liked—and that's because of the species we are. But in working to be accepted and valued, we have to *show ourselves* and take risks, and to recognize that sometimes someone is not going to value or approve of us. So how are we going to cope when that happens?

Problematically shy or socially anxious people can feel on the horns of a dilemma. On the one hand, you may wish to be valued, to have your contribution recognized and to feel accepted; on the other hand, to display yourself sufficiently for people to get to know you and to choose you can provoke a lot of anxiety. After all, you might say something or suggest something that others will criticize. Tricky, isn't it! If you think about your own shyness, can you sense that sometimes you feel in a bit of a dilemma, both wanting to be part of the social scene and at the same time anxious that you might do or say something that brings negative attention to yourself? Part of learning to cope with problematic shyness or social anxiety is learning how to cope with those risks, and facing up to setbacks if they arise.

HOW OUR EMOTIONS WORK: THREE SYSTEMS

If we feel shy a lot then, faced with the dilemma we've been looking at here, we may hedge our bets, go for the less risky options, hold back. Holding back until you warm up is fine; it simply reflects a cautious approach, what we called in chapter 1 a "prevention focus" rather than a "promotion focus." But if we hedge our bets and hold back so much that we don't engage in our lives, make friends, or take up activities we would really like to do, then the quality of our lives suffers.

One way of understanding what happens is to recognize that we humans have three different types of emotional systems, each of which can quite literally take control of our minds and direct how we behave. I'm going to look at these systems in some detail here, because it will help us to understand how we can help ourselves deal with anxiety by learning to treat ourselves with kindness and compassion, particularly when things don't always work out as we would like, and when we make mistakes.

So far in this book I've explained how anxieties are related to a sense of threat and trying to protect ourselves. Indeed, all living things need to have ways of detecting threats and responding to protect themselves. So it's important to understand that some of our shyness and social anxiety is linked to a threat system. It's also important to recognize that our threat system is regulated by another system, which I'm going to call a soothing system. So let's look at how emotions linked to threats, like anxiety, work through these systems.

The three systems can be summed up as follows. (You can read about them in more detail in Paul Gilbert's book, *The Compassionate Mind.)*

- First, there is a *threat/protection system,* which helps us to detect, track, and respond to things that threaten us. When this system is in charge, our attention is focused on the threats, and the typical emotion we feel is anxiety, anger, or disgust.
- Second, there is an *activating system* that stimulates and directs our desires and helps us pursue our goals. This is the system that prompts us to "go for it" when we want something. When this system is in the driver's seat, we feel motivated, anticipating pleasure, and if it arrives or we achieve something good, we get the buzz of excitement. When this system is too muted, we can lose feelings of motivation, energy, and vitality.
- Third, there is a system linked to positive feelings of contentment, peacefulness, safety, and well-being. When animals do not have to cope with threats and they are satisfied, they can become calm and relaxed; and humans are just the same. We're

going to call this a soothing system, partly because when it is uppermost, it can regulate the other two.

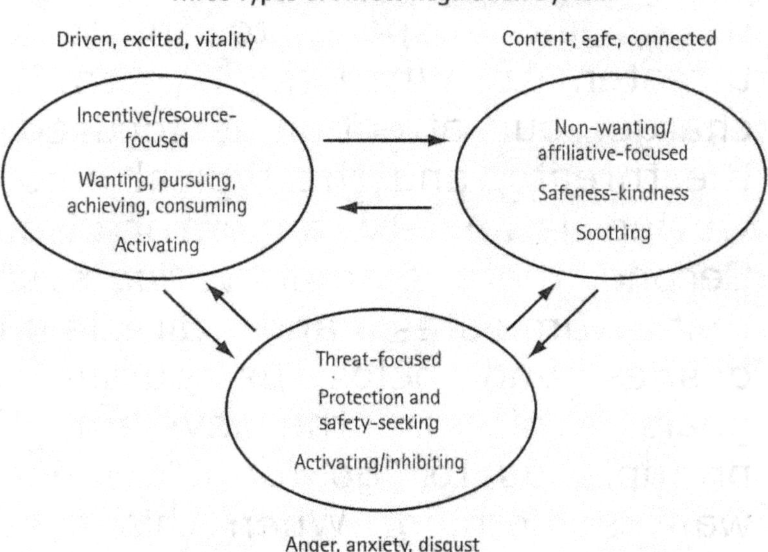

Figure 2.1 How our three major emotional systems interact Reprinted with kind permission from Paul Gilbert, The Compassionate Mind (London: Constable, 2009).

These systems are constantly interacting and giving rise to different states of mind, as you can see in figure 2.1. This means that it's a bit artificial to identify them as separate systems, but it is very useful to do so for the purposes of explanation. The one that's of special interest to us in this book is the third system, the one we're going to call a "soothing system."

All kinds of situations, including our own thoughts about ourselves, can stimulate the threat system. However, the key message is that the soothing system can calm it down again. One reason why it can do this is because it is sensitive to signals of kindness, care, and support, and can pick these up. It's not hard to think of an example of how kindness and affection from others can soothe the threat system. If we are distressed as children, we go to our parents, who give us reassurance, maybe a hug, and the distress comes down. Kindness of all forms has soothing properties, and this is because of how our brains, and in particular the emotional soothing system, work. Just as your threat system is sensitive to threats and will activate defensive emotions such as anger and anxiety, so your soothing system is sensitive to the kindness of others and will help settle your threat system.

The Importance of Kindness

Kindness, then, is very important because it helps stimulate that soothing system. This is easily demonstrated. Imagine that you are struggling with something, and that you have a partner or a teacher who is very competent and who is good at spotting errors, but is critical. If you ask that person for help, she will probably give it to you, but her nonverbal communication and some of the things she says imply that she sees your mistake as rather thoughtless or stupid. The chances are that you will be wary around this person and, even though she could be very helpful you, might be anxious about approaching her for help. In contrast, consider the same situation, but with a parent or teacher who shows delight in being able to help you, makes you feel he really understands your difficulty, points out your strengths and shows you how you can build on them, and how you can look for and correct potential errors, and encourages you to explore the problem further and bring it back to him so he can see if you need more help. Simply put, the second parent or teacher is *kind* to you. Imagine that you are very upset about something and go to a friend who listens for a bit and then switches subjects to talk about the things that are preoccupying him. This person is not *un* kind, but not kind either. Now imagine going to a friend who listens intensely, takes your feelings seriously, maybe puts an arm around you, and shows genuine care and concern for you. How do you feel in each situation? You probably thought of the second friend as kinder and more focused on you, and you probably felt better.

This soothing effect of kindness goes way back in evolutionary time. When animals are not in danger or needing to forage for food, they can rest. When we are not feeling driven or threatened and are just in the present moment, we feel calm and content. Take a moment or two to remember times when you have felt peaceful and content. Remember what was happening; spend a few moments really thinking about what it felt like, what it feels like now as you remember, and the difference between feeling like this and being excited. When we meditate regularly—something we'll explore how to do in later chapters of this book—we find that our feelings of peacefulness and calm increase.

As mammals evolved, the contentment system became strongly linked to affection and caring. When mammals began to care for their infants by grooming, feeding, and protecting them, these infants survived more often than those who were not groomed, fed, and protected, and so passed on the genes for care. Over millions of years, this evolved habit of protecting and caring for offspring spread around the world and was reflected in new brain designs. Now we can see all sorts of species, from tropical birds to our own family dogs, looking after their newly hatched chicks or recently delivered pups, nuzzling and caring for their babies as we do ours. We can also see that the babies are quiet and peaceful when they are cared for this way. This ability to soothe and bring about peace with kindness is part of our evolutionary heritage, and that's why you'll notice yourself and others looking for kindness in marital partners, doctors, friends, and teachers. The psychologist David Buss studied people from all over the world and found that the thing people everywhere thought most important in a partner was kindness, even ahead of reproductive success and control of resources.

The important thing to grasp here is that kindness really does influence our brains; it really does affect how we feel about ourselves and others, and it really does settle down our threat systems.

Being Kind to Yourself

Given that it is so clear that kindness from others stimulates a system in our brains that helps regulate the threat system, what happens when we show kindness to ourselves? Well, it turns out that the same patterns apply. If we are disappointed or make a mistake and start getting critical and angry with ourselves, that is only going to stimulate the sense of threat. In contrast, if we are kind and supportive to ourselves, this stimulates the soothing system.

Think about your own experience. If you were feeling uncomfortably shy or anxious about giving a presentation or going to a party, how would you feel if your partner or friend said, "Oh, for heaven's sake, it's not that big a deal; you'll be fine! Don't make such a production of it!" Or what if you heard, "I've got a tougher one next week, and you don't hear me making a fuss!" Now, what would it feel like if your partner or a friend listened carefully, empathized with your feelings, understood how you might feel that way, maybe touched your arm or your shoulder, or said, "I've felt scared about giving talks/going to parties, too." You can probably feel how calming that would feel and what a different response you would experience in your body. Feel the inner wisdom you have in knowing the difference. It's easy to get caught up in the fear and resentment of the threat system, and then to criticize and belittle, shame and bully ourselves. But equally, we can train our thoughts to be kind and understanding so that we feel calm and cared for—as you just experienced when you thought of how a compassionate friend or partner would speak to you. These good, calm feelings are associated with a hormone called *oxytocin,* on which a lot of research has recently been done and which is linked to feelings of trust and closeness. Kindness and trust go together. We can turn to people we trust who are kind, and soothe ourselves that way. We can also learn to turn to ourselves.

Again, the physical effects are easy to demonstrate. If you are hungry and see a meal, this will stimulate your saliva and stomach acids; but if it's late at night, you have no money, and the shops are closed, and you just fantasize a wonderful meal, your inner thoughts and images can do just the same thing, stimulating your stomach acids and saliva. If you see a sexual scene on TV, or you see someone on the street who is very sexually attractive to you, that may stimulate your pituitary hormones, which, when released into the body, cause sexual arousal. And we know that our own fantasies can do the same. If you see a baby or small child in a park, you may feel parental nurturing feelings. If you fantasize about having a child, you will probably experience the same nurturing feelings. Our fantasies can stimulate specific brain pathways, and through them, our bodies, in very specific ways.

Once we really understand this—that what goes through our minds, the things we think about and ruminate about and the fantasies we have, and our states of mind stimulate our brains in particular ways—then we begin truly to understand that we are able to take control of those ruminations and fantasies. Using the same principles, think about what happens in your brain if somebody is critical of you and rather unpleasant. That will stimulate your threat system and create anxiety and anger. Now think about how you feel if you are critical and unpleasant to yourself. Recent research has shown that when we are critical of ourselves, this stimulates areas of our brain linked to detecting errors and inhibiting our behavior. So not only are we acutely aware of doing something wrong, but we feel nervous and very cautious as well. So what you think about and how you treat yourself have a direct impact on how you feel and how you behave; and they do this by altering the balance between the three emotional systems.

So you can see the value of developing a habit of being kind and compassionate toward yourself. When you learn to switch to kind and compassionate images, thoughts, and feelings, you're going to be stimulating areas of your brain that are going to help you, rather than activating anxiety. It's like creating a friend in your head, rather than a bad-tempered critic.

HOW SHY PEOPLE'S EMOTIONS WORK

While we all have the three emotional systems, the balance among them differs from one type of person, and one individual, to another. In a painfully shy person, the threat system is particularly active. In a challenging situation, we feel scared and anxious; if we are isolated we become sad, tipping the balance even further. More threat feelings arise: we feel anxiety, anger, resentment and irritability, shame and pessimism; motivation and energy drop, we become prey to feelings of hopelessness, and contentment and peace seem far away.

When we understand how our brains work, we can step back and rebalance the three systems. Remember what I said about social fitness training being similar in many ways to physical fitness training? Well, in much the same way, working on our shy emotions by cultivating compassion is a kind of physiotherapy for the mind. We can learn and practice compassionate states that will help us to rebalance our brain systems, and we can reach out to others for help in doing that. We can work on behavior, thoughts, and feelings. Exercise, diet, and medication also help, though they are outside our focus in this book. The exercises we will discuss and practice in later chapters are designed to work alongside a health-promoting lifestyle.

We don't want to wipe out the threat system, because it has evolved for good reasons and is useful to us; but we don't want it to be too dominant either. It can get out of hand, and when it does, it can cause us problems. If our threat emotions are too easily triggered or get too intense, it is hard to keep the systems in balance. Trying to deal with the resulting emotional imbalance through rationality alone is not much help; our new, logical brains are saying that the party or the date is really not that dangerous and that the more we practice, the better we will feel, but our old brain patterns are saying the situation really *is* dangerous. We may not think or remember that these warning thoughts and feelings are part of our old brain patterns, so we try to suppress them and control them by pushing ourselves around and blaming ourselves. We feel ashamed of feeling socially anxious and vulnerable, and we try to manage and fight the feelings rather than accept them, try to understand them, comfort ourselves, and work with them.

The Automatic Shy Response

If we feel shy and walk into a party to find there's no one there we've met before besides our hostess, our threat system can become automatically activated and social anxiety can suddenly escalate, even though we know rationally that we have the skills to walk up to someone and start a conversation. We also know that the likelihood that people will be waiting to judge us harshly is very small, but the feelings go on rising nevertheless. Next, we can find that our legs are carrying us to our hostess's side to help pass trays of food so we don't have to make conversation with anyone. Or we might find ourselves gravitating to a spot behind the buffet table, where it is hard for people to start a conversation with us; when someone does approach, we turn the other way and look very absorbed in the roast-beef platter. Maybe we sweat a bit, feel shaky, and become aware of a rapid heartbeat. This activation of the threat/protection system happens so fast that we don't think through any of this; in fact, we don't think anything other than threat-related thoughts like *I look foolish* and *I must try not to do anything embarrassing,* while we try to fade into the wallpaper.

Or what about that time when you went to a job interview, having prepared carefully for it in advance, researching the company as well as the activities and duties the job required and going over your qualifications for it. You had made a list of questions the interviewers were likely to ask and were just going over your responses in your head as the elevator went up to the floor where the interview was to be held, when your mind suddenly went blank. You could feel the sudden rise of anxiety, and your mouth felt dry. Suddenly you felt panicky and wanted to cancel the interview. That is how fast social anxiety can hit when the threat system kicks in, and it can feel overwhelming.

Ruminating, Dwelling, and Brooding

Another problem is that our new self-aware brain can have a field day ruminating and worrying about potential threats and humiliations, and it's amazingly creative at thinking up all the horrible and catastrophic things that could possibly happen. Well, that's how threat systems work, always preparing for the worst: "Better safe than sorry," we say. That is what the brain is designed to do. I remember being so anxious just before an exam once that I wondered if I would pass out. You've probably had the experience of a shot of anxiety hitting you when you were meeting someone for the first time, perhaps as you said hello or shook hands. Looking back, you can feel how automatic the social anxiety is. It comes out of the blue: bang! And with it come automatic thoughts like *I won't be able to think of anything to say. I look anxious. I'll sound dumb. They'll think I'm stupid.* You can change this dwelling on how you might fall short of your expectations by challenging your automatic thoughts, saying more supportive things to yourself, focusing on what you find interesting about the other person, and looking for common interests. And again, this will be easier when you have learned to be kind to yourself instead of being so hard on yourself.

So much for when you first meet someone. What about when a meeting did not go as well as you had hoped? Did you find yourself brooding about it? Remember the self-blame/shame vicious cycle described in chapter 1? You also may find yourself feeling angry with the other person for not drawing you out more. Remember the resentment/other-blame cycle? Research has shown that this kind of brooding makes our social anxiety worse and is associated with sadness and lowered mood. Exercises in this book will help you to draw on your soothing system when you are feeling bad about yourself or other people, and help relieve your painful feelings. Buddhism, a spiritual tradition that places great emphasis on compassion, teaches that feeling kindness toward others and ourselves, especially when we feel disappointed or let down, leads to greater emotional well-being.

We know that intense shyness and social anxiety are part of the threat/protection response. When we are anxious, the amygdala, an almond-shaped organ in the center of the brain, becomes activated. If this occurs frequently—because of a very stressful environment, genetic predispositions, unresolved pain, trauma from the past, some combination of these, or other reasons—the amygdala becomes sensitized, so that it reacts to smaller threats, leading to more easily triggered and more intense anxiety. When we recognize that becoming anxious is part of a system that has evolved to protect us, but that our new brains can also climb on the bandwagon and exaggerate danger, then we can think about how to reduce the sensitivity. It is a great help toward this goal to be kind and compassionate toward ourselves, helping bring the threat system more into balance with the other systems.

Uncovering the Feel-Good Emotions

Your brain is designed so that your threat system will overrule and turn off your positive feelings in many situations. For example, imagine that you are enjoying a quiet walk through the woods, a picnic under a tree, or a romantic moment with your partner, and then suddenly you hear the siren of a police car or fire engine. Chances are your anxiety will switch on, and you will lose all interest in your meal or romantic possibilities. This is because you must attend to the threat, and to do so you must turn off your positive interests and emotions.

Sometimes, of course, we can be pulled in two directions at once, if the situation stimulates positive emotions but also carries risk or threat; for example, if we're thinking about making a date with someone, we may feel excited and hopeful about the possibility of a new relationship, but also fearful of rejection. In this situation we may have to learn to overrule anxiety in order to take the risk and ask the person out, so that we can at least have a chance of enjoying the date. If the balance tips in favor of anxiety, then we never make that phone call and never know whether the date would have gone well or badly.

Some people, of course, actually get pleasure and excitement from increasing their sense of risk; think of downhill skiers or skydivers! The point is that positive and negative emotions are constantly being balanced and traded off against each other, and we're making decisions about which of them we're going to act on, which of the three systems we're going to let govern our behavior. Anxiety can make us lose touch with two kinds of positive feelings, both of which are important to our well-being. One kind, the emotions produced by the activating system, has to do with going after what we want, energizing us. For example, we get excited when we compete at sports or work, or for a good grade on an exam, or go for a job we want. The other kind of positive feeling, the emotions produced by the soothing system, makes us feel calm and content, peaceful and safe.

When we feel painfully shy or socially anxious, we can lose touch with our positive feelings and desires as the threat/protection emotional system trumps the activating and soothing emotional systems. We forget about the pleasures of being with other people and how interesting they can be, because we are so focused on the fact that they might be critical of us or not accept us. Now, I'm not trying to belittle this fear. It can be very upsetting if people don't accept us. Rejection or exclusion can threaten anyone's sense of well-being as much as physical threat, and can cause us just as much pain. In fact, social exclusion activates systems in the brain associated with physical pain. The point is that when we feel socially anxious, we tend to focus too strongly on risks and be too sensitive to social threat, and to forget our own positive qualities and previous occasions when we've enjoyed talking to and being with other people. We also forget that liking others and enjoying their company, and letting them know this, helps them to get to know us a bit and from that position to come to like us. People can only like what they get to know.

You have probably also noticed that when people like you and show this, it is easy to like them back. After all, they can recognize quality when they see it! They may be intelligent, discerning people with great personalities. This works both ways: so it is helpful to show this when you like another person. It's also helpful to think of what it is that you find interesting and likable about the other person. This is a good way to find things you have in common, and focusing on the other person, rather than on your own anxious feelings, also pulls you away from ruminative thoughts and worry. Now, usually, what we notice when we continue to take risks—go to parties, meet new friends, take job interviews—is that we become more comfortable over time. That is, it's not facing the risks that makes us more anxious next time; it's *avoiding* them. So it makes sense to try to help ourselves face the situations that might, at the moment, seem too challenging, as a way of lessening our anxiety. And to do this, it would help to learn how to accept our anxiety, take a kind and supportive position with it, see it as naturally occurring because of our evolution, and then, as best we can, do the things we want to do anyway.

WHAT DO YOU REALLY WANT?

When you're anxious about doing something, it's always worth asking yourself, *If I weren't so anxious about this, would I* want *to do it?* Sometimes we have been so socially anxious for so long that we have forgotten what we actually want to do and who we would like to become. Learning to fantasize and imagine how things might be if you could find a way of dealing with your social anxiety can be an important first step in discovering this. After all, what's the point of taking on your anxiety—which can be difficult and hard going at first—if there is no reason to? It is important for us to think about *why* we want to change and what it is that really matters to us—what our values are. At the shyness clinic, we and our clients all ask ourselves during our work in group, Who *do I want to be?* How *do I want to be?* What we're trying to pinpoint is what things we would do that (within the law, of course!) could give us pleasure if we could do them, what sort of lives we would lead; this helps us to home in on what we really want and the way we would really like to be.

Avoiding Emotional Exhaustion

When people feel insecure, they can spend a lot of time either trying to impress other people with their achievements or just being nice and doing things for others. Because they don't feel secure and valuable within themselves, they are constantly trying to win approval or admiration from others. Unfortunately, this only works temporarily at best, so they can become exhausted and depressed by their repeated efforts to impress or please. When you talk to these people, it often becomes clear that they are not kind to themselves; in fact, they are typically quite critical of themselves, and believe they're not good enough and must prove themselves to others. Some, though by no means all, have a history of shyness and social anxiety, and have had bad experiences with others where they haven't really felt comfortable or accepted for themselves. So now they strive to impress others in order to avoid rejection. In therapy, the first step for them is often to learn how to develop kindness toward themselves and self-acceptance.

Constantly trying to impress other people and do things to please them can exhaust the activating emotional system in the brain. Once we recognize this—that a brain system can become exhausted—rather than just thinking all our efforts are getting nowhere, we can start to think of ways to help it become more active again. If we just criticize ourselves when we get tired of pushing so hard and think that others don't experience these things, it will just make things worse. Coming down hard on yourself is no way to restore your enthusiasm and renew your energy.

One way to restore an exhausted emotional system can be to rest, of course. If that doesn't help, another way is to create situations that can stimulate the activating system by going after positive stimuli, maybe taking walks or swimming (exercise always helps), or going to museums, films, or plays. Or we can concentrate on the soothing system by focusing on the little things we like day to day. This might be something as simple as the first cup of coffee in the morning—maybe as we look out the window at the birds at a feeder, or as we stop by the local coffee shop on the way to work and take a minute to look at the green lawns of the houses nearby or at flowers blooming in someone's front garden. It could be the feel of a warm spring day after cold weather, the sound or feel of rain, or thoughts of a friend or of how you feel when someone you love (young or old) gets tickled about a small thing, like a new toy or a joke. These things soothe us, and by homing in on them we can learn to refocus our attention on these when we're upset. Later on in this book, we'll talk about how to design a program that stimulates this system.

THE PERILS OF THINKING AHEAD

So now we can see how our brains work with these three different emotional systems, and how humans and other animals operate similarly in some ways. One of the key *differences* between humans and other animals, though, is that we can form mental images, think about the future, and plan. This is clearly helpful: it means we can identify goals and work toward them, study for exams, prepare for a job interview, or think what we would like in a suitable mate. Of course, there's a down side to this capacity to imagine and plan. We are sophisticated enough not only to invent computers and robots, but also to develop weapons that kill millions, often indiscriminately. On the positive side, we can plan with other people and dream of future scenarios with our partners. We can make adventurous expeditions, compose music, and invent plots for novels. We have a sense of being alive and being conscious. We can create identities for ourselves as urbanites or country dwellers, scientists or artists, sportspeople or politicians. However, we can also dream up very negative scenarios, such as being alone forever, never finding a mate, never having a good job. Our brains can generate, and focus on, either positive or negative feelings and thoughts.

Imagine a situation where you are feeling socially anxious at work, and someone in your group is always bullying and criticizing you. What happens inside you now is that you start to produce more of the stress hormone cortisol. This triggers the threat system in your brain and you feel more upset, perhaps shaky or even panicky. Now—and this is important!—our own self-critical thoughts, particularly when they are shaming and harsh, *can do the same thing* as that external bullying critic, with *the same physical results*—just as you can stimulate your own sexual system. If we're constantly criticizing or bullying ourselves, we are repeatedly stimulating our threat system. We may do this because we've been criticized in the past, and didn't stop to think whether the person cared about us, whether the criticism was accurate or reasonable, or whether that other person might have problems herself that were leading her to criticize others. If we are working hard to reach a particular standard or outcome and aren't where we would like to be, we may think we are letting ourselves down and criticize ourselves, as well as think that others will be critical and rejecting. Now we are stimulating our own threat system and affecting our brains. And the more frequent the criticism, the more that brain system is stimulated.

I'm reminded of a shy client, Anne, who worked in the IT department of a large corporation and felt threatened knowing that there were layoffs coming up. A lot of jobs were going to have to go, so it was natural to be nervous. Anne watched her colleagues like a hawk, thinking that any sign of rejection would mean that everyone thought she would be the one to go from her team. There was one person at work in particular, quite a dominant and critical person, who snapped at her, and that made it worse. Anne thought about her programming skills and dwelled on the fact that they weren't perfect. It was hard for her to resist going over and over all the ways in which she could be found wanting. When she remembered that her critic had put another team member down recently, it just made him seem even more powerful and threatening.

When Anne shared her fears with her shyness group, the other members understood her fear and could identify with it. They reminded her that she'd been working at the same corporation for nearly thirty years, and said that the conscientiousness they saw in her in the group must be visible at work as well. But because Anne's threat system was strongly activated, while she listened to what the others said, afterward her worries surfaced again. The group heard her out and then, once more, acknowledged the strength and capabilities they saw in her. They also said that the colleague who had snapped at her sounded more "stressed out" than she did, and wondered if that might be one of the reasons he was being irritable with people. They also suggested she might go to her human resources department and ask them where she would stand financially if she did get laid off, thinking that might calm her fears a little. She then said she did have a fair amount saved and that, if she did lose her job, she thought she would retrain as a librarian. She loved reading and was already a volunteer at a local library. Thus, as the group supported her, she began to feel soothed and was able to explore alternatives.

CULTIVATING COMPASSION

Using Anne's case, and the earlier hypothetical example of the kind teacher, we can see how we might be able to stimulate our own kindness and soothing system. If we can be kind and supportive to ourselves, focus on our strengths and successes when things are hard, and be gentle with ourselves when we need extra practice, we can stimulate those parts of our brain that respond to kindness, and soothe ourselves. As you read on through this book, you will learn how to deliberately use compassionate thinking, behavior, imagery, and emotion to soothe yourself and rebalance the emotional systems in your brain.

Sometimes, people who are highly critical of themselves can find the very idea of being compassionate to themselves threatening. To some of these people, being kind to yourself, even wanting kindness at all, seems to be a weakness or an indulgence. I've had these thoughts myself at times, particularly when I have felt I wasn't getting as much accomplished as I would have liked. When we feel this way, we need to start retraining our minds, working through our reluctance and fear.

There is a growing body of evidence that compassion and kindness toward yourself improve your ability to cope under stress and your wellbeing in general. Kristin Neff, one of the early researchers to study self-compassion, has a helpful website at www.self-compassion.org. There is a questionnaire on the site to measure how compassionate you are toward yourself, along with suggestions for increasing your self-compassion. In 2007 Paul Gilbert founded the Compassionate Mind Foundation in Derby, UK, to support the study of compassion. You can find details of the foundation's website and its work in the "Helpful Organizations and Websites" section at the back of this book.

Self-compassion is not the same thing as self-esteem. Self-esteem is a regard for yourself as a person, often boosted by achievement and performance. Self-compassion is a deep awareness of your own suffering, accompanied by the same wish to relieve it that you would feel if someone else were suffering. At the shyness clinic we distinguish between self-esteem and self-acceptance, and help clients focus on self-acceptance, because self-esteem tends to go up and down with whatever successes or failures people are having at the moment. One interesting point about self-esteem, by the way, is that there is *no relationship* between self-esteem and actual competence!

Many people who have high self-esteem are not actually supercompetent, but give themselves credit for what they do accomplish. And we all know people who are very self-confident and high in self-esteem with very little apparent reason to be so on the basis of any obvious measure of success or performance. On the other hand, I have seen many very accomplished people at the shyness clinic who are nonetheless low in self-esteem, partly because they have had very high expectations of themselves and, at the same time, have tended to underestimate themselves. So at the clinic we focus on self-acceptance, the ability to accept ourselves regardless of what we achieve, socially or otherwise, just as a good and loyal friend would do—because, let's face it, none of us does well all the time.

Self-compassion takes self-acceptance further, focusing on our shared humanity and shared struggles. Often, when people come to the clinic, they don't realize that their worries and self-criticisms are similar to everyone else's; they just don't think other people have the same thoughts and feelings. We know, though, that we all do, so the first thing we do as therapists is to share some of our own worries and negative thoughts, so clients can see that we are all in this together.

Our brains have been designed to respond to kindness. It is not self-indulgent to be kind to ourselves. Training our brains with kindness is very like social and physical fitness training, or taking vitamins. It just means we are giving the brain the practice and nourishment to help it function in the best possible way.

One of the ways of being kind to ourselves is not to let the pain in the world overwhelm us. This is not to say that we need to be indifferent to it; we may feel deep sorrow about it, and the sorrow can help us to cultivate compassion for others as well as for ourselves and motivate us to help and contribute in ways that we can. But getting too far into our own personal distress doesn't help anyone else, and it doesn't help us either. Focusing on the good both helps us to feel better and energizes us to do good in the world—to others and to ourselves.

Read this sentence to yourself: There are people everywhere who are working to make the world a better place and to build trust among all peoples. Allow your face to relax into a gentle smile and focus on the sentence for a few moments. Notice what happens to your mood and how you feel.

Now focus for a few moments on this sentence instead: All over the world, millions of people are engaging in cruel and horrible acts toward each other. Notice what happens to your mood and how you feel now.

There is so much bad news in the world that it's all too easy to feel oppressed by it, to no good end. Fortunately, there is now an online magazine that focuses on just the good things that people are doing around the world. Contributors tell readers about the good things they see around them and the good things they do. You can simply sign up to receive it, or you can also contribute to it if you like. People tell each other about the good things they see in their own worlds, and can talk about the good things they do as well. There is also a website that reports on the evolution of human goodness and how it operates in our lives.

Let's just go back to where we began this chapter for a moment and remember together that social anxiety is a natural emotion in evolution. It is not something we do wrong, something to criticize ourselves for; it's just part of the design of our evolved brains. So we just need to train our brains to work in ways that support us and are compassionate to us when we feel scared or discouraged. If we can do this, we function better and are happier. We accept our shyness when it becomes a problem, and we don't let it get in the way of our goals and relationships.

We are going to talk a lot in this book about how to work with our shyness when it gets in our way. We are also going to be much more compassionate toward ourselves as we go along. We can take responsibility for realizing our goals while accepting our feelings, and we can do this without blaming ourselves.

KEY POINTS

- We all find ourselves in this life with a brain that we didn't design.
- Part of this brain, which we share with other animals, follows patterns of motivation and emotion that were designed millions of years ago to protect us by responding automatically and prompting us into rapid action.
- A more recently evolved part of the brain is capable of complex thought, including reflecting, ruminating, and fantasizing. This allows us to develop a sense of self, along with concerns about how we exist in the minds of others.
- Our brains have three basic emotional systems: a system that detects and tracks threat and responds to it; a system that involves feelings of motivation and desire; and a system that promotes feeling content, safe, and happy, especially in

relationships where we feel cared for and supported.

- The balance among these systems is not fixed. When we're being self-critical, we tend to activate a threat system; learning the art of self-kindness helps to redress the balance and stimulate the soothing system.

CHAPTER 3

Developing Your Compassionate Mind

So far we have explored the nature of shyness and how it can be both a help and a hindrance. We have also taken a first look at something that can help us enormously in dealing with our shyness: com passion. This chapter will look at what we mean by compassion. We will then go on in the following chapters to explore how we can use compassion with painful shyness and social anxiety to build a compassionate mind.

It's important to say right away that the approach to shyness set out in this book does not require you to hold any religious or spiritual belief. However, it's worth noting that many spiritual traditions have long suggested that compassion plays a key role in being able to develop happy relationships with others and happiness within ourselves. Over twenty-five hundred years ago, the Buddha came to realize that our minds are often chaotic, under the push and pull of various desires and anxieties that cause us deep unhappiness. A key element of his solution to this difficulty was the development of a compassionate mind.

Modern research has shown that developing compassion for ourselves and others does indeed have real and substantial effects on how our brains work, on our emotions and on the quality of our relationships.

WHAT IS COMPASSION?

At its simplest, compassion is an openness to the suffering of ourselves and others, linked to a commitment and motivation to try to reduce that suffering. From the beginning, then, it involves two key qualities: *openness and sensitivity* plus *motivation* (to reduce suffering). In the Buddhist tradition, there is also an emphasis on *skillfulness:* the need to understand the nature of suffering and how we can work to relieve it.

The "compassionate mind" approach adopted in this book, on which compassion-focused therapy is based, draws on Buddhist thinking and gives a central place to these three aspects of compassion. However, it also draws on new scientific thinking about our minds, about how they work and how they are influenced by different processes linked to the way our human brains have evolved.

The Anxious Mind in Action

We can begin by recognizing that our brains are wired so that they can be in different states and take on or develop different patterns. When the brain or mind is in a particular state, our attention, thinking, behavior, and emotions are all affected, along with our motivation and imagination, so that they may all be different from how they will be when our mind is in a different state.

For example, look at figure 3.1. This sets out two types of brain patterns, that is, two types of mind, which we can compare and contrast. We can call these *threatened/anxious mind* and *compassionate mind.*

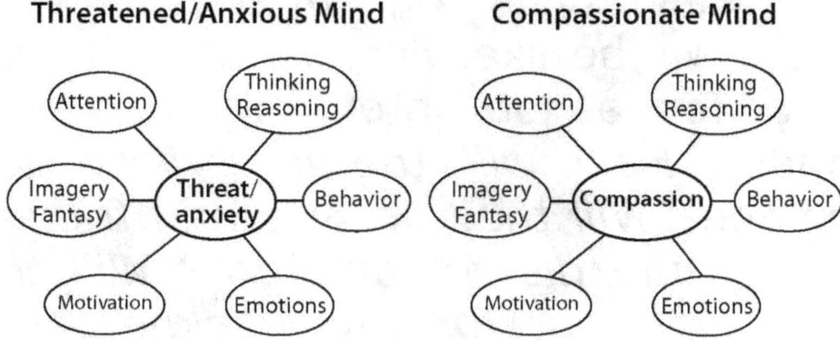

Figure 3.1 The threatened mind and the compassionate mind

Imagine that you are feeling very shy or socially anxious; perhaps you're getting ready for a party where there will be people you want to get to know, or perhaps you are going for a job interview. These kinds of events are naturally likely to bring our threat system into action because, remember, it's there to detect and help us respond quickly to threats or avoid them. So even before the party or interview takes place, our threat mind is working for us, and it may well start to switch on an anxious pattern. So let's look at how this pattern takes shape by going around the circle.

In an anxious pattern, what are the things we *attend to* and focus on? We may well focus on what the other people will be like. For example, if we're going for a job interview, we might wonder, *How will the interviewers be with me? Will they be nice and friendly, or cold and distant or stern? Will they be looking out for my weaknesses or difficulties, or will they listen and encourage me when I talk about my strengths?* We might have intrusive images or thoughts about previous occasions when things have not gone so well.

How are we *thinking and reasoning?* Are we thinking how well we will do, how good and impressive our presentation might be? Well, before the event, if we're very anxious, probably not. It's more likely that we're thinking that we might not come across very well or make a good impression, that we might not present ourselves at our best. Then we reason that other people might see that we're anxious and take a rather dim view of us as a result, or that someone else is bound to do better than we do and get the job. So our thinking, reasoning, and ruminating are focused on the possible *threats* in the situation.

What about what our bodies want to do? What *behavior* does our threat system push us toward? Now, you may want to go to that interview because it's a good job, just right for you with pay. However, another part of you would rather not have to face it and wants to avoid going. Indeed, if you suffer from a lot of shyness and anxiety, you might not even apply for the job in the first place or might wonder why on earth you did! So when the anxious mind is revved up, it can fill us with strong urges to run away and avoid things.

As for the *emotions* of our anxious minds, these can be simple or complex. If it is only social anxiety we feel, that is reasonably straightforward, albeit unpleasant; but sometimes we can have mixed emotions, both wanting to engage others and being frightened to engage, so that positive desires to meet and get to know other people pull against protective ones that push us away from social events. Indeed, it's often the case that the more badly we want to meet or to be with someone, the more anxious we are! You might also remember times when, after becoming anxious about things you wanted to do, you then became angry with yourself for getting anxious, or annoyed or disappointed with yourself for feeling shy in a social situation. We can get angry at that anxiety or shyness because we feel that it holds us back or that we are different from other people. It's easy to imagine how getting angry with ourselves gives an extra stimulus and push to our threat system. We now have two threat emotions to cope with—not only anxiety, but anger as well! We certainly don't feel comfortable, calm, or soothed.

The same applies to our *motives:* our basic desires, wants, and wishes. Here, too, we can be pushed in two different directions by two types of motives: the motive to deal with our immediate feelings and the situation we're encountering in the moment, and the motive to achieve our long-term goals and to have a better future. So our immediate motivation under the pressure of anxiety may be to run away and avoid the interview altogether. We are motivated to reduce our anxiety and remove any possible threat as quickly as possible. Afterward, though, we may well feel sad because we've missed an opportunity. And then, once again, we might go into self-recriminations and criticism.

In the last bubble in our pattern of the threatened and anxious mind, but by no means the least, are *imagery and fantasy,* that is, the images and pictures we create in our minds. When we become socially anxious, we might find images of previous anxiety-laden memories or future threatening possibilities flitting through our minds. For example, we might see a mental picture of ourselves sitting in a chair in front of the interview panel feeling a bit dumbstruck and looking awkward, as the interviewers look at us with cold and aloof, unreadable faces. When we are socially anxious, we do tend to imagine others taking negative views of us, and often imagine these negative perceptions in quite a lot of detail. We might, for example, imagine the interviewer saying, "Thanks for coming, but I don't think you are the person we need for this position." We'd get a sinking feeling just imagining this, and then dwell on those words and brood. The more these kinds of images play through our minds, the more our threat system will react to them.

So the threatened/anxious mind pulls on all these different aspects of our being to create a pattern. Notice, too, that different elements in this pattern feed each other. For example, the images that we create in our minds will affect what we pay attention to, what we think, how we feel, and how we behave; recall the example in the previous chapter of how our bodies react when we imagine something sexy. Likewise, the way we ruminate and reason about the feared situation will affect our attention, feelings, motivation, and behavior. This is why we can call this state of mind an anxious *mind,* because it is about many aspects of the mind working together with the sole purpose of trying to deal with what we perceive to be a threat. The fact that these elements can excite one another and push you along the road to more social anxiety is important: your thinking can drive and escalate your anxiety feelings, and your anxiety feelings can, in turn, drive more anxious thinking.

Now remember: *none of this is your fault.* We have very tricky brains to deal with, thanks to evolution. On top of that, you may have a propensity to social anxiety and problematic shyness because of things that happened or ways people treated you in your early life. Perhaps you had teachers or parents who were critical or harsh, or who tried to make you extroverted rather than introverted, or perhaps you were bullied at school or at work, or perhaps you had to deal with many setbacks. All these experiences may have made you especially sensitive to real or imagined criticism. However, the good news is that although your sensitivity and fear are not your fault, it is possible to begin to take more control and drive your mind in the direction you want it to go, rather than let your threat system run the show.

TAKING CONTROL: UNDERSTANDING AND COMPASSION

So how do we begin to take control, then? Well, you have already taken the first step by becoming more aware of how your threatened/anxious mind works in you. From there you can go on to recognize it—become "mindful" of it—as it arises in you, acknowledge it as part of the threat system, and learn to take steps to activate a different type of mind that can counteract the social anxiety produced and fed by the anxious mind.

You have probably guessed already what I'm going to say. This different type of mind that can really help us cope with the socially anxious and painfully shy mind is the *compassionate mind.* Now in some ways this has been understood for a very long time indeed. As I've mentioned we can trace these ideas back over twenty-five hundred years. The Buddha understood that the *cultivation of compassion* often had soothing effects on the mind and increased soothing qualities within the self. Much more recently in the West, a group of psychotherapists called *behavior therapists* (who focus on changing our behavior, including our thoughts) also came to realize that we can generate one emotion in order to dissipate another. That is, they suggested, if we learn to relax, we will become less anxious, because the state of relaxation cannot coexist with the state of high anxiety. This led to treatments for anxiety that include paying attention to breathing and deliberately slowing everything down while we imagine a stressful social situation. Thus, in the early days of working with anxiety, learning techniques for relaxation became part of learning to cope with anxiety.

Today we focus much more on learning to accept and tolerate anxiety, and on realizing that although it is unpleasant, there is no need to be frightened of it. But it is still sometimes helpful to learn that the way we breathe or tense our bodies—perhaps without even being aware of it—can increase our anxiety unnecessarily. The key point is that we can learn to generate helpful states of mind (in particular, compassion) that prevent the unhelpful, anxious mind from governing our feelings, behavior, and action. So our learning how to deal with anxiety goes along two paths. On one path we learn to understand anxiety—what contributes to our anxiety, what we can do to avoid contributing to it (such as dwelling on the threat-focused thoughts)—and to tolerate it; and on the second path we learn that tolerating and accepting anxiety become easier if we develop compassion for ourselves rather than become critical or irritable with ourselves for being anxious.

THE COMPASSIONATE MIND IN ACTION

So what do you think would happen if you learned how to compassionately refocus your mind whenever you felt very shy and anxious? Might this help? Could you train your mind to cope better with problematic and chronic shyness? And if so, what is the best way to refocus? What should you focus on? This section will help you form your answers to these questions.

First, though, you might like to stop and think about what a compassionate mind would be for you. Go back to figure 3.1 and look at the other half of it, the "compassion" circle, and think of each element in turn. This will build a picture of what your mind would be like if you focused it on compassion.

What would the compassionate mind pay *attention* to? You might bring to mind times when you were successful, times when you got along well with other people; you might remember a time when some people were kind.

Compassionate *reasoning* is focusing on understanding that chronic shyness and social anxiety are very common problems, and acknowledging that we all suffer from social anxiety to a greater or lesser degree because of the kind of brain we have; evolution has given us a really tricky brain to deal with. This is an important compassionate insight. We might also remember that although too much shyness can have a downside, there are also many positive aspects to shyness.

Compassionate *behavior* can often be about developing courage and learning how to engage with things even when we are frightened to do so. With compassion we can encourage ourselves to do things we want to do but are scared to do, and to learn more about problematic shyness, social anxiety, and coping. Focusing on the example of the job interview we looked at previously, we might learn job interview skills, to make sure we are as well prepared as possible for the next opportunity. Or we might focus on developing skills for social occasions or skills in public speaking. The key point here is that we are doing these things not to demand more of ourselves but to nurture ourselves. We might learn that it is best to practice slowly, to go one step at a time from trying out our new skills in lower-key situations at first and gradually working up to the most challenging situation we can imagine ourselves in. For example, we might acknowledge that it is best to get skills like assertiveness in place before we need them. After all, if you're learning to swim, it's not helpful to learn in the open sea in a storm—much better to gain confidence at the shallow end of a warm swimming pool. It seems obvious, but sometimes when we are very shy, we don't want to think about challenging situations in advance, so we don't prepare for them by rehearsing useful skills.

Compassionate *emotions* are linked to feelings of warmth, support, kindness, and connection. If you try to give yourself encouraging thoughts, are you able to hear them in your mind and feel kindness and warmth in them? For example, if you're going to an interview and you think to yourself, *I have done this before and if I'm not successful this time it will be disappointing, but I can cope,* do you hear that in a genuinely kind and concerned tone or in a kind of *Pull yourself together and stop being silly and getting into a state* tone? The emotions we generate can affect how helpful our thoughts are as we hear them in our minds. So it is well worth trying to create compassionate tones and feelings in our minds when we are trying to support ourselves. The exercises in this book will give you lots of practice in doing this.

Compassionate *motives* are those that contribute to the overarching aim of relieving suffering. Now, you might think that the best way to relieve suffering if you're anxious is simply to avoid what makes you anxious—then there will be no more anxiety! The problem is that this just sets up another source of suffering: the regret and frustration that you have not been able to achieve what you wanted or do what you wanted to do. Remember the section of chapter 2 where we discussed what you really want? With compassion you can give yourself the space to be honest, to think about what your true values are, what kind of person you really want to be, and how you might bring that about. Later on in the book, we will work through some exercises to help you in this, but for the moment, it's enough to recognize that compassionate motives are about harnessing the inner desire to reduce our suffering, whether that be social anxiety itself or the consequences of social anxiety, such as avoiding things you really want to do.

Compassionate *images* are supportive, understanding, kind, and encouraging. When we are anxious, it is very easy to generate frightening images and self-critical ones. But we can make deliberate and trained efforts to create different types of images in our minds, and in this way stimulate different brain systems, especially the soothing system that we discussed in chapter 2.

Holding our focus on compassion takes a bit of effort, of course, especially at first, because the threat mind will try to pull you back to feeling threatened and anxious. That's its job, of course, what evolution designed it to do, and it isn't your enemy—after all, it's only trying to protect you! But compassion offers you another way to protect yourself. Developing compassion doesn't necessarily get rid of anxious mind, but I believe it can help us cope better and find a better balance between the emotional systems in the brain. When the threat system is in charge, it's as if we're in a canoe without a paddle on a fast-flowing river with rapids; compassion can help us to find paddles and start to direct our canoe so that it is more under our control, even while we are anxious.

COMPASSIONATE MIND: THE BIGGER PICTURE

We are now ready to explore the notion of the compassionate mind in a little more detail. We have already touched on the interesting questions of why we should want to be compassionate. The short answer is that the impulse to show compassion comes from our capacities and motives to care for one another; and these have developed in us through evolution. We look after our babies and children because, over thousands of years, this has helped our species to reproduce and thrive. So we care for our children; we enjoy seeing them grow and develop, and we become unhappy if they are in pain or distress. As children we begin to recognize that we can have these feelings for other people outside our families, especially people we like, and these people become our friends. We enjoy seeing them happy and are distressed if they are hurt or unhappy.

This is not to say that at times some of us are also not very selfish, critical, and cruel, because clearly we can be and sometimes are. But the key point is that as a species, we are highly motivated to care for at least some others.

Interestingly, it is usually when the threat system raises its head that we might be most likely to turn away from caring. We are less likely to have caring feelings for those who frighten us, those we feel are more powerful than we are and are likely to abuse that power, or those we don't like. Our attitudes toward people in these categories are often wary, protective, and defensive, and that, of course, turns off our interest in compassionate caring! We bomb our enemies and do not care for or about them. As we will see later, the same is true when it comes to relating to and thinking about ourselves. If we are angry with ourselves and critical toward ourselves, we turn off our caring and soothing motives and emotions—the very feelings that we need to help combat our threat system!

Clearly, our motives for caring and not caring, for kindness and cruelty, are complex. However, all we need to do here is to understand that compassion has deep roots in the human mind, and to learn how to harness it and apply it to helping us deal with problem shyness and social anxiety. A useful mechanism here that I'm going to introduce to you now is the "compassion circle" developed by Paul Gilbert, who drew, in turn, on the research and ideas of many other people and traditions.

The full circle is shown in figure 3.2. Don't be put off if it looks a bit complicated: we've already gone through many of the key elements. The key new point is the separation between compassionate *attributes* and compassionate *skills.* The attributes are what power compassion along; the skills are the ways we learn to harness and apply those attributes. The skills (in the outer ellipse of the figure) fall into the categories we've discussed previously in looking at "The Compassionate Mind in

Action"; here I'm going to focus on the attributes.

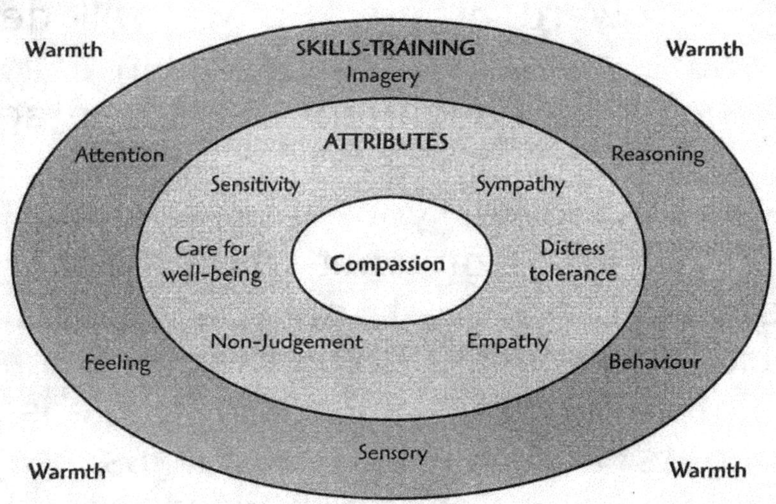

Figure 3.2 The Compassion Circle Adapted with kind permission from Paul Gilbert, The Compassionate Mind (London: Constable, 2009).

Motivation

Beginning on the left-hand side of the inner ellipse, we see "care for well-being." This phrase captures the *motives to be caring:* the decision and commitment that we do wish to relieve suffering, in ourselves and others. Clearly, there may be some of you who find it hard to imagine developing a caring and compassionate approach to your problematic shyness and social anxiety, or feel no interest in this approach, even though you may be caring toward others. So we will need to address that. You might begin to look at the advantages and disadvantages of becoming compassionate, to ask yourself whether you have anything to lose in trying; or whether perhaps you feel you can't do it, so you've already decided against it; whether you have so many angry or other unpleasant thoughts and fantasies you just can't imagine being caring toward yourself. And maybe you also find it hard to be caring toward others, although we've found that difficulty unusual at the shyness clinic: even when people were very aware of feeling angry, mistrustful, and resentful, their behavior toward others tended to be cooperative and not hurtful.

In any case, all humans have difficult feelings and fantasies; whatever applies in your own case, that does not make you in any way less *able* to be caring. It's just that you might have to focus on that ability and develop it.

Sensitivity

Moving clockwise round the inner ellipse of figure 3.2, we next come to *sensitivity,* which refers to the attribute of being open in your attention, learning to pay attention and notice when you or others are in distress. This is very characteristic of shy people, who, unless very distressed, tend to be very alive to the signs that others are in distress. But sometimes—this is more common when we feel depressed as well as shy—when we feel distressed ourselves, we try not to notice it. We try to avoid our painful feelings because we "don't want to go there." Also, when we become anxious, we can become angry with ourselves —*Oh, for heaven's sake, here I go again. Why am I so shy? What's the matter with me? Why can't I be likeother people?*—rather than being sensitive, gentle, and understanding. We sometimes say unpleasant things to ourselves that we wouldn't dream of saying to another person who was feeling painfully shy. In that case, if we're honest, we lack sensitivity to our shyness.

Sympathy

The next attribute in figure 3.2 is *sympathy.* Some people think this is a bad thing, that it's like indulging, feeling sorry for, or (even worse) pitying yourself or others. That is a *big* misunderstanding of sympathy. Sympathy is simply the ability to be emotionally moved. Suppose you see a three-year-old child happily toddling down the street with her mother. You smile at her happiness; but then she trips over and bangs her head hard and is really hurt. Her laughter turns to tears of intense pain. Immediately, we have a flash of sadness and anxiety that we feel in the stomach, and we want to rush out, hold her, and somehow make it better. Sympathy is that *emotional connection to pain.* It arises without thought; we are moved immediately. Developing self-sympathy can sound more difficult, but it's the same principle. Just as we can learn to be sensitive and open to our emotions, we can learn to allow ourselves to be moved by our difficulties. We can have sympathy for our social anxiety rather than feel angry with ourselves for feeling anxious and inferior.

Distress Tolerance

We've seen how, when the threat system controls us, it can push us into avoidance. We've also mentioned how avoiding challenges, though it might bring relief from anxiety in the short term, doesn't help in the long term. In fact, the inability to accept and tolerate painful or frightening emotions and the situations that ignite them—the lack of *distress tolerance*—is at the root of many of our difficulties. The problem is that if we avoid those feelings and situations, we don't learn to tolerate and work with our difficult feelings, and we don't learn the skills for coping with difficult situations. Worse still, a vicious cycle gets set up: it is in the cruel nature of things that avoidance actually *strengthens the power of anxiety.* That is, the more you avoid what makes you anxious, the more powerful your anxiety tends to become. So learning how to tolerate social anxiety can be very important in helping us cope with challenging situations.

It is important to remember that you can be highly anxious and perform well at the same time. The first thirteen weeks of social fitness training is devoted to role-playing situations *while* you feel anxious. We call this *exposure to feared situations,* and it's the most effective element of treatment for painful shyness and social anxiety disorder. We ask people to rate their anxiety levels before and after practicing with a challenging situation. Their ratings in highly challenging situations often start at around 90 on a scale that goes from 0 to 100. But by the time they have gone through a ten-minute practice session—for example, asking for a date, giving a talk, or interviewing for a job—the anxiety level has often come down to 20 or 30. What has happened is that the person has realized that he can function socially, even though the anxiety hasn't gone away.

Now, sometimes levels of anxiety don't drop so dramatically during an exercise. Sometimes they only come down five or ten points at first, and it might take a number of role-plays to bring them down any further. Sometimes they even go up before they come down, and we warn people that this can happen. But persistence pays off. What is happening is this: you are learning that *you can tolerate your social anxiety and perform well anyway.* People are often astonished to find that volunteers who are taking part in the role-play are often unaware of the level of anxiety they are feeling. The point I'm making here is that it is possible, with practice, to learn to tolerate distress. And compassion helps us with this by teaching us to accept our anxiety without anger or criticism.

Learning to tolerate distress may seem a strange idea if compassion is all about reducing suffering. So it's worth pausing to look at another example of why it matters, taking the example of parents and children, which will also remind us of how we can become intolerant of distress. You might remember from chapter 1 that very socially anxious children often have highly anxious parents. Usually to avoid their own anxiety, these parents are overprotective and try to prevent the child from any upset, anxiety, or pain. For example, a child may become anxious about going to a party with children she doesn't know very well, so the parents keep her at home. Unintentionally, they are teaching their child a number of things: first, that painful emotions are not to be tolerated; second, that painful emotions will overwhelm you; and third, that the right thing to do is avoid the event and thereby the painful feelings. To sum up, the child is taught that avoidance is the best strategy, instead of that going to more parties and getting to know new friends will lessen anxiety in the long run. Because the child avoided the first party, she didn't become familiar with the other children, so what is she likely to do the next time there's a party with those children? Moreover, what will the child who invited her feel? Will his feelings be hurt, or will he assume the child doesn't want to be friends and not invite her next time? And how will that make the overprotected child feel? Sadly, without intending to, these parents are not helping their child to understand how her own mind works, or how to face up to and cope with difficult feelings and situations. Sometimes parents have to learn to tolerate their own anxiety before they can help their children, which is sometimes very challenging. But you see the point: compassion is not about providing temporary relief through avoidance; it's about doing those things that are genuinely helpful in the long term. It is developing courage through our compassion.

I have a friend who, as a teenager, felt very shy at parties. He went to a boys' prep school and felt terrified when he had to talk to teenage girls. He would push himself to ask a girl to go out with him, and then when the time came, he would leave the house feeling nauseated and wondering if he was actually going to throw up. His mother would walk him to the door, and as he hesitated, she would simply say, "She's waiting." And, while parties continued to be a challenge—and sometimes they still are—he now knows he can manage and he usually enjoys them once he gets there. I know his mother, and I know it was hard for her to see him be anxious, but I can still see her determined calm face in my mind. She knew what would make him happier in the long run.

Another reason why it's worth emphasizing the importance of tolerating distress is because sometimes people think that compassion is about *soothing painful feelings away,* that is, getting rid of them. Now, of course, sometimes we can soothe painful feelings away, but that's not always possible or desirable. If we are very angry about something, we may need to learn how to deal with the anger, to be honest about our feelings and fantasies while being kind, and to be assertive. Compassion is not about refusing to address issues. The Dalai Lama, for example, has been very tough with the Chinese, who pushed him out of Tibet. Jesus Christ became very angry with the moneylenders who were using the church to make money. Sometimes we must learn how to tolerate our powerful feelings—even hateful thoughts and our feelings of hatred—rather than suppress or hide them or pretend we don't have them. While brutal honesty all the time is not helpful, neither are suppression and denial.

Of course, this is not an excuse to be rude or unpleasant. Angry feelings often need to be shared because they interfere with friendship and intimacy, and they can be shared in a loving way. There are many ways to be assertive, respectful, and strong at the same time. There are also times when an angry outburst just shoots out of our mouths unannounced, unexpected either by ourselves or others—and this usually happens when we have been suppressing feelings. Sometimes we don't know how strongly we feel about something until this happens. Outbursts like this don't have to be a disaster; afterward we can take a problem-solving approach and sort things out calmly, being assertive rather than aggressive. However, if we tend to let things build up like this, we can become very critical of ourselves for allowing the outburst to happen, so instead of addressing the underlying problem, we put the lid back on our feelings, which start to build up again. So we're into a vicious cycle. Compassion helps us recognize that conflicts are common and an important part of growth: they're not something to be avoided but something we can learn to tolerate and work with. When you suppress your emotions to avoid open conflict—because you find it very difficult to tolerate them or are frightened of them, and you try not to let others see them—you are stopping a potential growth process.

Empathy

Empathy is the ability to think about and understand the nature of our minds and those of others. Unlike other animals, we recognize that people do things for reasons: because they want things and have desires, because they're anxious or angry, because they might not know the full picture of a situation, because they are motivated to do them—sometimes unconsciously. We recognize that people can be mistaken in their views (particularly when they disagree with us!), and can have false beliefs or be ignorant in relation to something others know about.

And, just as we can understand the minds of others like this, we can come to understand our own. We can reflect on and think about how our minds work. Through empathy, we can understand the nature of shyness and how it can become problematic; we understand that it is a universal emotion that has evolved in us because it is useful to us, and it only gets in our way when it becomes too intense and constant. We can also understand how our own personal social anxiety may have developed, the situations that can make it worse, and the kinds of things we do when we feel uncomfortably shy or socially anxious. It's our empathy, our ability to grasp how our minds work and how social anxiety is operating within us, that forms the basis of our compassion.

Nonjudgment

Last but not least comes the attribute of nonjudgment. What this means is not rushing to condemn; it means letting go of that angry desire to attack and be critical. It is also an essential part of what we will call "mindfulness" (more on this in the next chapter). The more we ease back from charging in and criticizing, which can sometimes be our immediate reaction to things that happen within us and around us, the more chance we have for reflection and thinking about how best to deal with whatever has happened. The more we rush to judge our problematic shyness and social anxiety, the more difficult it may be to develop tolerance and acceptance and to work with it.

THE COMPASSION CIRCLE

So there you have it, the compassion circle. If you take a look back at figure 3.2 now, you will see all the compassionate attributes we have just been talking about in the inner ring, and the compassionate skills we explored in the first part of the chapter in the outer ring. You can probably see how the attributes all build on and help the development of one another. So the more motivation you have to become compassionate and the more you can develop, the more strongly the other attributes may emerge. Equally, the more sensitive or the more empathic you become to your problematic shyness and social anxiety, the more motivation you will have to be compassionate. So in the chapters to come, we will work on this family of attributes, encouraging them to build on each other.

The same is true of the compassionate skills. We can develop these skills in ourselves. We train ourselves to create and build images that are helpful and compassionate, and designed to stimulate the soothing system. We can develop our reasoning skills and our thinking to focus on experiences compassionately. We can train ourselves in compassionate behavior, that is, to act in ways that are in our long-term interests and are compassionate toward ourselves and others. We can train our bodies to experience compassionate sensations (for example, by using imagery in ways we will be exploring later). We can use our images and other ideas to generate compassionate feelings. And last but not least, we can practice compassionate attention; that is, we can *consciously direct our attention,* looking for our own helpful and supportive images and thoughts, and the helpful and supportive behavior of others, rather than letting the threat system continually direct us toward the things we are frightened of or angry about.

You have probably noticed by now that within the compassionate mind approach we are very interested in circles. This is because we want to get across the notion of interactions, with attributes and skills influencing and building on each other. But it's also appropriate because circles are symbolic of wholeness and compassion, as represented, for example, in the mandalas of the Buddhist tradition.

Although we have explored how different mind states can block out each other (so that, for example, an anxious mind can turn off compassion), this is not to say that even painfully shy people are not compassionate: they are as compassionate as anyone else when not caught up in intense social anxiety.

Indeed, shyness in children often goes with sympathy for schoolmates. What it does mean is that focusing on compassion can be helpful in coping with problematic shyness.

KEY POINTS

- This chapter has given you an overview of a way to think about compassion.
- We can see it simply in terms of an openness and sensitivity to our own and other people's distress, with a sense of commitment to relieve that distress.
- However, we can also see that it is made up of different elements, and that we can train ourselves to develop a compassionate mind.
- In the next chapters this is exactly what we are going to do, because we will explore all of these elements as they apply to helping you with painful shyness and social anxiety.

CHAPTER 4

Switching Our Minds to Kindness and Compassion

In this chapter I will describe how to begin the process of turning the mind toward compassion by introducing the idea of mindfulness and exploring how you can begin to use it in your everyday life.

This chapter and the ones that follow contain practical exercises for you to try that will help you to focus on compassion and prepare you to work compassionately with shyness. In this chapter we will begin with some straightforward exercises in mindful breathing, relaxation, and sensory focus.

SOME PRACTICAL PREPARATIONS

You may want to start by buying a notebook or folder in which you can keep notes about your reactions to exercises, your customary thoughts and any insights that emerge, and ways you might respond differently or are already responding differently to particular thoughts or events in your life. You can think of this as your "compassion journal." Writing things down helps us to "hear" ourselves better, and particularly allows us to pay attention to thoughts and feelings that are less close to the surface. It also helps us to clarify our values and attitudes.

You may also want to gather relevant poetry, articles, sayings, and pictures. It's important to collect not only those related to sensitivity, shyness, and social anxiety, but also those related to pleasant or exciting social interactions, and to the ways you want to be in life when you have reduced your problematic shyness and social anxiety and are kind and compassionate toward yourself. All these you can add to your folder or journal.

INTRODUCING MINDFULNESS

One of the most important skills we will learn in relation to developing compassion is *mindfulness.* Mindfulness simply means being aware in each moment. It means paying attention to whatever is in our field of awareness right now, whether it is something in our immediate environment or something that is happening internally, in our minds and bodies. You've probably experienced it when walking in the woods or pausing by a quiet pond or lake, perhaps sitting in the garden with your first cup of coffee in the morning, listening to the birds singing. You are suddenly completely absorbed. No thoughts or emotions distract you. The most important quality of mindfulness is being aware without judging, simply observing what is happening inside and outside our bodies and minds in this moment.

Take a few moments now and remember a time when you felt completely absorbed in the moment, with no distracting thoughts or emotions; when you felt in tune with your surroundings and fully present in the moment. As you come back to the present, notice your calm feelings, the sensations in your body, your quiet and steady breathing.

Developing a New Relationship with Our Old Brains

The idea is to develop a new relationship with the old brain and its emotions, senses, cravings, desires, and aversions. You probably notice that when we start to worry about problematic shyness and what is going to happen in the future (maybe that we won't be able to get a date with someone we like, or do well in that job interview), or focus on disappointments or sadness about past social situations (where we didn't say no to an unreasonable request or speak up in that meeting, or had nothing to say at a party), we lose the present moment. And the present moment is, after all, the only moment we ever have. This doesn't mean that we won't deliberately focus on the past or the present in order to learn from experience or practice and plan for the future; it simply means that we won't be automatically thrown backward and forward in time by our thoughts and feelings.

Becoming Aware of Our Thoughts, Emotions, and Bodily Sensations

Through mindfulness we can also learn to be aware of our thoughts, emotions, and bodily sensations while we are caught up in social anxiety, frustration, and fear. How many times have you checked in with your body and mind when you were in these states to see where the emotion was coming from? To see what part of the mind was directing the catastrophic fears and worry? For most of us, the capacity for mindfulness needs to be developed. Otherwise the old brain just takes off with us. Mindful awareness helps us not to resist or suppress our social anxiety and what is happening in our minds and bodies in a given moment. When we feel very shy or socially anxious, being aware, accepting, and not resisting our anxious emotions helps us understand them and be compassionate toward ourselves when we are facing challenges.

This takes some effort, of course, and we will need to set aside time to practice mindfulness each day, to get used to noticing what comes into our awareness moment by moment. In this way we are deliberately using our attention to develop new connections in the brain, to stimulate patterns of activity in our brain cells that help us calm our minds and compassionately soothe ourselves when we are very shy or socially anxious. Mindfulness involves learning to direct our attention in ways that help us with overall balance, ease, and serenity, so that we can cope in social situations even when we feel anxious or frustrated.

Try a simple exercise. If I ask you to focus on the back of your left hand and notice whatever sensations are present, you will notice certain perceptions of warmth or coolness, dryness or moistness, itchiness or scratchiness. As I focus on my left hand, I can feel the coolness of the air in the room and the rippling sensations in my skin as I type. If now I ask you to focus on your right ear, you will notice different sensations. As I notice my right ear, I can hear a slight ringing on the inside; on the outside I notice the feeling of the sidepieces of my glasses against the skin across the top and back of my ear.

Clarity and Focused Attention

Mindfulness also lends to the clarity with which we observe. Imagine yourself eating a grape and doing it mindfully (and when you can, try it with a real grape). As you choose a grape from the bunch, notice its color and texture. As you rinse it, notice the droplets of water that cling to it. Notice the smooth skin as you hold it between your fingers. Bring it to your nose to smell its freshness. If you like, peel it and notice the spongy flesh underneath the skin. Take your time. Put it in your mouth, feeling its texture. Bite into it and feel the juice squirt in your mouth. Resist rushing as you slowly chew the grape and taste its sweetness, noticing your mouth water. You are simply observing the properties of the grape. You are not judging. As your mind wanders to thoughts like *I wonder if I'm doing this correctly* or *Oh, gosh, how is this going tohelp my social anxiety? I need to put grapes on the grocery list,* simply note them and bring your awareness back to just exploring the characteristics of the grape. Focus on the taste and the sensations of swallowing. You have now explored by sight, touch, smell, texture, and taste.

Mindfulness is about simply being in the present. So often we are distracted: sometimes we daydream even when we are driving, so that we can't remember the route we took driving home. We also get distracted by worrying about whether we'll be able to assert ourselves in a business meeting, or whether we should make an appointment with our manager to let her know about the helpful things we are doing on a project or the recent successes we've had. You have probably noticed the result of this, too: you may put something in the wrong place in your office without being aware of it, or suddenly someone in a meeting directs a question or comment at you when you haven't been paying attention to what is being said. That will trigger an adrenaline rush, which will make your heart beat faster and may bring on panicky feelings, increasing your anxiety. If you are focused on the moment, however, you will not be "ambushed" in this way.

Exercise: Mindful Breathing

Now we'll focus on our breathing, bringing our awareness to our breath as we brought our awareness to eating the grape. We'll practice ordinary breathing, and as thoughts pop into our minds, such as ***What if I'm not doing it right? or How can breathing help with my painful shyness?*** or ***This could take for ever; I need to get results faster,*** again we simply notice them with compassion and gently bring our awareness back to our breath.

Mindful breathing forms the basis of meditation practice. As you become familiar with the process by practicing the breathing exercises described in this book, you may also want to find a meditation teacher and a group of people who meditate together, usually called a ***sangha,*** in order to learn the practice in more depth and be with others who are also practicing. You can also look for groups that teach mindfulness-based stress reduction, particularly those focused on social anxiety. A group such as this provides a gentle and safe container within which you can continue to develop this very important skill of calming yourself so that you can easily call on it when you are worrying about a social situation in the future, or when you are actually in a situation that triggers your shyness.

To begin with, find a quiet place where you won't be disturbed. You can sit in a straight-backed chair with your feet flat on the floor and your back straight. Your hands can rest on your knees or in your lap. You can also sit on a meditation cushion or bench (a meditation cushion is very firm, a meditation bench low and compact). If you choose a cushion, you may wish to cross your legs on the floor in front of you. If you're using a meditation bench, you can kneel and straddle the bench with your feet under the bench behind you, or with your calves outside the bench on either side of it. You can also lie on the floor on your back; this may be most comfortable, but you may fall asleep, whereas the purpose is to develop a kind of alert focus and awareness, which is best done while you are comfortable with your back straight.

Now, just focus on breathing through your nose, being aware of your breath at the tip of the nose or in the belly. You can feel the belly expand on each inhalation and subside on each exhalation. Put your hand on your diaphragm, just under the rib cage, with your thumb pointing upward. Notice how your diaphragm expands with each inbreath and contracts with each outbreath. Do this for a few breaths until you feel comfortable and your breathing feels natural and easy. Feel a half smile in the back of your throat, and then become aware of your face settling into a gentle, compassionate expression.

Now place one hand on either side of your rib cage with your elbows pointed outward. This may feel a bit more awkward, but don't worry. Breathing gently, notice how your rib cage expands to the sides. Your lungs are like bellows. You can feel them expanding inside you. Your breath comes in through the nose and down through the diaphragm, expanding your rib cage to the sides. Your breathing should feel comfortable; you don't need to force it, but you may notice it deepen. Yoga instructors suggest about three to eight seconds on the inbreath and the same on the outbreath. It is important to find the rhythm that suits you and doesn't feel strained. As you breathe you may notice that you breathe a little faster or slower until you find your own natural rhythm. Once you have found a settled rhythm, you'll feel yourself slowing down. Your body is setting the pace and you're paying attention to it.

It helps to look down at an angle of about 45 degrees. Some people close their eyes, but this may make you sleepy or encourage your mind to wander more. If you wish, you can put your hand on your diaphragm again, and then both hands on the sides of your rib cage. Simply notice the sensations in your body as your breath flows in and out through the nose. Some people like to focus on the tip of the nose as the air flows in and out. Others like to focus on the belly, feeling it expand and subside with inhalation and exhalation. The important thing is to find a focus that is comfortable for you, rather than impose one on yourself.

After you have found your rhythm and spent some time focusing on your breath, and when it feels right, gently allow your eyes to open fully. Now take a few moments to absorb the exercise. If you stand up, move about gently. You may want to start by meditating for just a few minutes, and then extend the time as you practice each day until you reach twenty to thirty minutes, if possible.

WHAT DID YOU NOTICE?

Sometimes this initial practice actually raises feelings of anxiety. If that is the case for you, don't worry; it will help to practice, even if you do it for only a few seconds at first and then gradually do more over the next few weeks. As you practice, you will find you become more comfortable with these sensations.

If you didn't find yourself feeling anxious, how did the breathing go for you? What did you notice? Did you have feelings of slowing down and feeling slightly heavier, and did you notice the chair holding you up? How were the distracting thoughts? What did it feel like to gently and kindly bring your awareness back to the breath? Distracting thoughts (often called "monkey mind" in mindfulness practice), distracting body aches, itches, and whatnot, are all part of meditation practice. You may have found yourself drifting off into worry about an upcoming social occasion, maybe for some moments. If this happens, simply become aware of where your mind has gone, and then gently bring your awareness back to the breath. You might start to blame yourself about being distracted by your worries. If this happens, again, just notice that this is where your mind has gone, and gently bring your awareness back to the breath. Pema Chödrön, a well-known meditation teacher who has written several books, giggles on one of her CDs as she jokes about the hilarity of saying "bad meditation" after a sitting, because the idea is that meditation is just "what it is": there is no such thing as a "bad meditation." The practice is what matters. You are not trying to relax, to change anything or achieve anything in each moment. Yes, we know that in the long run, mindful breathing and meditation practice will lead to reduced social anxiety, greater mental control, and well-being; but that is outside the moment. For now, all you need to focus on is gently, playfully bringing the awareness back to the breath each time you notice the craziness of your monkey mind: where it goes, what it thinks, and imagines, and what it conjures up as you simply sit there, meditating.

Exercise: Mindful Breathing and Social Anxiety

Now, if you feel ready, think of a situation that triggers a mild level (no more) of social anxiety. Take a few moments to imagine it in your mind. Notice your anxiety rising a bit now, thinking about it. Now do the mindful breathing exercise again, simply noting your anxious thoughts and bringing your awareness back to the breath, again and again. If you have done the breathing exercise in a calm state first, it will help in doing this exercise. If you find it triggers strong anxiety, allow yourself not to do it, without blaming yourself. You can do it later, when you are more practiced.

WHAT DID YOU NOTICE?

If you did the exercise, what did you notice? Did you notice your anxiety reducing a bit as you established mindful breathing? Did you feel a little calmer? Did your body settle down a little? If not, it is not a problem. You can try it again after you have practiced mindful breathing for a while. Eventually you will notice the effects.

DEVELOPING A MINDFUL STATE

Mindfulness in Everyday Life

You can develop a mindful state at any time, bringing your awareness to the breath and the present moment. Try it in the car at a red traffic light, waiting for a bus, in the bath or shower, waiting for the children at school, or in the waiting room at the doctor's or dentist's office. It is helpful to build from a couple of minutes to five, then ten, and maybe at some point even twenty to thirty minutes a day at a regular time. With our busy lives this can be challenging, and it can be difficult to be consistent. If you can't find twenty to thirty minutes, do five or ten in the morning. I notice, when I can't fit in thirty minutes, that I do more than I think when I add up all the small snippets I've done at different times during a day.

Aids to Encourage Mindfulness

Some people like to focus their attention with the help of a mantra, a word or a phrase said again and again to stimulate a particular state of mind, for example, "peace," "calm," or "love." Others might focus on a candle or a flower. Zen meditators often count continuously from one to ten and then start over again: one on the inbreath, two on the outbreath, three on the next inbreath, four on the outbreath, and so on. Focusing the attention in this way helps the mind not to get caught up so readily in socially anxious thoughts and emotions, in worries about upcoming social events or presentations, or speaking up in a group. There are CDs of singing bells or bowls that involve sounds that facilitate meditation; Karma Moffett calls one such CD *Golden Bowls of Compassion.* An image I use is that of a sturdy oak tree with its roots planted deeply in the ground and its branches moving gently in the wind. My thoughts and feelings are the leaves that flutter gently to the ground in an autumn breeze while I simply watch.

Walking Meditation

Another way to deepen the awareness of the present moment is to focus the attention on bodily sensations while moving or walking. This is usually called a walking meditation. Feel the heel as it touches the ground, then the sole of the foot, then the toes, as you pick up the foot while you are setting the other foot down, all in the same manner with the same awareness. Get up and try it now if you like, just being aware of the sensations of walking around the room. See what you notice. If you like, and if you have pleasant weather at the moment, step outside for a few minutes and feel what it's like to do the mindful walking outdoors. Notice how your senses feel awakened, to colors, to sounds, to the air against your skin. Do all of this at your own pace in a way that feels comfortable to you. You may notice your shyness and social anxiety rising; you will certainly notice distracting thoughts, as we all do, and these may be particularly about your shyness. Again, just gently bring your awareness back to simply walking in the present moment.

SOOTHING BREATHING AND RELAXATION

Now, after you have practiced mindful breathing and walking for a bit—perhaps up to ten to fifteen minutes—try focusing on a deliberately soothing breathing rhythm. Your mindful breathing and walking may have left you in a calm state, or if your distracting thoughts were very active, perhaps it didn't, which is just a natural part of mindfulness practice. So this time you are going to focus deliberately on soothing yourself with a soothing breathing rhythm. Imagine a social situation that is challenging for you or one that you avoid, perhaps a party, a small group meeting, a gathering of friends and neighbors, going to the bar with a group of people after work. Just choose one situation that is challenging for you. Then read through the following exercise, maybe just once, maybe a couple of times. Then put the book down and try the exercise for yourself, following the sequence described. If you forget a stage, don't worry; just remind yourself by looking at the book, and try again.

Exercise: Deliberate Relaxation

We don't need to see tension as a bad thing or an enemy to be rid of, but only as an understandable way the body has learned to protect us and to prepare us for action. We are helping our bodies begin to understand that at this moment, they can rest, that it is safe to rest right now. At this moment there are no social demands; there's nothing social that you have to gear up for, no need to work to assert yourself.

You can practice relaxing in your sitting position or lying down. So, now, take the position that feels comfortable to you, and gently move your awareness to your breath. If you feel tense or slightly uncomfortable, don't worry; just breathe as comfortably as you can. Spend a few moments finding your own rhythm. Then gently move your awareness to your legs, noting for a moment how they feel. Now imagine that the tension in your legs is flowing down into the floor and away. Just let it go. As you breathe in, note any tension; as you breathe out, imagine the tension flowing down through the legs and down into the floor. Imagine your legs feeling pleased and grateful as they let go, and even smiling back at you. Just let the tension go, with kindness. Now focus on your torso, from your shoulders to your lower back. As you breathe in, notice the tension; as you breathe out, feel the tension slipping away down through the floor. Your body feels grateful and you feel kindness toward it. Feel the body's pleasure.

Now focus on the tips of your fingers and move your attention from there up through your wrists, forearms, elbows, upper arms, and shoulders. Imagine the tension releasing. Gently let the tension go, feeling it slip away from your body and down through the floor. Now imagine the tension in your head and neck. This area is one of your early warning systems in shyness, perhaps tensing with the thought of an upcoming social situation in which you need to perform, and you would like it to be released now to rest. As you breathe out, imagine the tension slipping away down through your body and into the floor.

Now focus on the whole body, breathing in, and as you breathe out, focus on the word "relax," feeling your whole body becoming more relaxed.

If you can, spend five minutes doing this exercise. If a shorter time feels better to start with, that is fine. As you end the exercise, you can take an even deeper breath, moving around, perhaps holding your arms out from your shoulders and stretching. Notice how the body feels and how gently grateful it is that you spent time releasing its tension.

Practicing the Deliberate Relaxation Exercise

You can practice this exercise as often as you like. It can help you sleep when you're tense at the end of the day or when you have leftover tension, perhaps after a conflict at work or with your spouse, or when you felt anxious speaking in a group or did not behave as assertively as you wanted to. Remember that your mind will wander as you do it. Just gently bring your awareness back to your breath and to releasing tension from your body. Your slight compassionate smile will help ground you. As you focus on your body, you will become more aware of where you hold tension, and as you become aware of it, you will automatically start to release it.

Focusing on your body in this way may be difficult in itself if you feel shame about your body, for example, if you believe that others see you as too fat, too skinny, or somehow just not the right shape. Thoughts of this kind sometimes go with feeling very shy and socially inadequate. Sometimes, when you feel very shy, you may want to reject your own body. If you find that you think in this way, this exercise can be very helpful with practice, even if it is difficult at first. Over time you will come to think of your body as a friend in whom you take an interest, whom you can nurture, care for, and help relax. You may then find that, because you accept it and care for it, you feel less anxious about its shape. It is also the case, interestingly, that if you are not terribly self-conscious and critical of your own body, others will be much less likely to notice or indeed care very much; they will be interacting with you, not with your self-consciousness or self-preoccupation.

It is also useful to practice the deliberate relaxation exercise by linking it to the times when you feel tense because of shyness and social anxiety. Think of the last time you experienced anxiety before a conversation with someone you'd just met, or before a work meeting where you'd promised yourself you would speak up at least once or twice. Or think of the leftover tension after you went through a conflict with someone, the shame you perhaps felt after a challenging social interaction that didn't go as well as you had hoped, or when you felt you left a situation too quickly, to avoid your anxiety. Remember how your body felt, your emotions, your thoughts. When you can imagine the incident, follow the previous instructions to release tension in your body. If you find yourself becoming more anxious, try to imagine a less challenging situation than the one you chose. It can help to start with situations that are mildly upsetting and practice with those before you move to more challenging ones.

Relaxing Activity

Sometimes sitting or lying down and focusing on the breath seems impossible, particularly if we are agitated and upset after a disappointing meeting with a manager, a conflict with a coworker, or a disagreement with a spouse or friend. At these times it may help to do something physical. I find it helpful to do the dishes or the laundry; or sometimes to do simple tasks like paying bills or shopping that will also give me a sense of accomplishment; or to tend and water my plants, go for a walk, or ride my bike.

SENSORY FOCUSING

Paul Gilbert and Sue Proctor found when treating patients with depression that focusing on something concrete besides the breath or the body helped people get started in mindfulness practices. They handed out tennis balls, encouraging patients to focus on the texture, the shape, and the way the ball felt in the hand as they practiced soothing breathing and attention. You might like to try holding a tennis ball too, or you can use objects like worry beads or smooth stones, which you can hold while practicing soothing breathing.

We call this *sensory focusing* because it encourages us to home in not just on our breath but also on information from our senses. Another way to ground yourself by sensory focusing is through smells. Some people burn incense while they meditate; this is often done in meditation halls. Others use scented oils like lavender. You can also use sounds, household or outdoor sounds, such as the wind through the trees or perhaps one of the CDs mentioned earlier. Psychological research has taught us that the more senses we use, the more likely we are to attend to what we are doing and to facilitate developing new states of mind.

Exercise: Sensory Focusing

Using the ideas in the previous paragraphs, pick something that will help you focus and try a simple exercise in sensory focusing. Simply bring your attention to the object, sound, or smell as you find your natural breathing rhythm, while in your meditation posture with a straight back, on a chair, cushion, or bench. You can also move from one object to another when you practice mindful breathing, perhaps spending a few minutes on each.

You can also try the sensory focusing exercise when you are feeling shy or socially anxious, perhaps in anticipation of meeting someone for coffee you find interesting, whether a date or a new friend. Do the exercise in advance of the event so your anxiety is not too intense. Choose just one of the objects to start. Just be aware of your anxiety, without suppressing it (as far as you can). Then focus on your chosen object while you practice mindful breathing. If your anxiety becomes too intense while doing this, just do the exercise without connecting it to your social anxiety.

CARING FOR YOURSELF IN EVERYDAY LIFE

Quiet time alone to care for yourself and rejuvenate is important, though it's often hard to find in our hurried and often harried and stressful lives. It can take the form of a quiet bath, maybe with candles, or a few minutes of listening to music, reading a book, or just sitting and looking out the window at something green. Try caring for yourself in one of these ways the night before a challenging social task, such as meeting new people at a party, giving a presentation at work, or asserting yourself with a colleague. You can also try it after an event that has triggered your shyness or social anxiety. Giving yourself a few moments to recover after an upsetting social event such as a first date, approaching a small group at a party, a presentation at a conference or a business meeting—even if you did well enough, but feel leftover stress—helps enormously with balance.

Watching Thoughts and Emotions, and Using More Self-Supportive Statements

Watch your thoughts and emotions as they go flying by in socially demanding and challenging situations:

> *I can't believe what that guy just said to me! I am so completely fed up with being a team player while he just waltzes in, expects me to do everything, and then takes the credit!*
>
> *I'm never going to get through this job interview. I can't express myself well. They will never hire me!*

Try putting them into different words, words that acknowledge and accept your feelings in a calmer way:

> *Wow, I'm angry and frustrated, really scared, but I know threat-based automatic thoughts and emotions don't necessarily reflect reality; in fact they seldom do. I*

can think and feel these things and do what I need to do anyway for my long-term best interest. I can practice self-assertion with my colleague.

I will learn from this job interview whether I get the job or not.

Mindful Sex

When we feel shy, sex is an area where we often feel particularly self-conscious, whether we are with a new partner or in a long-term relationship. We often feel under pressure to perform, and in these circumstances our automatic negative thoughts and fear of failure can be so distracting that we feel separated from our bodies and our sexual pleasure. It was very interesting to me to learn that what actually interferes with sexual arousal is not so much anxiety, but distracting thoughts and worry about our performance. We can feel anxious and enjoy sex at the same time because our senses are still functioning. To many people who feel very shy, that realization comes as a huge relief. When we're hoping that a new relationship may become something more lasting, we want sex to be as good as it possibly can be, and we don't want to be distracted by worry about how our anxiety might interfere!

A man's sexual arousal, or lack of it, is visible, but to discerning partners, it is usually apparent whether or not a partner of either sex is relaxed and enjoying a sexual experience. Learning to be mindful means that we can savor both our own and our partner's enjoyment and pleasure moment by moment. Instead of racing for the orgasm and worrying about whether the arousal will last until then, we can simply focus on the pleasures of each moment and let the orgasm take care of itself. Approaching sex in this way also provides the opportunity to learn that orgasm is only a part of sex, that touch and closeness are vastly rewarding even without an orgasm in any particular lovemaking session. Affectionate touching and closeness stimulate the brain to produce oxytocin, the hormone we encountered earlier;

this hormone is associated with trust and love, and thereby facilitates arousal because we feel safe. Even if we don't arrive at an orgasm, the pleasurable arousal we've experienced is likely to make the next lovemaking session even more arousing and satisfying. That is the basis of tantric sex, something you may want to learn about to help you understand the process and help reduce your social anxiety in regard to lovemaking.

Exercise: The Half-Full Glass

Another way of caring for yourself through everyday life is appreciating all the small good things throughout the day, all the little things you enjoy. This is like putting into practice the old proverb about whether you see half a glass of water as a half-full or half-empty glass. If you've been shy for a long time and lonely, you may well be in a mild chronic depressive state with a pessimistic outlook. You will then usually be looking at the glass half empty. This is a common experience in chronic shyness, and if you recognize it as your own experience, this exercise may be particularly valuable for you.

First, focus on the little things that matter to you, whether it is the first cup of coffee or tea, the morning shower, the evening bath, toast with butter and jam, flowers in the garden outside the door, or plants in pots in the house. Focus on a few minutes of reading your favorite writer in the newspaper, watching your favorite TV program, or reading a particular book you like.

Just breathe in and out and notice these things in detail. As much as possible, leave behind all those preoccupations about the future and social performance, and regrets about past disappointing social interactions; focus instead on enjoyable moments of here and now. As you get used to doing this, the state of awareness becomes more and more pleasurable and tends to last longer. Just learning to notice stimulates the brain in new ways and builds new patterns in the brain.

On another day, focus on all the things you appreciate about people in your life, your family, those you love, your colleagues, your friends. Take time to appreciate the qualities they have that you like or admire. Think about all the things other people do for you to make your life easier, from the car mechanic to the person who delivers the newspaper, to the people who run the local market so you can enjoy fresh fruit as you start your day. What about telling people the things you appreciate or admire about them? You might be pleasantly surprised at the results. I remember as a young mother, I lived on a cul-de-sac where one of my neighbors was a woman who was very capable and could be a good friend, but tended to be very bossy and critical. I discovered that she softened considerably when I started to acknowledge her strengths explicitly and compliment her on them; it seemed to reduce her driven intensity, her determination to put everyone—and everything!—right.

Often, if you're feeling uncomfortably and chronically shy, you are so anxious about your own social performance, as you rehearse before every worrying event and rehash afterward, that you don't focus on the things you appreciate and love about others, your surroundings, and your everyday pleasures. By practicing the "half-full glass" exercise, whether with things or with people, you are practicing overruling your threat/protection system. That system is seeking to protect you by warning you constantly that your glass is half empty; but now you are deliberately using your attention to stimulate that other emotional system in the brain that produces pleasurable feelings, soothing feelings, and calm states of mind.

Remember, too, that these exercises are about being playful and kind to yourself, and experiencing natural pleasures. They are not about "shoulds" and "oughts," what you "ought" to feel or think. All you're doing is kindly training your brain to develop your natural capacities for joy and pleasure.

FEELINGS THAT MAY ARISE DURING MINDFULNESS EXERCISES

Sometimes, as we do these exercises, uncomfortable feelings may surface: sadness, fear, social anxiety, hurt, or anger. This is completely natural and simply part of the process of your growing self-awareness. You don't need to worry about them; just note what they are, listen to them for a moment, and then gently bring your awareness back to your breath. When you do this as part of your sitting or walking practice, you will find that you experience sudden insights, often after your practice session has ended, and often when particular thoughts and feelings have arisen consistently for a few days in your sessions. You may well find that your shyness experiences make more sense to you. When you note the memories that arise and then move your awareness back to your breath, you may see links between your shy and socially anxious feelings now and your earlier experiences.

I think of this process as developing mindful social fitness. We talked in chapter 1 about physical and social fitness; well, now we are developing emotional fitness, emotion regulation, and balance through daily practice.

It's a good idea to practice the exercises when you are relatively calm, because in this state it is easier to develop your awareness, as well as the practice of noting your thoughts and feelings and then returning to the breath. The more you practice mindfulness, the more you will notice that a rush of intense thoughts and feelings is usually followed over time by a reduction in intensity and a more quiet, observing state. If the feelings that arise are intense, it is very helpful to talk to someone you trust; if you don't have someone you know and trust whom you can talk to, it might be a good idea to find a therapist or a meditation teacher. You can also look for mindfulness-based stress reduction classes in your community and read other self-help books, such as the recent one by Steve Flowers, *The Mindful Path Through Shyness.*

We are now on the road to developing the compassionate and balanced mind. In the next chapter, I will describe how to work with interfering painful thoughts and feelings using balancing and compassion focusing. Working with shyness in this manner helps us to trust and accept ourselves while also taking responsibility for our own behavior so that we can work toward meeting our goals in life. We'll also talk about the importance of writing, using exercises from compassion-focused therapy.

KEY POINTS

- A notebook or journal is helpful as you develop your mindfulness and relaxation practice—and indeed for recording your thoughts on the rest of the exercises in this book.
- A daily mindfulness practice is very helpful in learning to accept your social anxiety without resisting or suppressing your emotions and while developing your compassionate focus.
- Watching thoughts and emotions while using self-supporting thoughts

helps us to balance our minds and show ourselves compassion toward our shyness.

CHAPTER 5

Compassionate Mind Training Using Imagery

In this chapter we will practice developing our compassionate minds using imagery (one of our compassionate skills, as you may remember from chapter 3) to soothe ourselves and to develop compassionate patterns in our brains. We will develop our self-soothing systems to help us cope with and learn from our experiences. This will help us to gain control over some of the old brain patterns that can interfere with pursuing what we really want in life.

Through the exercises set out in this chapter, we will be stimulating mind-body states that help us cope with life's challenges, including the fear of getting close to others, and dealing with our own human vulnerability as we do that. When we feel shy, we are afraid of being disappointed and hurt as we reach out to others. We are afraid that others will criticize us or find us wanting, that we'll fail to make that impression we so desperately want to make in that job interview or on that first date. Although our fear is a natural part of the threat/protection system, being close to others is a prerequisite for a satisfying and fulfilling life. Without human closeness we can wither and sometimes even die. Through both nature and nurture, we are exquisitely aware of the consequences of human rejection. Our sensitivity can be both a gift and a burden.

Let's be honest with ourselves: we *will* be disappointed sometimes. We will be hurt, and we will be rejected. But it's just as important, if not more important, to understand that if we pick ourselves up and try again, if we continue to participate, to reach out, to learn, we will go on to lead rich and rewarding lives and to understand others and ourselves better. We will feel truly alive and connected to others and ourselves, and we will flourish.

As you try out these exercises, you may experience self-kindness and warmth relatively quickly, but don't worry if you don't. People vary in how quickly these exercises have an effect. It doesn't matter if it takes a while, or if some exercises work for you and others don't. What is most important is to be in touch with your own timing and pace, and to find the exercises that work the best for you.

It is important to remember, as you use your imagination to do these exercises, that the imagery we are using is not like a well-developed photograph or video. It usually just involves fleeting impressions, often including sensations, voice tones, sounds, or feelings. It is the sense or feeling that is created in you that is important. So be kind and gentle with yourself, and accepting toward whatever images come to you.

THE DESIRE TO BE HAPPY

Exercise: Desire to Be at Peace

This exercise is about focusing on the desire to be at peace and free from suffering, which includes any kind of mental unease or pain, particularly related to shyness and social anxiety.

Find a quiet place where you can adopt your preferred posture for mindful breathing, calm but alert, sitting on a chair, cushion, or bench. Your back should be straight, and your body comfortable. You can also lie down in the beginning, if that feels better. Feel a half smile in the back of your throat and then become aware of your face taking on a gentle, compassionate expression. Take a few moments to settle into this feeling. If it is difficult for you at first, you might like to play some gentle calming sound in the background, either quiet music or one of the CDs I mentioned in chapter 4.

Now say to yourself silently, ***May I be happy, may I be well, and may***

I be free from suffering. This is the basic Buddhist loving-kindness meditation. Focus on being free from suffering and in a state of well-being, while you become familiar with your desire to be peaceful. Notice that the self in which the desire for peace is located is wise and caring; it is not ruminating, brooding, and exhausted from worry about being criticized or judged. There may be a voice inside you saying, ***Anything for a rest from social anxiety and worry,*** but the wise, peaceful self is not worrying. It is calm.

If you are happy to memorize another, slightly more involved, meditation, you might like to focus on this one, which I like: ***May I be happy, may I be free from sources of inner and outer harm, may I be strong and healthy and live with ease, may I be free from suffering, may I be at peace.*** But if you prefer, stay with the first, simple meditation. Try both and see what suits you best.

Try to spend around five minutes focusing on these phrases, saying them again and again in your mind, and then write down your thoughts and reactions in your compassion journal. This will help you to remember your experience of doing the exercise, and also encourage you to reflect on your experience and insights. For example, did you notice any resistance to doing the exercise, such as thoughts that you don't deserve to be peaceful, that it is hard, that you might miss out on something, that you may not be worthy in others' eyes, that this won't help painful shyness, that you must not let your guard down, or that you will be too vulnerable? Just note with interest ***any*** of your thoughts and feelings, including what it feels like to be aware of your genuine desire for well-being, and take a moment afterward to write down what you noticed.

Exercise: Peaceful Joyfulness

This exercise is about focusing on the desire to feel happy and joyful as well as peaceful. Bringing joy into the picture adds a link to the activating system and stimulates a slightly different pattern in the brain from that associated with the soothing system alone. Try saying to yourself silently, ***May I be happy, may I be joyful and peaceful.*** As you do the exercise you will again notice your mind wandering. Simply bring it back to your focus on peace and joyfulness. You may notice thoughts related to feeling upset about your shyness or social anxiety, or find yourself dwelling on perceived social failures that block the path to self-compassion and well-being. Once again, just note those thoughts and gently bring your awareness back to peace and joyfulness.

I have sometimes been afraid to be peaceful and joyful for fear that in focusing on these things, I might neglect my responsibilities. I have been afraid that I might lose my achievement drive or neglect doing something that was important. How many of us, particularly in the Western world with its extreme focus on individual achievement, feel afraid of contentment, afraid that we won't be motivated, that we'll lose our drive, or that we won't continue to work toward reaching out to people and making friends; or that we won't be alert to cues that signal potential social threats? If you can, release, with your inward smile, any worry about these fears of contentment and, at this moment, just allow yourself to feel grateful that you are learning how you work internally. You can also think about how you want to proceed anyway in the face of your resistance to cultivating the peaceful and joyful states. Write these feelings down in your compassion journal after the exercise.

CONTENTMENT AND PURSUING GOALS

It's worth pausing here to reflect for a moment on what contentment does and doesn't mean. Being content does not imply a lack of commitment to pursuing important goals in our lives, whether these goals involve a cause, a meaningful way of life, or simply our own interpersonal relationships. The Dalai Lama provides a good example here. The head of the global Buddhist community is deeply committed to increasing compassion in the world and travels extensively to work to that end. At the same time he is deeply peaceful and content, while acknowledging that he, too, still struggles with an unruly mind. The Dalai Lama is also committed to integrating Eastern mindfulness practices and Western science. He devotes enormous amounts of time, as well as using his considerable influence with monks experienced in very long-term meditation, to enable Western psychological researchers to study how meditation affects the brain and body. Some of these studies have shown that participation in an eight-week program of mindfulness-based stress reduction can reduce social anxiety. Those results are now being widely disseminated in England and the United States, and are having a noticeable influence on Western thinking, as shown by the increasing numbers of people attending meditation retreat centers in both countries, and the numbers of people integrating these practices into sustainable businesses and nonprofit organizations.

We need to be careful, however, not to make being peaceful dependent on reaching our social goals, such as speaking up at work, asking someone over for dinner, striking up a social conversation in the office, or speaking to that neighbor we've often seen but never greeted. For example, I may think I can only be peaceful if I succeed in getting that job, in dating a particular person, or having a certain person become my partner. I remember vividly when I realized that going flat out for what I wanted, while at the same time understanding that I might never get it or achieve what I hoped to, was for me the secret to a meaningful life. What mattered was really trying for the goal, so that whether I reached it or not, I would always know that I had done the best I could. I didn't realize then that peace, as well as joy, could be a big part of that pursuit. I learned that joy could be, but it took longer to grasp that peacefulness and contentment could also be present while I worked hard to achieve my goals.

So you might like to consider the following: What are your goals and values? What do you want for yourself in life, and what really matters to you? What do you want to contribute? Or, as we say at the shyness clinic: *Who* do you want to be? And *how* do you want to be? You may want to jot down some notes in your compassion journal on these themes to help clarify your thinking and perhaps guide your practice.

Exercise: Using Memory

This exercise will help you create compassionate feelings toward yourself using your memory. Using the same or similar posture, with a straight back, that you have been using for previous exercises, allow yourself to become aware of your breathing and notice as it deepens for a few moments before you begin.

Try to recall a time when someone was kind, caring, and warm toward you. If you can, focus on a particular event, including its specific details. It may be a time when you felt shy and someone reached out to you, perhaps drawing you into a conversation with a small group. Pick something that was not too distressing, or your attention may be pulled toward the distress itself. What you are trying to do is r e-create how you felt when you experienced another's kindness. Focus on facial expressions, voice tones, and general manner. Remember as much specific detail as you can. What were the feelings, your own and your perception of the other person's? Can you sense them in your body? Feel them flow into yourself. Take a few minutes to really experience what it was like. After you have finished, make a few notes in your journal about your experience and how it felt to return to that experience.

Now recall a time when you felt kindness toward someone else, compassion arising in you and flowing out to another individual. Recall a time when you felt warm, kind, and caring toward another person in distress, maybe someone else who felt shy or who was embarrassed by forgetting someone's name. Again, avoid major distress because it will pull up more complex feelings and you could be reminded of too much anxiety and uncertainty. The focus here is on your own feelings of warmth and kindness. You want others to experience well-being and warmth, and kindness is flowing from you to them. Bring the memory back in as much detail as possible. Include sounds, facial expressions, and feelings, and try to focus on sensory details. It doesn't matter if nothing arises; just note if something does. Again, when you have finished, write down your thoughts and feelings in your journal.

Now reflect on the two elements of this exercise. Was one easier than the other? Was it easier to recall kindness flowing in or flowing out? It doesn't matter what triggered the kindness in each case; the important thing is feeling the warmth associated with kindness and caring.

Exercise: Desire for the Happiness of Others

Now you can try an imagery exercise in the present. Start with people you care about, using the same phrases from the first exercise in this chapter: ***May you be happy, may you be well, and may you be free from suffering.*** Try to see your loved ones' faces and imagine their smiles, how they move, and how their voices sound. Explore the feelings that arise from your desire for them to be happy, peaceful, and free from suffering. Remember that they simply find themselves here, like you, and are doing the best they can. You may feel warm toward them, or you may find other feelings arising. You may be worried about them or sad for a loss they have suffered. If you can, make notes in your journal about the different feelings that arise. As you continue to practice in these ways and look back over your journal entries, you will see how particular emotional states stimulate different brain patterns as well as serve as meaningful experiences in themselves.

If you wish, you could begin with someone you look up to or are grateful to—perhaps a mentor, maybe someone who has guided you in your life, encouraged and supported you, or perhaps someone who has helped you with your shyness—and then move to more intimate loved ones. Try to take a few minutes to focus on each of these people.

Having started by focusing on those we look up to and are grateful to, and those who are closest to us, we can then extend loving-kindness to our friends. Imagine your friends' faces and their other qualities, their smiles and funny quirks, in as much detail as you can, and hold out to them your loving-kindness and wishes for them to be happy, to be well, and to be free from suffering. Take a few moments with each individual so you can feel your wish for that person to be content and happy. As much as you can, visualize the person's happiness and peacefulness. As your mind wanders, note where it has gone, and gently bring your awareness back to your loving-kindness meditation.

Now focus on people you don't know so well. These are people for whom you have neutral feelings: neighbors and acquaintances, maybe people you see at the post office or supermarket, in passing at work, or on the tennis court or playing field. Extend to them your loving-kindness and your wishes for them to be happy, to be peaceful, and to be free from suffering. Visualize their happiness and peacefulness. When the mind wanders, note where it has gone again, and gently bring the awareness back to loving-kindness toward people for whom you have neutral feelings.

Having focused for a few minutes on people you feel neutral about, extend your loving-kindness to people you disagree with, people who have hurt you or put you down, and people toward whom you harbor angry or resentful feelings, or see as outright enemies. This part of the exercise is more challenging for most of us, but it can be very enlightening and helpful. Like us, these people did not choose to be here, and have not chosen their genes or their early environments; they are doing the best they can, given their circumstances and understanding. We hurt each other through ignorance and a lack of mindful control of our thoughts and behavior. It can be particularly helpful to feel this acceptance, this ability to offer loving-kindness, toward people who have embarrassed you, rejected you, put you down, or even humiliated you, even though it may take many attempts at the exercise over quite some time to arrive at that point.

Take a few moments now, after your first attempt at the exercise, to write down your experiences. Note where you felt resistance or any point where you felt self-critical during the exercise; write down how you dealt with your resistance or negative emotions and whether you could bring your awareness back to loving-kindness.

It takes effort to acquire this skill, this ability to extend loving-kindness to people who have hurt us or opposed us; so give yourself time for practice and learning. It will be worth it. Sometimes people report sudden moments of liberation from painful states of anger, resentment and hurt that have been constant, painful companions throughout their lives. These moments of liberation come with the realization that responsibility for what the other person has done is theirs and not ours. It can be a relief to recognize that the consequences of others' deeds in the world will be theirs to manage.

We just need to attend to what is our responsibility, the consequences of our own words and deeds. Practicing loving-kindness helps us to forgive each other and ourselves. We are not trying to get rid of our negative emotions in relation to others' acts, only to transcend them: to live happy lives of our own in the face of past and current hurts.

After practicing loving-kindness toward people who have hurt you and people you consider to be your enemies, you can then extend loving-kindness to all people in the world—and beyond, to all sentient beings: plants and animals, all forms of life, including all those unknown, beyond our planet and throughout the whole universe. Do this for a few minutes, and then write down your thoughts and feelings.

Loving-Kindness Toward Others: An Example

A professor from whom I took some classes used to talk about a friend of his, a man who had gone through the Holocaust and spent time in a concentration camp. In spite of the terrible trauma he had endured, this man was one of the happiest people my professor knew. The professor finally asked him "Why, given what you've been through, are you so happy all the time and not bitter? Don't you struggle with anger at what happened to you?"

His friend replied, "Given everything I've been through, the things that people around here consider to be really upsetting aren't that upsetting to me. I know what constitutes really upsetting, and it is concerned with the life and death of loved ones and people you know. This is small potatoes. I thank my lucky stars every day that I am here. I know what constitutes a good life and this is it. Why should I spend time on anger and bitterness?"

Some Reflections on Loving-Kindness Meditation

Some depressed clients have trouble with the words "free from suffering" and prefer instead to say, *May I have compassion for my suffering.* They find that they can identify with these words more easily and that this form of the phrase helps them muster the courage to face difficult things. If you have been painfully shy and socially anxious for a long time and have experienced great suffering, you may find this as well. The point is just to find the particular words that work best for you. It may be useful to write in your journal which meditation wordings and which music work best for you in stimulating the soothing/contentment system and calm feelings.

When we extend loving-kindness to all beings, we may feel sadness and experience a sense of sharing the sorrow of the world. Practicing with music, particularly in minor keys, may facilitate this sense of sorrow and thereby the wish to help heal your own suffering and that of others. You may already be starting to collect poetry that speaks to these feelings. There is a wonderful poem by Mary Oliver that talks about living fully in the face of the losses and sorrows of life, and ends with an idea that may be particularly valuable and inspiring when you struggle with shyness.

When Death Comes

When death comes
like the hungry bear in autumn
when death comes and takes all the
 bright coins from his purse

to buy me, and snaps his purse shut;
when death comes
like the measle pox;

when death comes
like an iceberg between the shoulder
 blades,

I want to step through the door full of
 curiosity, wondering;
what is it going to be like, that cottage
 of darkness?

And therefore I look upon everything
as a brotherhood and a sisterhood,
and I look upon time as no more than
 an idea,
and I consider eternity as another
 possibility,

and I think of each life as a flower, as
 common
as a field daisy, and as singular,

and each name a comfortable music in the mouth
tending as all music does, toward silence,

and each body a lion of courage, and something
precious to the earth.

When it's over, I want to say: all my life
I was a bride married to amazement.
I was a bridegroom, taking the world into my arms.

When it's over, I don't want to wonder
if I have made of my life something particular, and real.
I don't want to find myself sighing and frightened
or full of argument.

I don't want to end up simply having visited this world.

Mary Oliver

LIVING FULLY: LOVE WITHOUT SELF-SACRIFICE

When we are shy, the biggest temptation is to avoid interpersonal risks and to miss out on our lives because we are afraid of being rejected and hurt—to miss out on all the beauty and warmth that is available to us if we extend warmth and love to others. This is one of the ways we might, as Mary Oliver says, "end up simply having visited" the world.

Sometimes, in contrast, when we feel shy, we see ourselves as too loving and submissive and, as a result, exploited. I think the solution here lies in being not less loving, but less self-sacrificing. People who exploit you act from ignorance and their own insecurity, their own resentment over past hurts and pain. There is no need to tolerate exploitation in order to love. There will be people to love you who do not exploit you and who take joy in your caring for yourself. Often your natural warmth will draw them to you. When we are shy, our sensitivity and highly developed instincts for detecting danger can be very helpful. We can take risks and at the same time be wise about choosing people to whom we open up or make ourselves vulnerable. These are people who listen carefully to our feelings and remember our values and needs, and who are there when we need them.

If you're going to take risks, it helps to have a safe place to which you can retreat if you feel under too much threat, a place where you can recover your calm and contentment. The next exercise focuses on establishing a place like this in your mind so that it is always there for you to take refuge in when you need to.

Exercise: Your Safe Place

Begin with the breathing and relaxation exercise we've been practicing. After you have been breathing calmly for a few moments, imagine a place that gives you feelings of safety, calm, and contentment, a place where you feel comfortable and at peace with yourself. It may vary with your mood or the situation in which you find yourself. It doesn't always have to be the same one every time you do this exercise, but you will probably notice that you have one or more favorites that you choose again and again. There may be some benefit to you in having one or only a few, because they will come quickly to mind and will become more strongly associated with feeling safe and calm.

Sometimes people choose indoor spaces, perhaps a quiet room facing a garden, or a cozy room with favorite paintings or photographs on the walls. Maybe there is a log fire burning in the fireplace. Often the safe spaces are outdoors, places like your favorite beach where you like to walk in the first rays of sunshine in the morning, watching the waves come in over sand or pebbles in the brightness and warmth. Or perhaps your safe place is at the beach in the evening, where the slanting sun colors the waves a darker blue and the air has the poignant melting quality of a long summer day's ending. My painter mother used to call this the time of the long shadows, and it was the time she most liked to paint because of the subtlety of color as the shadows moved slowly over the trees and sand. Or maybe your safe place is a favorite place in the woods where you go walking or an open spot where you like to pause and look over the distant hills. Feel the air. Smell the pine trees and the wildflowers if they are in bloom. Are there white, fluffy clouds overhead? Are there budding rain clouds in the distance? Try to develop as many sensory images in as much detail as you can. This is your safe place, which welcomes you and enjoys having you there. It helps to focus on your sense of belonging there. It is your own and unique. Feel the welcome of the place.

You can use this exercise whenever you feel shy, socially anxious, lonely and sad, or frustrated and resentful. If it is not easy at first, don't worry. Developing the capacity for imagery is like any other skill you work on. At first it can feel awkward, strange, even silly, but over time the experience usually turns into a feeling of being safe and feeling soothed. You can take yourself to your safe place anytime, even just before you make a call to that friend you have promised yourself you will ask to go out walking with you or to meet you for coffee after work. In fact it can be particularly helpful then, because you are calling from your own internal safe place, a place where it is safe and accepted to be shy or socially anxious, a place to which you can always return, whether your friend can make it this time or not.

IMAGINING A COMPASSIONATE PERFECT NURTURER

We are usually aware of compassion coming from others when they are kind to us, and of compassion going out from ourselves toward others when we feel sympathy and empathy for the suffering of people we encounter in our lives, whether they are people we love or know, or don't know so well. Now we are going to deliberately create and develop your ideal compassionate nurturer so you can soothe yourself.

This idea was developed by psychologist Deborah Lee.

The important thing here is that you are going to create a unique image that is special to you. This image belongs to you alone, just like your safe place; it doesn't need to be an ideal nurturer to anyone besides you. You don't have to hold back in any way. You can give your nurturer every attribute or quality of compassion that is desirable to you. Try to include among these attributes these four basic qualities:

- a wise mind that is fully human, familiar with powerful emotions, both wanted and unwanted, and knows how to cope with them
- strength and fortitude to endure and tolerate painful emotions and conditions, and strength to defend and protect you if required
- overflowing warmth and kindness extended to you
- a nonjudgmental attitude toward you, desiring, above all, your well-being and flourishing

Imagining your compassionate nurturer is another way of imagining and getting used to the feeling of compassion flowing into you. This image, and the sense of compassion from another being directed toward us, will help us in working with the problems arising from shyness.

Exercise: Imagining a Compassionate Perfect Nurturer

Once more, move to a comfortable, quiet place where you won't be disturbed, and assume your comfortable position with a straight back, with quiet music or chanting in the background if that helps you feel calm. Become aware of your breathing. You can look downward at around a 45-degree angle so that your gaze rests on the floor, or you can close your eyes if you prefer. Notice your breathing becoming more even and soothing, bringing a gentle smile and compassionate expression to your face. Now begin to imagine your compassionate nurturer. When the mind wanders, just gently bring it back to your image of your compassionate nurturer.

When you think of a compassionate nurturer, what comes to your mind? Do you notice fleeting images, colors, sounds, or textures? You might want to imagine a color related to compassion flowing into your heart area, and then expanding throughout your chest and body, so that you can feel the warmth of it in your chest. Take a minute to become aware of these images and reflect on them. Imagine your compassionate nurturer in as much detail as you can, using all five senses. What does your compassionate nurturer look like? What is the style and color of this figure's dress and hair? How is this person poised? How does this person move? How old and what sex is your compassionate nurturer? Are there sounds that come to mind or voice tones? Is there a smell, like the smell of a particular shaving lotion or perfume, the smell of grass after rain, or the smell of the woods on an early morning walk? Is there a particular cooking smell? There may be images of a group or spiritual community where you feel you belong. The images may change, or new images may arise as your emotional state changes. Individuals of different gender, or aspects of different people from different parts of your life, may be related to different feelings of compassion flowing into you.

If you have difficulty forming a visual image, you can look at pictures from magazines, whether of people or scenes that represent nurturing or compassion to you. Some shy people don't want to create an ideal; they prefer the image of a real person. It may help you to remember people who have been kind to you or focus on the idea that your perfect nurturer wants to relate to you. Focusing on the facial expression of a real person helps because it triggers responses in the amygdala and other parts of the brain.

If you were abused or treated badly in childhood, human images may feel threatening to you, so you may want to choose an animal, perhaps a horse or a dog, or a scene from nature. This could be a lake, the ocean, mountains, or sky. Imagine it in as much sensory detail as you can. Focus on the water, how it glistens and how it feels as it slides along your body, whether it is warm or cool. Or focus on the sun warming your body, the smells of hawthorn and hay on a country walk, or the birdcalls and sound of the wind in the reeds on a marsh. You can imagine that this part of nature completely accepts you and knows your struggles and pain. It has been around for all of life on earth and seen everything, including species evolving and becoming extinct. Feel a sense of connection to something incredibly old and wise that welcomes and accepts you as part of the flow of life.

Imagine your perfect nurturer speaking to you slowly, in a kind and gentle voice, full of wisdom and understanding. This person, animal, or place is strong and steady, and cares deeply about your welfare. You feel cared for and understood as you listen. Your perfect nurturer understands and accepts your shyness, social anxiety, and feelings of inadequacy, and will be there for you as you reach out to people and assert yourself when you need to.

It doesn't matter whether or not you feel that there is a really nurturing person there for you in your life right now. It's imagining and creating a perfect nurturer in your mind that counts. You will use this image to help with the times when you feel shy and socially inadequate, to help you accept those feelings as well as feelings of shame when they occur and to reassure you of your inner worth.

You can practice imagining your perfect nurturer as often as you want to, in the shower or bath, starting your day, waiting for a meeting, or lingering at the table after dinner. The important thing is to really imagine the qualities of your perfect nurturer, so you can bring them strongly into your awareness.

Exercise: The Compassionate Perfect Nurturer in Action

This exercise builds on the previous one to bring your compassionate perfect nurturer into closer contact with you when you're feeling uncomfortably shy or socially anxious. Spend some moments engaging your soothing breathing rhythm and then spend a minute imagining your perfect nurturer as right by your side, understanding you and your shyness, accepting and caring for you.

When you can feel this care, imagine that you are watching a video or DVD of yourself. You are starting your morning and preparing for the day. Then see yourself in a situation that activates your shyness and social anxiety. Look at the person—you—experiencing your nervousness or anxiety, maybe embarrassment or inadequacy. Notice those feelings in the person you are watching, the concern about whether or not this person is making a good impression, the wish to withdraw.

Now, from the position of feeling your perfect nurturer at that person's side—your side—understanding the person's emotions, cheering the person on, caring deeply about the person, and confirming the person's worth, feel the nurturer's great compassion for that person—you—whom you are watching on your inner DVD.

If you find yourself becoming too anxious or sad, take a few soothing breaths, let the image fade, and, when you are calm once more, begin the process again.

This exercise is designed to help you have a sense of your perfect nurturer showing compassion, wisdom, and deep care, and to help you feel the person's care flowing into you, where that care helps you counteract your anxiety, concern, and self-criticism, and the frustration and anger that come from the sense of threat.

THE COMPASSIONATE IDEAL SELF

Another exercise using imagery in compassionate mind training is one designed to help you assume the role of a wise and compassionate person—the one who is there already inside you, but who needs to be accessed and released. In this exercise we practice the body postures and body states of compassion. Like a good actor, you are going to study and take on the role of becoming your perfect, ideal, compassionate person. A role model may come to mind, which can help, but in the end, it is the wise, compassionate person inside *you* that you are developing in order to become the most compassionate person you can be, in your own way, in your own time. We've already noted that one of the many strengths of shyness, which comes into its own when you are not feeling socially anxious, is a natural tendency to sympathize and empathize with other people. This can be the foundation for your compassionate image, the image of the compassionate person you are and can be.

The important thing to learn now is how to extend this compassion *to yourself.* I have seen shy people in my groups extend loving compassion to others in their words and behavior, but have a hard time offering it to themselves. Your compassionate person needs to feel compassion toward you, including your social anxiety and worry about being judged.

Exercise: Imagining the Compassionate Ideal Self

Take up your familiar relaxed, alert posture and gently engage your soothing breathing rhythm for a while. Feel your rib cage expanding to the sides as you breathe in. Take a few moments until you feel somewhat slowed down. Now, breathing steadily, imagine that you are a deeply compassionate and wise person. Take some time to think of all the ideal qualities you would love to have as a compassionate person, and imagine that you have them. Imagine yourself as strong, assured, deeply kind, warm, and gentle. You are calm and tolerant in the face of hostility, and you have the wisdom that comes from hard-won experience. Spend time playing with these images and imagine yourself having each of these qualities. Allow your face to settle into a compassionate expression. Imagine yourself speaking. As you speak, your words are slow, kind, and gentle, full of wisdom and understanding.

Whether you think you actually have these qualities or not is not important. You are focusing on visualizing them, imagining them, thinking about them and their dimensions, and being aware of how much you would like to develop these qualities, as well as experiencing them as being a natural part of you. It's the pretending and imagining that are important because, remember, you are getting into a role; you're creating a particular sense of self, and you will use this self to help you with your shyness and social anxiety.

You can think about your age, what you look like, your posture and stance, your facial expressions, and your inner feelings, such as warmth and gentleness. Experience you, the actor, beginning to take on the role, and notice yourself becoming these qualities. Allow your facial expression to be gentle and compassionate, and feel your gentle, warm smile. You are a wise person who has seen a lot in life, and you have perspective, deep understanding, and tolerance. You are a forgiving person who doesn't hold grudges. Think about the qualities you value in compassion and become them as you imagine yourself in the role.

Spend as long as you like on this. Play with the exercise and enjoy it. How does it affect your body, your posture, and your breathing? How does it affect your muscle tone? Are you more tense? More relaxed? Do you notice warmth or coolness anywhere?

This is another exercise you can practice anytime during the day or night and anywhere, in the shower or bath, waiting for a bus, cycling home, lying in bed. As you move through your day, you can do it whenever you think of it. It may be particularly helpful to do it as you move from one activity or task to another. Try it in the morning before work or school, to set the tone for your day. If you notice in the beginning that it feels strange, or even brings up old and painful feelings, whether related to shyness or not, just note what the feelings are and return to the imagining. Take your time, but don't force it. You may start with just a very few moments. Later on, when you practice it again, you may find you can stay with the image longer. The important thing is to really get into imagining those qualities in yourself.

Exercise: The Compassionate Ideal Self in Action

Now we're going to bring the compassionate ideal self into contact with our shyness. To begin this exercise, spend a few moments engaging your soothing breathing rhythm and then once more imagine yourself as your wise, strong, compassionate self. Take whatever time you need to get into the role.

When you feel that you have access to your compassionate self, imagine you're watching a video or DVD of your ordinary self. Perhaps you can see yourself getting out of bed in the morning and starting your day. Then see yourself encountering a situation that activates your shyness. From your compassionate self, simply feel great compassion for that person who is you, the person you are watching on your inner DVD.

If you notice yourself being pulled into feeling too anxious or sad while watching yourself from your compassionate-mind state, take a few soothing breaths, let the image fade, and then, when you feel calm again, begin the process again.

This exercise is designed to help you develop a compassionate attitude toward your shyness and social anxiety, and to help you learn to experience compassion for your anxiety and fear and the difficulties they cause you. This compassion will counteract the self-criticism, anger, and resentment that come from social anxiety and the sense of threat that brings.

A NOTE ON INTRUSIVE IMAGES

If your shyness and social anxiety stem from physical abuse you have suffered, you may notice that very upsetting images arise as you practice these exercises. If you do have traumatic memories of physical abuse and extreme rejection, it is when you remember them and can talk about them that you can come to terms with the pain and find it soothed. If we avoid traumatic memories and the fears they engendered, they may come up in the form of intrusive and very frightening images, flashbacks, or diffuse anxiety, that is, anxiety that is not linked to any obvious immediate cause. If you think that your painful shyness started with physical abuse, whether inflicted at school by bullies or at home by a family member, you may want to look at the website of Edna Foa's "Center for the Treatment and Study of Anxiety" at the University of Pennsylvania. The therapists there specialize in helping you to desensitize to these kinds of traumatic memories, which may also help in reducing your social anxiety. That is, they help you to reduce your fear of having the memories and reduce the anxiety that arises when you do remember painful events, so that you can feel calmer as you remember and calmer in situations that may not be actually threatening now, but stimulate fear because they are similar in some way to the original situation. For details of this center and other resources you may find helpful, see the notes section at the back of this book.

SHOWING YOURSELF COMPASSION UNDER THREAT OR IN DISTRESS

Next time you feel upset about something—perhaps fearful about an upcoming encounter with someone, or sad, ashamed, or resentful because a situation didn't go as well as you'd hoped—try this exercise.

Exercise: Responding to Threat or Distress with the Compassionate Self

Sitting in a chair or in your meditation posture, become aware of your breathing; notice as it deepens and becomes more regular. Now begin to take on that role of your ideal compassionate self. Imagine yourself as a deeply compassionate, warm person who never condemns and is very wise. Imagine the anxious or sad part of you in front of the compassionate you. From your compassionate self, look at the face and behavior of your anxious or sad self: imagine what you are thinking and feeling, and simply send compassion to that part of you, without trying to change anything. Suppressing emotions actually makes them more intense and painful, so we want to experience them and send compassion to the suffering parts of ourselves at the same time. Recognize that these painful emotions come from the threat/protection system and have a purpose, namely, to help you be aware of what you want and don't want. If you hold your compassionate stance and look at your anxious, sad, or angry self, you may notice different experiences that are helpful to you.

Exercise: Responding to Threat or Distress with the Compassionate Perfect Nurturer

Now do the same exercise, but this time imagine that your ideal compassionate perfect nurturer is by your side and you are looking at those parts of yourself together. If dismissive, judging, contemptuous feelings creep in, just note them and return to your compassionate, empathic focus.

While you're doing these exercises, you might like to hold your worry beads, smooth stones, or something else that helps to soothe and ground you, perhaps a bird feather you picked up while out on a favorite walk or a shell from your favorite beach. You can then carry these things around with you and touch them whenever you feel the need to link to your ideal compassionate image and the compassionate feelings you've been practicing. Smells, such as incense or hand cream, can also be helpful in this way because they trigger responses in the emotion centers of the brain. Aromatherapists can suggest scents that are thought to have soothing qualities. Other ways of grounding or centering yourself while you are doing the exercise include using a mantra or adopting a particular posture; for example, you might like to keep the index finger and thumb touching on each hand as your hands rest in your lap.

TRAINING OURSELVES IN THE USE OF IMAGERY

I think of compassionate mind training as being similar to social fitness training: a constant process of learning how to be the people we want to be. We are always in training as we go through life, learning to take risks by meeting new people and beginning to like those we don't know, to maintain our commitments, and to love those around us, including ourselves, as well as we can in each moment. I find the notion of commitment to continuing training a deeply comforting, reassuring, and soothing idea. It means that when we don't do something as well as we want to, whether it's our compassion exercises or social fitness exercises, or meeting people and speaking up for ourselves, if we are committed to it, we always have another chance to try again, and gradually we get better at it.

Imagery is a powerful, well-researched tool that helps many high performers, for example, athletes, actors, and musicians, to prepare for action. We know, too, from social fitness training, that imagery helps us to reduce our social fears. We practice our talks in front of mirrors, while imagining giving them to a real audience. We imagine opening gambits for conversations, such as "Do you live around here?" We rehearse in our minds entire conversations, particularly ones like asking for dates, where we want to help ourselves to remember to nail down the actual date and time when we'll meet someone. These exercises calm us and help us remember what we really want to do, in spite of our nervousness. With practice, imagery helps us develop confidence, first in our exercises and then in behavior out in the everyday world. The ultimate goal in working to overcome problematic shyness and social anxiety is to become less fearful in actual social situations; so while imagining social interactions is not a substitute for actual exposure to challenging situations, these exercises do help us to feel the compassion, warmth, and understanding for ourselves and others that we need to live our lives to the fullest among others.

KEY POINTS

- We can use images to stimulate particular states of mind and emotion in ourselves. We have focused on the soothing system to help balance the threat/protection system and to reduce social anxiety and painful arousal.
- You can use the exercises in this chapter to feel soothed and compassionate toward yourself more often and to reduce distress when the world triggers it.
- If it is hard to find time for the exercises, you can do them before falling asleep, when you first wake up, in the bath or shower, or even waiting at traffic lights and in the supermarket.
- If you practice these exercises regularly, for a brief time every day, for half an hour or so several times a week, or both, you will notice that you begin to feel better and more

empowered as you become able to create particular mind states.

• As in social fitness training, this is an ongoing lifelong process, creating the life and the emotions you want to feel, as you accept and master the challenges life hands you.

• Be compassionate about your practice of these exercises, too. Don't judge yourself, but be curious and enjoy them!

CHAPTER 6

Developing Compassionate Ways of Thinking

WHAT IS COMPASSIONATE THINKING?

Compassionate thinking involves empathy and understanding toward our painful shyness and distress, being kind and warm rather than self-critical in the face of setbacks, and seeing shyness as a part of the human condition, rather than isolating or shaming ourselves for being shy. Thinking compassionately increases our mental and social fitness, enabling us both to accept and support ourselves as we are, and to transform ourselves into the people we wish to be as we strive to reach our goals in life.

WAYS OF SEEING THE WORLD AND OURSELVES

Thinking with compassion as we cope with our emotions and passions is a great help in living humane and constructive lives. Indeed, the importance of compassion in the way we think is a basic tenet of most psychotherapy. However, once again we come up against the way our old brains have evolved. If we're in a potentially threatening situation, we need to make a decision about what to do quickly. So we tend to make judgments on the basis of opposites. George Kelly was one of the first psychologists to demonstrate that we construct models of the world based on our own experience and social relationships. He suggested that we do this using pairs of contrasting values or judgments: good versus bad, nice versus nasty, attractive versus unattractive, complex versus simple, hard versus easy, and so on. We don't often stop to consider that there are many alternative constructions or views of an event or thing, none of which can be viewed as simply right or wrong. These judgments about things, or "constructions," as psychologists call them, are important because they form the basis of our actions; and once we hold a belief, we seek evidence to confirm it rather than refute it. Life is just a whole lot easier if we can categorize incoming information quickly, and is less demanding than if we always take a reflective and contemplative view, assessing each person, situation, or event from scratch.

We also develop beliefs about things from what we have learned and experienced. Some beliefs are about the world, such as that the sun makes you hot or that vegetables are good for you. Others relate to ourselves, other people, and our relationships: *I am good at tennis but not good at golf; I am attractive and fit* or *unattractive and need to exercise; other people are nice* or *other people are likely to be critical.* These beliefs about ourselves and others form the basis of our sense of identity and also shape the relationships we have with other people. It is these beliefs about ourselves and others that are especially important in shyness. It's worth taking a few moments to think about how you see yourself as a *social* being: as a person moving among other people, whether your family, your work colleagues, or people you don't know, in shops and on public transport, for example. What beliefs do you hold about how you are in new situations, for example?

I mentioned just now that once we hold a belief, we tend to look for evidence that confirms it. So when we're faced with evidence that contradicts our basic beliefs about ourselves, we often reject the evidence and cling to the old beliefs, even though this might sound illogical. We do this because as humans, we crave stability, a settled sense of who we are. If we were constantly having to change our beliefs about ourselves, that clear sense of identity would be under threat, and research shows that people find this very unsettling. So people hang on to beliefs about themselves and others—even when these beliefs are not entirely accurate—because this gives them a sense of stability and predictability.

What is more, because we form relationships based on our beliefs, we also reinforce *each others'* beliefs about ourselves and other people. Our human need to belong to a group, to share an identity with others, also means that sometimes we will support beliefs even when we know they are wrong, in order to avoid being shamed or ostracized by other members of the group.

George Kelly believed that people needed to see and acknowledge plausible alternative beliefs about themselves, the world, and other people, and many kinds of psychotherapy now work on this basis. If we can overcome our instinctive reluctance to change established beliefs and become willing to explore potential new ways of seeing and thinking about themselves, the world, and others, we open up new possibilities for ourselves, including that of increased health and well-being. This is what we will learn how to do with the help of our compassionate mind.

The tendency to hold on to established, basic beliefs about ourselves and others is particularly relevant for very shy and socially anxious people. When we are painfully shy, we form beliefs that accentuate those feelings of shyness and anxiety rather than help us to cope with them. These include beliefs based on our fears that we will be judged and found wanting, that we won't be able to make a good impression on others, that others will be critical of us or, even if they are pleasant on the surface, will simply not be interested in us. These beliefs may be linked in turn to further beliefs that we are inadequate or basically unappealing. These beliefs about ourselves can become quite complicated and elaborate, forming many pathways and interconnections in our brains, and because we dwell on them a lot and constantly refer to them, they become deeply entrenched. We become so well practiced at looking out for social threats, putting ourselves down, doubting ourselves, and predicting the worst that our brains automatically run in this style of thinking.

SHAME AND SELF-CRITICISM

When you believe that you are inadequate or unappealing, you experience shame. All human beings experience shame associated with feeling bad, inadequate, or undesirable in some way. This shame can be internal or external.

When we feel external shame, we think others are judging us and coming to the conclusion that we're not adequate or that we're falling short in some way. So external shame is about how we think we exist in the minds of others. We believe others regard us with feelings such as disgust, anger, indifference, or contempt, and think that this is our fault. As a result, we want to hide, shut down, and avoid being close to others. We may be frightened that others might find out something about us they don't like and then reject us.

When we feel internal shame, we are judging ourselves and coming to the conclusion that we are inadequate, inferior, or flawed. In this state of mind we tend to criticize and attack ourselves harshly, and believe we are bad or a failure. When we feel shy, we think we are alone in these feelings, but in fact they are very common in Western cultures. Such feelings keep the threat/protection system continually in overdrive and make it very hard for us to sustain a sense of contentment and well-being. The feelings produced by internal shame are the opposite of those produced by compassion toward ourselves: when things go wrong, instead of feeling kind, supportive, and determinedly hopeful for ourselves, we feel frustration, anger, and contempt for ourselves. So where does internal shame come from? What you think of yourself is based on early experiences with other people, and if these people weren't able to care for and support you, or treated you harshly, you probably took this as a message that you weren't worth caring for and supporting. So you can see that external as well as internal shame can actually have more to do with other people's problems and emotional difficulties than with our own.

Good Shame and Bad Shame

Shame and the self-blame that accompanies it seem to be what makes extreme and painful shyness so different from ordinary shyness, which all humans feel from time to time. Shame is a highly distressing experience that can take the joy out of life and make us want to withdraw from human contact.

It's important to understand, though, that not *all* shame is necessarily a bad thing to be overcome. The crippling, chronic shame we are talking about here is about our whole selves. When we feel this kind of severe shame, we have a sense of ourselves as deeply inadequate and flawed, at worst simply and irretrievably worthless, beyond our ability to control or change, sometimes beyond help or hope.

There is a milder form of shame, however, called *signal shame,* that is useful to us and helps us to be aware of the state of our relationships. This arises if we feel that we or others have been exposed or violated in some way, ignored or rejected. We can acknowledge our feelings of signal shame and resolve them in trusting relationships. This kind of shame indicates to us not only our own vulnerabilities, but those of others as well, and reminds us that we are all simply human and alike. Thus in its mild form, it helps us to feel compassion for others and, ultimately, for ourselves.

For example, suppose you ignored a friend at a party because you didn't want to open up a conversation you were having with someone else. Maybe you just didn't want to share the attention. That is natural; it's not a big deal, and your friend didn't even notice; but you know that your friend has been a little lonely lately and would have enjoyed talking to the other person. So you feel a little ashamed of yourself.

This kind of shame is triggered by anything that signals to us that we are not living up to our own standards or those of the people we respect. In response to the signal, we often try a little harder to be considerate—for example, to be sure to invite the friend into the conversation next time something similar happens—even though we have done the person no real harm.

Parents, Children, and Shame

Cheri Huber, a well-known Zen teacher in California, in a great book titled *There Is Nothing Wrong with You,* lists a lot of the things that are routinely said to children. Here are just a few of them:

> *Don't do that ... Stop that ... Put that down ... I told you not to do that ... Why don't you ever listen? ... Wipe that look off your face ... I'll give you something to cry about ... You shouldn't feel that way ... You should have known better ... You should be ashamed of yourself ... Shame on you ... Are you ever going to get it? ... You ruin everything ... You have no sense ... You're nuts ... I've sacrificed everything for you, and what do I get? ... Give you an inch,*

you take a mile ... Anybody would know that ... You're not funny ... Who do you think you are? ... You were born bad ... What will the neighbors say? ... I could beat the living daylights out of you ... It's all your fault ... You make me sick ... If you cry, I'll slap you...

The list goes on and on. Cheri Huber argues that a constant stream of critical remarks like these lays a strong foundation for self-criticism, even self-loathing. At some point, on the receiving end of this kind of commentary, a child will conclude that there is something wrong with him.

Now, most of us heard some of these comments coming our way as we were growing up. Sometimes they are said with good intentions by parents and teachers anxious to train us in good behavior; but sometimes they come from parents who, struggling with emotional problems of their own, are unable to give their children the love and support they need. Regardless of the circumstances, this kind of statement leads to both internal shame and external shame, to severe self-criticism, and to the belief that others are looking at us critically. I wonder how many of you remember your parents saying, "What will the neighbors think?" as though your worth in your parents' eyes were determined by what the neighbors thought of you.

We are all born with the need to connect with others, to feel cared for and supported, so we all want to be wanted, appreciated, and valued, so that we are confident of getting that support when we need it and our world feels safe. If our relationships with our parents were warm and caring, we feel accepted and thus safe; but if they were rejecting, critical, or verbally or physically abusive, we are vulnerable to both internal and external shame. Parents of painfully shy children are often either overcontrolling and too protective (as in the example we discussed in chapter 1) or critical, hurtful, or neglectful. People who grow up in either kind of environment become very sensitive to any kind of even mild criticism and prone to interpret anything as indicating something bad about themselves.

Exercise: External and Internal Shame

Here is an exercise to help you become aware of the two streams of thought related to shame, one about what others are thinking and one about what you are thinking about yourself. To help see how this goes, let's look at an example.

You have asked a couple you'd like to get to know better over for dinner. They both work at the company where your spouse works. Both are known to be well organized and efficient. You have carefully planned dinner and made as much of the meal as you could before the guests arrive. You are cooking salmon with a special sauce, and sautéed asparagus. The salad is in the refrigerator, and the rice is in the microwave. You are having hors d'œuvres and wine while waiting and, while you are a little nervous, you are enjoying a get-acquainted chat. Your timer rings to remind you to remove the salmon from the oven and the asparagus from the pan. You put things into serving dishes and remove the rice from the microwave. You discover, to your horror, that you have overdone the rice and it is glued to the microwave container, which has partially melted. What do you think the couple is thinking and feeling about you? What self-critical and judgmental thoughts are going through your mind?

Table 6.1 sets out in the first column the external shame thoughts that might result ("How I think others feel and view me"), and in the second column, the internal shame thoughts ("What I feel and think about myself"). Looking at the two columns, you can see how they echo each other, how when we feel self-critical, we also assume that others are criticizing us. We assume that they are thinking about us what we are thinking about ourselves. In this case, although your guests behaved as though they understood and it was fun to improvise a pasta dish together to substitute for the rice, you worry that this wasn't what they were really thinking and that they'll talk about you on the way home. You see both the outside world and your inner world as critical and rejecting, so you feel threatened from both outside and inside and there is nowhere to go that is safe, calming, soothing, or kind. No wonder you feel stressed and threatened!

Table 6.1 Self-Critical Thoughts and Fears

External shame thoughts:	Internal shame thoughts:
How I think others feel about me and view me	What I feel and think about myself
These people will think I'm careless and can't focus. They'll see I'm nervous and look down on me.	I can't believe I didn't check the time more carefully. What an idiot! I'm always too shy and too anxious to pay attention. I'll never change!
They won't be impressed with my entertaining skills. They'll think I'm inept.	What's wrong with me? Why can't I focus? I get so distracted when I get anxious.
They won't want to come again. I made my husband look bad, too, just being married to me.	The meal would have been nice. I really mess things up when I feel self-conscious.
They won't want to be friends with someone like me.	I've blown it with my carelessness and my social anxiety.
It will reflect on my husband. They'll think I'm an airhead.	When will I learn to pay attention? I hate myself for not being able to control my anxiety and self-consciousness!

My key fear about how others will think of me is: I won't be able to make friends and find people who like and respect me.	My key fear about my own feelings of inadequacy is: I won't be able to make good friends. I'll be lonely and an outsider.

One thing you can do is stand back and recognize what you are thinking; then you are in a position to balance your critical, shaming thoughts. Engage your soothing breathing rhythm, refocus your attention, and try to gradually balance your thoughts with some questions, being sure to keep your tone kind and gentle.

- Did either of your guests seem that bothered about the burned rice?
- Did either of them express empathy or give a personal example of something similar that happened to them?
- Did either of them reassure you?
- Did they seem to enjoy your company and have a good time?
- Is this really going to prevent you from being friends?
- Is this really going to interfere with your husband's relationship with them?

- If the roles were reversed, would you reject them?
- Do you think the incident with the rice might have even broken the ice and helped everyone relax and be themselves?

Ask yourself these questions with as much warmth, kindness, and gentleness as you can muster, and compassionately pay attention to any positive aspects of your guests' reactions to which your answers direct you. This might not be easy; focusing on the negative comes so much more readily to you because your threat/protection system is in charge; that is how it works. So, if either of your guests seemed even faintly surprised or questioning, you'll immediately focus on that. However, in response to your compassionate questions, you'll remember that one of them said, "Oh gosh, I've done that too. Do you have any pasta? We can do that quickly." And you'll remember how you said, "Oh yes, I do—good idea. Let's do that." And then you'll recall how companionable it was for the two of you to boil the pasta together, rummage through the fridge, and add some pesto sauce and broccoli while the other two just went on chatting happily in the other room. If this happened at someone else's house, you'd think, ***Whew, it's not just me,*** and probably be relieved. Indeed, people like us better when we make a few mistakes here and there; you'll probably know from your own experience that someone who is "too perfect" can be a bit off-putting, even intimidating, which doesn't encourage ease and friendship.

How did you answer the question about how you'd react if this happened to someone else? Almost certainly you said that you wouldn't reject them. Gently allow yourself to think of the possibility that other people might also be kind and forgiving. When we're very shy and self-critical, we tend to have a skewed idea of what matters to other people. In fact, people tend to like you if you are warm, open, and caring, and show that you like them, not because you never make a mistake in the kitchen (or anywhere else). Nor do people dislike others just because they are shy: recent research shows that signs of social anxiety are irrelevant in determining whether people respond positively to being approached by someone. You can look a bit nervous while you approach others and people are likely to respond positively anyway. People respond when you reach out to them.

It is our fear of being judged as wanting and rejected that drives our self-criticism. If you genuinely believed that your guests weren't bothered about your slipup and maybe even felt more comfortable with you for it, would you be that self-critical? That is why table 6.1 contains at the end of each column a box headed "My key fear ... is." You can ask yourself this question whenever you become self-critical and feel disappointed, angry, or contemptuous toward yourself. Once you have identified your real fear, you can use your compassionate, balancing questioning to challenge it; but self-criticism tends to block your path to acknowledging that fear, so that if you can't acknowledge it, then you can't work on it. So try to gently challenge your self-critical thoughts, using the questioning process described here, then really notice and acknowledge your fear. Treat your fearful self compassionately as you do this so that you don't slip back into berating yourself and hurting yourself emotionally.

Safety Strategies: Submission, Withdrawal, Self-Blame, and Anger

You may find that you have developed what are called "safety strategies" to cope with external shame. We all use these strategies to try to protect ourselves in various ways. For example, to avoid physical injury we avoid dangerous sports and keep out of the way of people we think are aggressive. In just the same way, to avoid disappointment and even worse feelings of shame and inadequacy, we behave submissively, try to do nothing that might provoke anger or ridicule, and stay withdrawn and uncommunicative, taking care not to reveal anything about ourselves that we think others will laugh at or reject. Our minds are set to be self-protective. Indeed, it is very common for humans to overestimate threats. So when people feel shy, they can experience the social world as more threatening than it actually is and turn to submissive behavior and withdrawal from social contact in efforts to protect themselves. Also, when people feel shy, they tend to blame themselves for anything they think has gone wrong, in part as a defense against having others blame them. You blame yourself in the hope of getting in before they do.

Backing down and being submissive is one of the main ways we deal with situations that we find socially threatening, but it isn't the only one. Ironically, perhaps, as many of us associate threat with aggression, anger is another key defensive emotion. Have you perhaps sometimes felt humiliated and, as a result, become more aggressive and attacking toward others, possibly being arrogant, critical, and condescending?

We don't consciously choose these safety strategies. Which ones come most readily to us depend on our temperaments, physiques, and intellectual abilities, and on our environments, both now and in early life. The main problem with safety strategies is that they don't give us a chance to learn that things can be different. If you are shy and avoid others, you may never learn how to cope with your anxiety and gradually reduce it. So it can be very useful to gradually develop ways of doing things differently, confronting your social anxiety and shyness and not letting them dictate what you do. So, for example, you may make a conscious effort to look people in the eye, initiate social contact, stand up for yourself when necessary, invite people to do things with you, and develop intimacy in friendships by sharing your thoughts and feelings. This can be stressful in the beginning, but highly rewarding with persistence. We will discuss how to work on your behavior with compassion in making these changes in chapter 8.

Sharing Vulnerability as an Antidote to Shame

Far better than cutting ourselves off with safety strategies is learning to be more open with others about our vulnerabilities. The rewards this offers will in turn help us to work on reducing shyness and social anxiety. If we can be open about our vulnerabilities in a safe environment, where others are accepting and nonjudgmental, and acknowledge our feelings of shame, we will build trust and the freedom to experiment, to fail, and to laugh with our trusted friends and family about the absurdity of life's situations and our own reactions. When we can begin to tell each other in a warm and accepting relationship the things we feel ashamed about, we begin to build the foundation for real intimacy and trust.

A KEY PRINCIPLE: YOU ARE NOT FORCING YOURSELF TO GIVE UP ANYTHING

Having said all this, it's important here to emphasize one of the key principles of the compassion-focused approach: namely, that *you are not forcing yourself to give up anything.* If you choose to, you can go back to the way you were. If you feel that you are trying to force yourself to give up things that until now have seemed to work for you and keep you safe, this might actually increase your anxiety at first. So remember: you don't need to throw away your "better safe than sorry" strategies all at once. You can use them as long as they seem useful. Indeed, all of us use them from time to time. Let change come gradually; as you find your self-compassion and develop courage, knowing that you can count on yourself to support and accept you in the face of setbacks, you will find, too, that you no longer need safety strategies so much and can let them go without effort or anxiety. Your developing self-compassion will help you to become kinder, gentler, and more accepting toward yourself as you reach out, and to realize that there is no mistake or embarrassing characteristic that millions of others have not experienced.

HOW COMPASSION CAN HELP US THINK DIFFERENTLY

Imagine what might happen if we began to practice compassionate thinking every day in order to change the old beliefs we have about ourselves and other people. What might happen if we deliberately tried to refocus our attention on things that are helpful to us, if we tried not to accept at face value our old beliefs just because we always have before? Imagine what would happen if we started to look at how we are with other people, and deliberately focused on what we did well. This isn't to ask ourselves to pretend that everything always goes well—there are always, for all of us, things that don't go so well—but with practice we can refocus our attention on what we *did* do well, which we've probably tended to overlook in the past. Imagine also what would happen if we began to think about our shyness in different ways, seeing its strengths as well as its vulnerabilities, and practicing alternative ways of thinking about ourselves and other people.

Automatic Thoughts and How We Can Challenge Them

Aaron Beck, a psychiatrist working with depression during the 1960s, was one of the first to pay attention to the kinds of thought that run through our minds and how we judge ourselves when we're in certain moods or feeling certain ways. For example, on our first day in a new job or at a party, we may think things like *I hope I'm making a good impression. What if I say something stupid?* Beck noted that these thoughts interfered with people's attention to what was happening in a given moment, whether this was a task they were carrying out or a conversation with another person. Beck also noticed that when people were struggling with anger, anxiety, or depression, their thoughts tended to be about threats and potential losses of one kind or another, according to their emotional state. For example, when people were angry, their thoughts focused on whether their needs or goals were being obstructed; when generally anxious, on whether a skipped heartbeat meant an incipient heart condition; when depressed, on being inadequate and hopeless.

You can see from these examples how common this pattern of thinking, this tendency to judge ourselves unfavorably, is in all of us. When we feel shy, it is particularly strong; and we also monitor ourselves, trying to spot mistakes or problems (rather than noticing good things), worrying that others will think we are boring, unattractive, undesirable, or stupid. We have thoughts like *I don't sound good, I can't think of anything clever or interesting to say, Other people here are much more entertaining than I am, This person would rather be talking to someone else* (you probably know only too well how a stream of thoughts like this runs through your mind). These thoughts distract us and preoccupy us, getting in the way of our enjoyment of being with other people and our natural interest in them—the very things that tend to prompt others to like us. Beck called these anxious, judging thoughts *automatic thoughts* because they occur instantaneously, without conscious thought or careful reasoning; we don't even know where they've come from.

Albert Ellis, another psychologist working around the same time as Beck, noticed that people were often driven by thoughts that took the form of "should" and "ought." He focused on turning these mental instructions into preferences, encouraging people to think of what they *could* do rather than what they *must* do. He also noted that people often tell themselves that they can't possibly cope with certain emotions, that if they don't avoid these feelings, things will be just too awful, indeed unbearable. The trouble is, as he noted, that if you think along these lines, you have no incentive to try to tolerate and cope with those difficult emotions, but will strive to avoid them or, if they start to arise, to escape from them as soon as possible. It's very difficult to learn how to cope with emotions if we keep telling ourselves that they are unbearable, rather than unpleasant and difficult.

The ideas of Beck, Ellis, and others, about learning to challenge automatic thoughts and entrenched beliefs and to come up with alternatives, spread quickly and were tested through research. A psychotherapeutic approach called *cognitive behavioral therapy* (CBT) was developed, which specifically focuses on the thoughts that go through our minds when we are anxious, and the ways we feel and behave as a result. Further research has shown that this approach works well with people who are shy, helpfully challenging the belief that we will be judged unfavorably and rejected by others. CBT involves gently and gradually facing our fears through a technique called "exposure," in which we take active part in social contacts and develop alternatives to our automatic threat-based thoughts that seem more realistic, helpful, and self-supportive.

Thinking About How We Think: An Example

By now you can see how, when life confronts us with difficulties, our minds can add to our pain by jumping to certain kinds of interpretations and particular kinds of thinking. We can't avoid feeling shy or socially anxious from time to time, any more than we can avoid setbacks, loss, and trauma, but we can change the ways we think about these things, so that instead of feeling fearful and disheartened, we feel supported and encouraged to pick ourselves up and move on.

For example, let's say you have been developing a romantic relationship with someone who then changes her mind about being closer to you and just wants to be friends. If you make sense of the situation by thinking that perhaps you didn't have as much in common as you'd hoped, or that the relationship just didn't have the right chemistry and that it takes time to find someone who is a good fit, you will be disappointed, but not devastated. You might even be a bit gratified that the person values you enough to still want to be friends. Alternatively, if you are painfully shy, you might think that you are to blame for the other person's change of view, and are unlovable and inadequate and that you'll never find a partner. If you focus on these thoughts, you could find yourself discouraged, sad, and even ashamed. So in the first case, you look at the situation in broad-brush terms, taking a semidetached view, as it were, looking at your partner, yourself, and the interaction in some kind of perspective; whereas in the second situation you're trapped inside your own fears and threat-based thoughts, so closely focused on these that the possibilities that the two of you weren't particularly a good fit or that the other person had decided she didn't want any type of close relationship because of issues in her own life or background may not have occurred to you.

When our automatic thoughts are self-focused and self-blaming, they will be particularly painful and obstructive when we try to reach out to meet new people or to find a partner, because they undermine our confidence; it's difficult to take risks and learn new ways of relating to others if we're simply criticizing ourselves all the time. These thoughts and feelings can also get in between us and the other person, so that we find it hard to trust him enough to ask directly what he thinks went wrong or what he thinks the important differences between us are. It can be really helpful to be able to ask questions such as, "What made you decide that we weren't a good fit?" Sometimes what the person says is a relief, because you can see what he means and agree. Sometimes you may learn that you are doing something you're not aware of that does push people away, which is valuable feedback for the next time you embark on a relationship.

Thinking About How We Think: Automatic and Intrusive Thoughts

Automatic thoughts are triggered by many things besides specific incidents. These triggers include physical brain states, bodily states, such as fatigue, and background mood states, such as frequently feeling shy. Thoughts, sensations, and emotions that may feel as if they come from nowhere are usually related to something that is not in our awareness at the moment.

Take an unusual physical sensation like a skipped heartbeat. Variations in heartbeat are natural, and can occur anytime, but if we automatically think that this skipped beat is a symptom of a heart problem, perhaps even a signal that heart failure is imminent, we may panic, causing the heart to beat very fast and breathing to become quick and shallow; this can make us feel we are choking or about to die, and our anxiety then becomes a full-blown panic attack. Someone who has had that frightening experience may then begin to treat herself as very fragile, avoiding any situations that might increase the heart rate, like exercise, which is actually very good for the heart.

In the same way, people who are very socially anxious may experience panic symptoms or a panic attack in a social situation; thereafter they may treat themselves as very fragile socially and avoid any situations where they might become socially anxious, in order not to risk a recurrence of the alarming panic symptoms.

Another kind of automatic thought is the unwelcome intrusive thought, maybe of a violent or sexual nature. These thoughts are also common in all of us; sexual thoughts occur many times a day in males, and violent thoughts are not uncommon. If we interpret these as an indication that there is something bad in ourselves, we can become very upset and develop a psychological problem called "obsessive thinking." We cannot stop thinking about the intrusive thoughts, are frightened of them, and believe there is something wrong with us for having the thoughts. If we are very shy as well, this fear and anxiety add to the discomfort caused by our threat-based thoughts and encourage us to avoid social situations and other people even more. A compassionate mind approach reminds us that our "old brains" throw off odd, unpleasant feelings, fantasies, and thoughts as a matter of course. All of us have these odd intrusions. It is only our interpretation of them that determines how frightened we become of them.

The Compassionate Alternative

You can probably see by now that it makes sense to become more aware of the kinds of thoughts we have, and to learn not to take them at face value, while at the same time learning how to tolerate and accept emotions so that we can deal with them more effectively.

Compassionate reasoning builds on these principles—and adds one extra key element. If we're going to develop real alternatives to those shy thoughts that increase anxiety, just coming up with "facts" about how our thoughts might be distorted is sometimes not all that helpful. For example, how often have you said to yourself, *Well, I know I don't really need to feel anxious and shy; and I know that I am probably better than I think I am, ... but I can't* feel *it.* So the extra key element we need is a way to help you *feel* your alternatives, so they don't just seem true to you at an intellectual level but convince you more deeply. This is where putting compassion into those thoughts can help.

Consider also that, if we're going to develop acceptance and tolerance of difficult emotions, trying to do this "cold" may be a struggle. So, what if we learn how to generate feelings of kindness, understanding, validation, and support while we come up with alternative thoughts to our threat-based, socially-anxious thoughts? What if, when learning to be accepting and tolerant of our painful emotions, we create a kind, gentle, understanding voice that encourages and supports us in this effort? Do you think that if people develop kindness toward themselves in the face of these sorts of challenges, they're more likely to succeed? I think so, and that's the whole basis of compassionate thinking. We learn to be as open and as objective as we can while keeping the focus on kindness and support. This is the spirit of compassionate thinking, and learning to generate that emotional quality in your thoughts is a key part of the compassionate approach. So, in learning to think compassionately, we are learning to be objective, but also to develop our emotional tone and the caring motivation behind it.

Exercise: Attending to and Monitoring Feelings

Imagine you are becoming friends with someone you feel could become a lifetime partner. You are becoming closer and are having deeper and more intimate conversations. You love your time together with this person, just the two of you. The person invites you over for the evening and you are delighted—and then you learn, before the day arrives, that other people will be there, too: other friends and a cousin who's visiting from out of town.

You may feel disappointed, anxious, angry, sad, or a bit shut down and emotionally withdrawn, because you thought it would be an evening for just the two of you.

Pay attention to the thoughts and interpretations going through your mind when you think about this event. Write down your thoughts and emotions by completing this sentence:

When I heard that it was not going to be just the two of us, I felt

____

Be prepared for the answer to involve several different emotions, such as anxiety, anger, disappointment, and confusion. If you can identify different emotions, then think about the thoughts that go with each emotion:

My angry part thinks

____

My anxious part thinks

____

My "I don't want to go" part thinks

____

Do this for each emotion you can identify.

Spend some time gently, even playfully if you can, exploring these areas of your mind, becoming more familiar with the different thoughts and feelings that can go through it. Be respectful to these different parts, as if you're really interested in what they are thinking. Writing down the feelings and thoughts and really focusing on these different parts helps your mind to slow down and notice them. What you are doing here is ***monitoring*** your thoughts and feelings, so that you can see how different thoughts and interpretations go along with different emotions.

We can play with a few ideas here too, to get the hang of things. If you are feeling shy or anxious, you might think that the other person's having invited other people along means that he is getting bored with you, a signal that your relationship is "cooling off." You might then feel anxious and worried. If you do, you can reassure yourself by creating alternative thoughts and explanations. Here is what to do:

Take a moment or two to engage in your soothing breathing rhythm (review chapter 4). This will slow you down a little and help you begin to focus. Then imagine that compassionate ideal self, that part of you that deeply understands you and everything you feel.

Next recognize and accept your feelings of anxiety and concern; that is, don't try to tell yourself you are being silly or shouldn't feel like this. You can say to yourself, ***It's understandable that I feel like this because ...*** (for example, ***because I really want a romantic relationship with this person, because I have been hurt in the past I so want things to be different this time,*** or ***because it is natural to feel a bit anxious when someone really important to me may not feel the way I do).***

Next, however, recognize that your thoughts are linked to your anxiety, and because of this they may not be objective and certainly are unlikely to be helpful.

Next, using your compassion focus, begin to think of as many alter native interpretations as you can. For example, your friend may like to socialize more than you and want to include you in that wider social circle; although this might make you anxious, it also might give you an opportunity to develop a little confidence with new people. Perhaps the person's cousin wants to meet you, and your friend thought the visit would be a good opportunity to introduce you. Focus on generating a real feeling of warmth and understanding in these alternatives.

Now let's look at a different emotion. Maybe you are feeling frustrated and resentful. Maybe you're thinking, ***Inviting me was just an afterthought; my friend is just being polite in including me. Maybe he's found someone else and can't be decent enough to tell me. He knows I am shy with other people; how can he be soinconsiderate and make things so hard for me?*** By this time you may feel ready to dump the other person first or do something equally "inconsiderate" to him. As you ruminate about this, your emotions will be in turmoil, your stomach tight, and your muscles tense.

So let's come up with some compassionate ways of thinking about this.

First, as always, recognize and accept your feelings. Is it likely that your anger is coming out because you feel threatened? Is a degree of anxiety behind this? We can slow down and be honest about that without feeling ashamed. Feel compassionate toward yourself, maybe bringing to mind your compassionate ideal self, who is wise and warm and who accepts you. Once you have recognized that some of this resentment is linked to a feeling of threat and your anger is a reaction to that threat, then you can use some of the alternative ideas we just sketched out.

Perhaps the anger is still there when you've done this? If so, consider the following thoughts:

> ***All relationships involve different points of view, values, and things people want to do; so it seems only natural that at times there will be some friction or conflict in my relationship. There will be things I want to***

do that my partner doesn't and vice versa. Caring for people sometimes means doing things they want to do even though you don't particularly want to because you know it's important to them. So, by facing my anxiety and going along with this more social evening, I may actually be caring both for myself and for my friend, and it may help me go to the get-together. At the same time, learning to be assertive and express my concerns or dissatisfaction is also part of learning to be honest in the relationship. So perhaps it will be possible for me to take part in this event, but if the right opportunity comes up at another time, I can also mention to the other person that I really enjoy times together with no one else present. This might be difficult for me if I'm feeling very shy or socially anxious, but step by step, if I'm kind and as honest as I can be, it can be helpful.

If you spot yourself ruminating on your frustration and resentment, you can try to refocus your attention on more helpful thoughts; maybe refocus again on the compassionate ideal self and start to work out what is helpful to think about and focus on in this situation.

Let's look at yet another emotion that could occur in this situation: sadness. Maybe you are focused on thoughts that say, well, of course, the other person isn't really interested in you—you're probably boring and inadequate as a date. Maybe you suddenly feel ashamed that you were really interested in this person as a potential partner. After all, you may think, it doesn't usually work out for you. Maybe you suddenly start remembering previous conversations and looking for earlier signals of withdrawal that you might not have seen. You remember things you said that could have sounded stupid or silly, and you blame yourself for any little thing that might have gone wrong during previous times together. By this time shame is pulling you into deeper sadness, and you want to withdraw and never approach the person again. If this is the case, remember that it is not your fault that you're feeling like this: this is how human brains and emotions have evolved.

Once again, the first thing to do is to accept your sadness and recognize that it is understandable. Establish your soothing breathing rhythm and extend your compassion to this sadness. Your feelings may be based on a lot of difficult previous experiences where you have felt excluded or hurt.

Now try to identify the thoughts that go with the sadness, perhaps the idea that you'd hoped your friend would always only want to be with you one to one, or feeling a bit pushed out by having to share. You may well also be having anxious thoughts; anxiety is often part of sadness because of the link to previous rejection. It may be that, far from having lost interest in you, your friend wants to include you in other aspects of his life. Is it possible that your sadness is linked to the thought that your shyness or social anxiety might stop you from going down that road with your friend?

Once again, focus on your compassionate ideal self. Allow yourself to feel the kindness and support this self offers you for engaging with this emotion, so that you're not going to run away from it. At the same time, try not to feed it with brooding or anxious thoughts that will only make it more intense. For example, you might imagine yourself coping quite well with the situation, struggling with some anxiety perhaps, but coming through. You might imagine yourself being quietly pleased with your efforts, praising yourself for your courage because it wasn't easy.

We've dealt with three possible emotional responses separately here, but this is just to make the exercise clearer; remember, all these emotions can arise at the same time. If you feel that you're surrounded and weighed down by several negative emotions, this is when your compassionate ideal self can be a real help to you.

The exact thoughts and exact imaginations are for you to work out as best fits you and the situation facing you. Once you are clear in your mind that your threat-based thoughts will pull you into more threat-based emotions, whereas your compassionate desires and efforts will pull you toward more engagement and coping, you can become your own guide and mentor. Your motivation to be kind to yourself, and to develop your objective wisdom and growth in engaging with your shy and socially anxious thoughts, rather than to allow your shyness to go on interfering with or even stopping your life, will help you to develop these alternative ideas.

DEVELOPING COMPASSIONATE THINKING

In the exercise described previously, we've set out some basic ideas about monitoring your thoughts and generating compassionate alternatives. Let's go into this now in more detail.

Self-Monitoring

We've seen how our minds go wandering off all over the place at the drop of a hat, and we've seen, too, how our emotions easily suck us up like a whirlwind, whisking us into increasingly intense feelings before we're fully aware of what's happening. We're not at the mercy of our automatic thoughts and instinctive feelings, however; our "new brains" can help us by simply observing or watching what we think, feel, and do. This is really important. Only once we can see what we're thinking, feeling, and doing can we begin to change.

Exercise: Watching Your Own Mind

The purpose of this exercise is simple: just to watch the flow of thoughts and emotions as they go through your mind. First do it during an ordinary day, and then you might try doing it at another time, when you are worrying or brooding that a situation might come up where you think you will feel shy or when one has just passed that you are going over and blaming yourself about because you think you didn't do well or it didn't turn out as you wanted. Remember to engage your soothing breathing rhythm as you watch the flow of your thinking, with kindness and compassion, and notice which emotions and brain systems are stimulated as the thoughts come and go: threat-focused protection, drive/excitement, or soothing/contentment.

There are various things you can do to help you with this exercise:

- Set your watch or an alarm on your mobile phone to go off at random intervals throughout the day, if possible, more than once an hour (you can turn it off when you don't feel you can be interrupted). When it sounds, simply pay attention to your thoughts, feelings, and bodily sensations for a few seconds, and then bring your awareness back to the present moment. If you like gadgets, you can find a variety of them on the Internet to assist you in doing this. I think it really helps to carry a small notebook in your shirt pocket, purse, or backpack so that you can write down your thoughts as they arise in the moment. (You can, of course, use your compassion journal, but this may be too big to carry around with you everywhere.) Many bookstores sell very attractive, slim notebooks with a band around them, and you can choose a color you like. This can be very helpful when something happens that triggers your shyness unexpectedly or when you have strong feelings in response to an event. It can be calming in the moment to write down your reactions, as well as helpful in understanding yourself and your automatic responses in more depth.

- You can also use a small voice recorder and speak your thoughts into it.
- Some people like to write down their thoughts on postcards with paintings or photographs they are drawn to.

Exercise: Imagining Yourself as a Sympathetic Interviewer

In this exercise you imagine yourself as an observer interviewing the shy or socially anxious you. Start with your soothing breathing for a moment or two, imagine your ideal compassionate self, and interview yourself gently and warmly for a few minutes.

Using our example in the earlier "Attending to and Monitoring Feelings" exercise, you could say something like: ***You seem upset; can you tell me a little about what you are thinking and feeling?*** with a warm, gentle tone.

Your shy self might reply, ***Well, I'm feeling shy and anxious right now. My body feels tense, and I'm beginning to worry about whether my friend is interested in me or cares about me. I'm beginning to think I've been mistaken about this person's interest and that she's trying to distance herself or let me down politely. I'm feeling a little suspicious about gossip or her cousin's not approving of our relationship and I'm feeling the urge to withdraw, and maybe tell her I can't come.***

Now see if you can go on with the interview, asking yourself in a warm, caring, and wise way about the specific thoughts and feelings you have. Take particular care to acknowledge and accept these feelings, saying, ***It is understandable that you feel this way because ...*** It's particularly helpful to note any new thoughts of your own. If you feel angry, tell your gentle observer how your anger is related to your anxiety and feelings of threat.

This exercise helps you to be aware in the moment of your thoughts and how they relate to your sensations, emotions, fantasies, and images. You can also notice whether your brain becomes particularly flighty and overactive in any situation that brings on feelings of shyness and social anxiety.

Being Aware Without Trying to Change Anything

In this process of observation, you're not trying to change anything; you just notice your reactions. That's the nice thing about this compassion-focused exercise: it doesn't ask you to challenge any of your thoughts, to point out that they might not be accurate or helpful. All you're being asked to do is to be curious about your thoughts and feelings, and gently to investigate them with kindness and warmth. Remember that key principle we emphasized earlier in this chapter? You're not forcing yourself to give up anything. Your job is simply to describe to yourself as carefully and clearly as possible what is happening in your mind and body. The interviewer is yourself—your kind, compassionate, unshockable self—who is not going to blame you or shame you, but is simply curious, genuinely interested in what is going on for you.

Exercise: Compassionate Writing

We noted earlier that writing things down is very helpful in personal growth and in therapy. It helps you identify themes in your life and make connections that you hadn't seen before. It also helps you to identify the more universal threats that we all feel.

It often helps to write in the form of a letter to yourself, and that is what we do in this exercise. To give you an idea of the themes that such a letter might cover and how you might write to yourself about them, we can think back to the example we discussed in the earlier exercise "Attending to and Monitoring Feelings."

- Anxiety: ***My friend invited other people to come along with us on what I thought was a more intimate time alone together. I'm afraid it means she is losing interest in me. It's interesting; it reminds me of a time in high school when I was dating someone and she had become involved with someone else without telling me. She said she would see me at a school party and showed up with someone else. Everyone seemed to know but me. They had their arms around each other all evening. I thought I'd be sick, and finally I just left. No wonder I feel anxious. No wonder I am afraid of people just leaving me and not caring enough even to tell me.***
- Anger: ***My friend invited other people to come along with us on what I thought was a more intimate time alone together. I'm wondering if more interesting***

people have come along and my friend decided I'm not a good catch or not impressive enough. It made methink of a time in junior-high school when my friend ditched me for a group of kids who were more lively and popular. It gave me satisfaction later when the popular group ditched him. Now, I don't let anyone do that to me first. I'll jump before I'm pushed. No wonder I want to pull away now before he can do that to me.

- Sadness: ***My friend invited other people to come along with us on what I thought was a more intimate time alone together. This feels hard because I was so enjoying being with her and having someone to really talk to. I suppose I'm just not that interesting. I'm not as exciting as other people and I don't jump into conversations like others do. I also probably follow too much and don't initiate enough. I can see that this is reminding me of my friend in school who always***

dominated the conversations—and me too. Next to her, I looked like a mouse, and no one paid that much attention to me. No wonder I feel sad and neglected.

Doing the Exercises in a Kind and Gentle Way

Taking a compassionate approach means doing these exercises in a kind and gentle way that simply reflects on an experience without either avoiding it or judging it—or yourself. Have another look at the compassion circle in figure 3.2, and you'll see how you're using the compassionate attributes in these exercises. By taking time to understand what you are thinking, you are showing that you genuinely wish to be caring toward yourself and to be sensitive to what you really think and feel, without either pushing it away or criticizing yourself for it. You feel sympathy for yourself, acknowledging that it is natural to feel some concern or distress in this situation. When you stay with your experience and write it down, you are tolerating your emotions, and when you give yourself time to think about them, you are developing understanding and empathy for yourself. You are being open, kind, focused, and accepting.

You've probably noticed—I certainly have—that our thoughts, fantasies, and emotions run in many directions all at once. In any situation we can find ourselves feeling anxious, angry, and sad all at once or in quick succession. That is why I am encouraging you through these exercises to begin to notice different parts of yourself, different internal voices. We all have these different voices, some of which seem to scream at us and some of which are much quieter. When the threat/protection system is activated, for example, when we are (or think we are) being criticized, all three emotions tend to be activated because we don't know yet how we're going to respond. At the same time, the positive emotions are inhibited so we can't hear those voices as clearly.

We often have competing concerns inside us; as well as being unsure how we are actually thinking and feeling, we're juggling how we'd like to be, how we think we should be, how we feel we're able to be, and all the things that might inhibit us. Viewing these inner conflicts as natural and normal can help us make sensible decisions based on the reality of each situation we find ourselves in. When we can stand back from our experience, we can see how we have learned to cope in a particular way and value it, even if it's not ideal.

Taking the same example again, we can see the ambiguity of the situation. We can't read the mind of a friend, and there are many different possibilities. But we *can* decide to be compassionate with ourselves, as a warm friend would be, and also to be compassionate to our friends, giving them the benefit of the doubt. We can get together with a friend and see how it goes. We can also practice assertiveness skills by doing what we call a "perception check" at a later date, asking the friend how he sees our relationship and where he sees it going. At the shyness clinic we call this "strengthening our emotional muscles." The people who come to the clinic, of course, have the group for emotional support while they are trying out these things; by reading this book and practicing these skills, you are gathering around you empathy, support, and wise counsel from your compassionate ideal self and your perfect nurturing image as well as your friends. However, if you don't feel you can turn to friends or family, and need some outside support, then a therapist can be really helpful here.

BALANCING YOUR THOUGHTS

Cognitive behavioral therapists originally focused on whether or not our thoughts are rational. At the shyness clinic we have focused on whether or not our thoughts are useful to us, or supportive of our efforts. The compassion-focused approach adds a strong appreciation of our right to be irrational. This makes sense because, in fact, human beings are deeply irrational. We fall in love, we have children and nurture them throughout life, we do dangerous things we don't have to, like driving race cars, climbing mountains, and sailing round the world—and sometimes we smoke, eat, and drink too much even though we know it is bad for us!

So we can ask ourselves: Is our thinking helping us or sabotaging us by threatening us? Is our thinking raising our social anxiety and shyness, or our shame and sadness? Can we soothe ourselves a bit and balance our thinking by simply observing it? In essence, our new minds can create a counterbalancing force by focusing on kindness and gentleness, and on emotional support and encouragement.

Exercise: Validating Feelings

In the example we've followed through this sequence of exercises, we acknowledged our feelings of social anxiety, shyness, anger, and sadness, and saw them as understandable. We also noticed how our feelings could be linked to specific incidents earlier in life. We could feel empathy and validate our feelings: acknowledge them, respect them, see how they make sense in our situation. This is an important skill, because many of us have come from families where feelings, particularly shyness and vulnerable feelings like sadness and social anxiety, and perhaps shame, were considered weak, pathetic, stupid, or wrong. Some of us may have been called "too sensitive" all of our lives. It leaves us in the position of invalidating ourselves, trying not to feel socially anxious, hurt, vulnerable, sad, ashamed, resentful, or angry. So the first compassion task is to say, ***Whatever I feel is okay.*** Feelings may hurt, they may be unwelcome, and you may not want to act on them, given the realities of a situation. You may even discover that you don't need to feel the way you do as you explore the possibilities. But the feelings themselves are acceptable and understandable. You are just human, like all of us.

This is a great time to take out your journal or notebook, because the starting point of this exercise is to write down the statement: ***It's understandable that I feel like this because*** ... Write that statement at the top of the page—or on a postcard with a picture that means something to you, if you prefer—and then take a moment or two to engage your soothing breathing rhythm. Imagine your compassionate ideal self, or maybe your ideal perfect nurturer, who is deeply understanding, or a compassionate friend. Next, listen, understand, and validate your feelings. If you notice that you are telling yourself you're being silly or you shouldn't feel like this, just note the thought and gently move your awareness back to the exercise. Take a few minutes to do this.

Once you feel that you can accept your feelings or that you have begun to accept them, you can engage your soothing breathing rhythm and imagine your ideal compassionate self feeling great warmth and understanding toward your feelings, just being with you as you experience them. If a lot of pain comes up, that is completely understandable because you are opening up to emotions that you may have tried to suppress or avoid. They can be very powerful. If your feelings seem too strong, just stay for a moment with what you've written so far, and then stop the exercise, engage your soothing breathing, and imagine your ideal compassionate self by your side sending you warmth and understanding. You can come back to this exercise later, practicing exploring all your different feelings in the same way if it is helpful to you. This process takes time to develop. There's no need to rush.

KEY POINTS

- In this chapter we have focused on how the compassionate approach can be applied to our ways of thinking and reasoning. Once we have established beliefs about ourselves and others, we tend to notice only evidence that confirms them, not evidence that challenges or refutes them. With compassion, we can gently encourage ourselves toward alternative ways of seeing and thinking about ourselves and the world.
- While mild shame can be useful in making us aware of the state of our relationships, chronic and crippling shame are unhelpful and can be damaging. Severe shame often has its roots in critical things said to us as children.

• By learning to observe, attend to, and monitor our thoughts and feelings, we become able to observe our thoughts without getting caught up in them and confusing them with an absolute, fixed reality.

• We can use compassion to balance the thoughts that arise from our threat/protection system with new thoughts and feelings from our soothing, calming system.

• You are not trying to force yourself to give up anything. As you gradually develop new ways of thinking and acting, you can still go back to older ways of being at any time.

CHAPTER 7

Taking Compassionate Thinking Further

In this chapter we will practice more ways of developing compassionate thinking, balancing our thoughts by generating alternatives to threat-based thoughts, and building on our strengths and capacities. It is helpful to continue to remind ourselves that we are all doing the best we can in often difficult circumstances, struggling to cope with our shyness and social anxiety, and sometimes shame too, while we are developing our compassion and learning how to balance our thoughts. You have probably begun to notice as you experiment with the exercises in this book that some work better for you than others. This chapter will introduce you to some more options. We'll also notice possible blocks to compassionate thinking and get some more practice at writing things down.

GENERATING ALTERNATIVES TO THREAT-BASED THOUGHTS

Let's return once more to our example from chapter 6. You're developing a relationship with a friend and potential partner, and looking forward to an occasion together; then you discover that the person has invited others along too. This may arouse feelings of anxiety, sadness, anger, or all of these emotions. You may think that the friend is putting some distance between you, or has changed her mind about the relationship.

In social fitness training we as therapists or group leaders would begin by helping you challenge some of your thoughts, by asking whether they are helpful to you in this situation. We would also ask questions such as:

> *'Does your friend's behavior necessarily mean she is distancing herself from you?*

Could there be any other explanations for your friend's behavior?'

We would listen to whatever alternative explanations occurred to you and then prompt you with a few possibilities that occurred to us; for example, maybe your friend wants you to get to know the important people in his life because he thinks you will like each other, or because you are getting closer. Even if your friend is pulling away, would that necessarily mean that you weren't good enough or that you can't cope and reach out to other people? You've coped before with this kind of situation.

Thoughts and emotions can be viewed at times as theories to be tested. We can ask if they are helpful to us, whether they motivate us to reach out to others, to tell others what we need and what we think and feel. We can look at something we say to ourselves, and ask ourselves whether we would say this to a good friend who was struggling with feeling shy. We generate possible alternatives because they help balance our minds and help us to develop well-being and to flourish. We don't want to be pushed around by our "old brain" fears and superstitions. We want to be able to choose. The compassionate approach builds on these ideas, adding an emphasis on finding a kind and sympathetic tone of voice and really feeling our alternative, self-supporting thoughts as well as acknowledging them intellectually.

Exercise: Asking Questions with Compassion

Can we ask ourselves questions and generate alternative thoughts in a warm, kind, gentle, caring way? This exercise asks you to move away from the example we've been working with and think of a situation in your own life right now that is triggering your social anxiety or painful shyness. The idea is to give you some practice in asking questions with compassion on a subject that is close to you personally, so that you can see how you might adapt this format to be as relevant to you as possible.

As you do this exercise, see if you can hear the questions in your mind as gentle, kind, and compassionate. You might like to imagine the questions being asked by your compassionate ideal self, your perfect nurturing other, or an ideal therapist.

Adopt your compassionate facial expression and gentle smile, and breathe deeply for a few moments, feeling the soothing rhythm.

Now think of a situation in your own life right now that is triggering your social anxiety or painful shyness. Imagine yourself in that situation and write down in your notebook or journal whatever thoughts occur to you.

Now ask yourself some of these questions, picking the ones that are most appropriate to the situation you have been thinking about and filling in the gaps with the relevant details:

- ***Do I know for certain that _____?***
- ***Does _____ have to equal or lead to _____?***
- ***What is the actual likelihood that _____?***

- ***Even _____ if, would this person's opinion reflect that of everyone else?***
- ***Is this the only opportunity to _____?***
- ***What is the worst that could happen? How bad is that?***
- ***I've coped in the past; do I know for certain that I cannot cope now?***

Write down your answers.

If you notice that as you ask yourself some of these questions, you find yourself saying, ***Well, no, but...,*** just acknowledge that this is what the mind does when feeling socially anxious, fearful, hurt, or irritated; note the thoughts and gently bring yourself back to the task.

We saw in chapter 6 how important it is in working with these fears from problematic shyness not to fight with them or tell ourselves that we are stupid to feel them. We need to validate our feelings, as best we can, while opening our attention and thinking of alternatives. So, thinking back to the example of the friend who has invited other people along to the occasion we hoped would be a *tête-à-tête,* we can ask:

- *How would I see this situation if I were in a different state of mind, for example, if I were happy and relaxed?*
- *How might these feelings that I know have arisen to protect me not actually be accurate?*
- *Although I can look to the past for some evidence, what evidence do I have right now in this situation to support the view I'm taking?*
- *What other possible reasons could there be that my friend has invited other people? Are any of them reasonable or more likely than the ones I fear?*

We can ask ourselves different kinds of questions to focus on different aspects of how we think. For example, we might use the principles identified by Albert Ellis. As we saw in chapter 6, he worked out that many people think in absolutes, with "rules" about what they and other people "ought," "should," or "must" do or not do, and believe that certain feelings are intolerable and should not be risked. Or we might ask questions that focus on bringing out our capabilities, to balance the fearful thoughts of inadequacy. We might also take an empathic stance, trying to think of things from our friend's point of view. And we might ask questions that gently try to identify what it is that is preventing us from really accepting alternative thoughts and possibilities. The four brief exercises that follow suggest some questions you might ask from each of these angles.

Exercise: Asking Questions Using Albert Ellis's Principles

- ***If my friend does withdraw, am I saying that this is totally unacceptable and that I can't stand it? I've had setbacks and disappointments before and come through. I wouldn't be the only person who's experienced something like this.***
- ***Am I saying that people must or must not behave as I want them to rather than accept them as fallible, as we all are? Maybe they***

have different wishes and ways of living. Maybe I just get into "musts" when I get anxious.

- ***Do I have a rule that says people should never disappoint me or always check things out with me before they do anything? If so, that's probably not reasonable.***

Exercise: Focusing on Strengths and Capacities

- ***I've coped with things like this in the past and come through; they are part of life. I've usually learned something in the process. I now have my compassionate image to back me up, and I am developing compassionate skills like warmth and understanding toward myself to help me in the process.***
- ***Do I really believe I can't cope? Do I tend to underestimate myself? Do I know for certain that I can't make a plan?***
- ***If I were supporting a friend in this situation, what would I say?***

What would I like a friend to say to me? On what would we focus?

Exercise: The Empathic Stance

- ***Let me take a second to think about what could be happening with my friend. We are different and have different concerns. What might my friend think about asking, or not asking, others to join us?***
- ***What if it's not really about me? What if it's just my friend's style?***

Exercise: Noticing Blocks and Resistance to Change

- ***What is getting in the way of my giving my friend the benefit of the doubt and listening to my own wisdom about different possibilities?***
- ***I see myself as really shy, and have for a while. What worries me about changing? What kind of a person do I think I'll be if I am less shy? Is there anything***

that scares me about being in a relationship or being happy? Am I worried that being in a relationship means that my partner will expect more of me than I can give and that I won't meet my partner's increased expectations?

FINDING OUT WHERE FEAR AND ANGER COME FROM: ANOTHER EXAMPLE

Sometimes these issues are complicated. One of our clients at the shyness clinic—I'll call him David—was struggling with mixed feelings about becoming more intimate with a woman he was close to, and talking about some of their differences. For example, they had slightly different habits and lifestyles. She rose early for a daily run and loved the early morning with her coffee and the newspaper. He stayed up late and liked to sleep late; when he exercised, he went to the gym late in the day. He worried that he would need to conform to her schedule because he was afraid of conflict or letting her down. He was also frightened of her expectations that he talk more about his thoughts and feelings, and that he tell her when he felt frustrated or angry with her rather than keep it to himself; and he was afraid the relationship would become sexual, because he'd had very little sexual experience and feared he'd get nervous and be sexually inadequate. He was afraid she'd be frustrated with him and not give him time to learn. He suddenly realized that he had made a commitment to himself in childhood, a decision really, not to depend on people because it wasn't safe. They had let him down. Sometimes they hadn't shown up, sometimes they had neglected him, and they hadn't reacted well when he had told them what he really felt. His parents had been very busy and worked hard, but never seemed to have the energy to deal with children. His older siblings had been competitive and never had much time for him, the youngest; like his parents, they had provided little support for him.

David realized that an intimate relationship would involve depending on another person. He felt angry and fearful at the prospect of having to open himself up like that again, and afraid of the possibility of disappointment. His fear scared him because he thought it meant he was weak. His anger scared him because he was afraid he'd lash out and hurt someone. Actually, David was consistently even tempered and reliable with other people, including other members of his group at the clinic, because he knew how important these characteristics were to him. Consequently, it wasn't too hard for him to begin to understand that his feelings were natural, given his life history and temperament, and were, indeed, the concerns that most people have in new relationships, that other group members shared them, that it might be important to others to be there for him, and even that working things out together might be interesting and empowering, and help him to reduce his shyness in other areas of his life.

David also realized that the woman with whom he was becoming involved was pretty reliable and open with her friends and family. He decided to pursue the relationship and to talk to her about their differences, and to tell her he felt nervous about becoming sexually intimate.

He found that she also had concerns about being in a close relationship and about being let down or abandoned. Discussing their concerns helped them both to realize that these thoughts and feelings were a normal part of the process of moving deeper into a relationship. They both began to relax a bit, and he began to enjoy their relationship in a way he'd not been able to do with anyone before. David still felt sad that his fear had kept him trapped for so long, but now he could also laugh a little about how his fear was beginning to feel a bit more like excitement, with just a tinge of exhilaration.

Exercise: Writing Down Compassionate Alternatives

Have you noticed how writing down your thoughts helps you look at them a bit differently? Writing engages a different part of the brain from that used in just speaking or thinking internally. This exercise shows you one way of organizing your thoughts on paper that may be helpful in generating alternative, compassionate thoughts.

Divide a page of your notebook or journal into two columns. In one, write down your upsetting thoughts and your major fears, one by one. Opposite each one, in the other column, write your alternative thoughts and possibilities.

If you record your alternative thoughts in your notebook or journal it is easy to look back over them, but you can also preserve them in other ways: you might put them in a folder, for example, perhaps with photo graphs or magazine pictures that you find calming or inspirational; or you might write them on postcards that you can carry around with you.

Here is a sample collection of shy thoughts and compassionate alter natives to get you started.

Shy thoughts	Compassionate alternatives
There is something wrong with me for being shy.	Although shyness can be unpleasant, it's not abnormal. Remember, hardly anyone says they have never been shy, and outstanding leaders and really famous people experience shyness too. Shyness is a universal emotion linked to how our brains have evolved, so feeling shy is part of life and not my fault. As I learn to think more compassionately, I will be freer to take steps to learn how to deal with my shyness.
I'm boring and not worth talking to.	No. I have a lot of interesting things to say. It's just that when I feel socially anxious and self-conscious, I get distracted and focused on myself, and this makes it difficult to get the words out. That's something I can learn to do if I am kind to myself and go one step at a time.

When I get into new situations, I can't think of what to say.	That's very understandable because anxiety makes us focus on threat-based thoughts, which distract me. I might also be trying too hard to impress people and thus putting pressure on myself, rather than just talking about everyday things. I can also ask people questions about themselves and find out what we have in common to talk about. The focus doesn't have to be on me. I can be quiet, but smile and look friendly and interested in other people.
If I tried to ask somebody out and they said no I couldn't bear it.	Well, it's disappointing and upsetting to be rejected, but it's not actually true that I couldn't bear it. Learning how to bear and tolerate my feelings would really help me, because then I wouldn't be so frightened of them. After all, I only need to go out with one person, and if nine people out of ten reject me, that means I only have to ask ten people!
But it's just me who gets rejected.	If I talk to friends, they also tell stories about people who didn't want to go out with them or about broken love affairs. This is part of life. It's not abnormal or just about me. I can give myself a chance by learning how to cope with these feelings and continuing to ask people out.

If I disagree with other people, they won't like me.	Yes, emotions can be aroused in disagreements, but this does not mean people don't like me. I have seen many TV programs where people have disagreements but still like and care for each other. I have also seen people disagree and stay friends. So maybe I just feel they may not like me, but I have not tested this out. If people do seem to get cross or withdraw when I disagree with them, I can ask them if I upset them, ask them what I did to upset them, or push them away. If what they say seems reasonable, I can learn to act differently. I can also observe what they do when others disagree with them. Conflicts can be difficult, but productive, in that we learn about each other and about what works and what doesn't work with each person. Again, learning to bear and tolerate these feelings can be helpful. If I think I've been aggressive, avoidant, sulky, or withdrawn, I can acknowledge that and learn instead to disagree in a kind but firm manner. I can think about whether I am choosing the "wrong" kind of people to be around, that is, people who are critical, need to be right, and don't like others to disagree.

I have to give a presentation and I am very anxious about it.	A fear of public speaking is the most common fear of all. However, I notice that I tend to imagine that things will go badly, and dwell on how this might happen rather than on things going well or at least okay. So I'm probably encouraging my mind to feel anxious the whole time. No wonder I feel bad. I can learn to notice when I do this and then make a deliberate decision to use my soothing breathing rhythm. I can focus on speaking slowly and imagine myself going through a presentation step by step. I can remind myself that three major points are enough in a presentation. I can imagine that there will be some people in the audience who will be interested in what I have to say and focus on them. So when I notice my mind switching to anxiety and predicting catastrophe, I can gently notice this and, with kindness, refocus my mind on more supportive, coping thoughts. I can also practice at home in front of a mirror or with a friend.

When I go back to work after the weekend, others will have interesting things they've done, and I haven't done anything interesting. They will think I am boring.	Sometimes people have done interesting things, but if I listen carefully, I can see that it's not always the case. Rather than focus on myself, I can focus on others and show pleasure in what they've achieved or done. I can see if it's my envy that prevents me from showing them that I'm glad for them and from drawing them out about what interests them. It's understandable to feel envious, of course; that's not my fault, but it's not helpful to me to act on it. So coping with this means taking an interest in other people. I might even get some ideas for what I could do on the weekends if I really wanted to. Anyhow, we all prefer just to putter about sometimes and there is absolutely nothing wrong with that!
I sometimes have aggressive or frightening feelings that I'm sure other people don't have. must not let people know what I feel.	Our brains have evolved over millions of years and are full of all kinds of things that we didn't put there ourselves. Actually, sometimes people write down their feelings and fantasies and make a lot of money from novels or horror stories! There is nothing wrong with me for having these feelings, even though they can be unpleasant for me. All of us have private lives and areas that we keep to ourselves. The main thing is I'm working to be compassionate and helpful to others and myself.

These are just ideas for you. The key thing is to write down some of your worrying thoughts and then imagine your compassionate self or your compassionate other talking with you and helping you take a kind and supportive perspective on coping with the problem you're dealing with. Here you're learning not to devalue yourself and, at the same time, to work with what can be difficult situations and emotions.

The key is to put as much compassionate feeling as you can into these alternative thoughts. So, after you have done the previous exercise, look through the comments you have written in the righthand column and read each one in turn, slowly, with your soothing breathing rhythm, focusing on them with as much kindness and understanding as you can. Don't worry yet about whether or not you believe in the alternative thoughts; just go through them in your mind with a sense of kindness. See what happens when you go over them, focusing on the warmth and kindness in the words, the real desire to be helpful. You will also probably come up with some other alternative thoughts that work better for you. Write these down too.

THE COMPASSION COPING CARD

If you come up with certain ideas that seem particularly helpful to you, then try this. Find a postcard that has on it a picture that seems soothing or compassionate in some way. Then on the back of the card, write down your compassionate coping thoughts. Spend a few moments reading through these thoughts in a kind, supportive, gentle way. This will be your "compassion coping card." You can keep it with you and take it out to read when your anxiety gets unpleasant. When you use it, always remember to keep, as best you can, this supportive, understanding, and kind tone when you're reading your alternatives.

COMPASSIONATE SELF-CORRECTION

In trying to overcome problem shyness, we are learning to observe and monitor ourselves, and to identify alternative ways of thinking. We are trying to change, which involves trying to correct unhelpful ways of thinking and behaving that have become familiar to us. So it's important that we understand the difference between what we may call compassionate self-correction—gently, supportively, patiently directing ourselves toward more helpful ways of being and doing—and the kinds of self-attacking criticism that lead to shame and humiliation, which are profoundly unhelpful. To begin with, let's summarize the differences among guilt, shame, and humiliation.

- When we feel *guilty,* our attention is focused on the hurt we have caused to another person. We feel sadness and remorse for our behavior, and we feel sympathy and empathy for the other person's pain. We try to put ourselves in the person's shoes and see the hurt from that person's point of view. We apologize for our behavior and make amends as best we can.

- When we feel *ashamed,* our attention is focused on potential damage to our reputations and our standing with ourselves and others. We feel very anxious, sometimes paralyzed, confused, empty, and angry with ourselves. We think about how others will judge us as bad, incompetent, or evil. Our behavior is submissive, focused on appeasing the other person, and we want to escape. We may apologetically deny what we've done, try to avoid responsibility, and even emotionally or physically harm ourselves if the shame is very intense.
- If we feel *humiliated,* we blame the other person and see that person as having caused us harm. We feel very angry, and want justice and revenge. We think about the unfairness, how we have been hurt, and we judge the other person harshly. Our

behavior is focused on justifying ourselves and seeking revenge.

You can see from this brief summary how more extreme shame and humiliation are part of our activated threat/protection system, which intensifies our fear, anxiety, and pain in the attempt to protect us, and how guilt is associated with the soothing system, which encourages us to apologize and soothe the other person, show comfort and restore the person's sense of safety with us.

If we have done something wrong, we feel guilty; we feel sorrow and remorse, and we want to make things better. If we are intensely ashamed, on the other hand, we focus on condemning and punishing ourselves, usually for past errors or transgressions, and we treat ourselves with contempt, anger, frustration, and disappointment. We focus on what we think is wrong with us and we are afraid of being exposed. Our shame is global and focuses on our whole selves and our fear of failure. We are likely to withdraw and avoid people. If we think we have done something wrong, we feel afraid, our hearts sink, our mood plummets, and sometimes we behave aggressively. If, in addition, we feel humiliated, we feel angry and are likely to ruminate over what we think has been done to us.

Compassionate self-correction is focused on a desire to improve and on our emotional growth. We think about how we can do better next time, so we encourage ourselves and treat ourselves kindly. We try to see what we did well and build on that. We focus on particular attributes and qualities we'd like to improve on, and our hope for success, which makes us want to stay engaged and continue to learn. So we learn to deal kindly and swiftly with guilt, and to work to improve without inflicting shame and humiliation on ourselves.

The Teacher in Your Head: Critic or Compassionate Guide?

Imagine a child who is learning, but struggling and making mistakes. A critical teacher focuses on the mistakes, points out what is wrong, and sounds irritated, implying the child isn't paying attention or could do better if he tried. Fear and shame are what the teacher is trying to make the child feel, believing that these will motivate the child to do better. A compassionate teacher, on the other hand, recognizes how hard it can be to learn new things. The teacher focuses on what the child does well and builds on that, praising effort, trying to find out where the difficulty is, giving accurate and clear feedback on how to improve, and then providing opportunities for practice in a supportive, kind environment where making mistakes is considered a natural part of learning.

What kind of "teacher" do you have in your head? If you notice that you are self-critical when you make mistakes or experience a setback, then just being aware of this and shifting again and again to compassionate self-correction will help you gradually shift from shaming yourself, which is harmful and unhelpful, to compassionately correcting yourself. It is part of the step-by-step, balancing development of self-compassion throughout life.

Compassionate Self-Correction vs. Shame-Based Self-Criticism: An Example

Imagine a woman—we'll call her Sarah—who has been involved in an important project at work. It was her job to give a presentation summarizing the project's results. She worked hard to put the presentation together, especially because she felt very anxious about standing up in front of a roomful of people on such a significant occasion for her team. On the morning of the presentation, however, she felt so anxious that she left the house without some of the latest slides and handouts, which she'd taken home the night before to check over one more time. As a result she felt distracted and didn't give as good a presentation as she had intended.

In the following table, you can see, in the left-hand column, Sarah's automatic, self-critical thoughts, and in the right-hand column, the alternative perspective that goes with compassionate self-correction.

Shame-based, self-attacking criticism	Compassionate self-correction
People are disappointed and frustrated; they think I'm not up to the job, that I'm not confident enough, that I get rattled too easily.	It's understandable that I feel this way, because I only felt safe when people approved of me and weren't mad at me. I felt alone at home and at school. I have done good work on this project, and others know that. My boss complimented me last week. A couple of people were supportive after the presentation, saying they had forgotten things too, and that I had presented most of the important points. Next time I will lay everything out by the door the night before, and double-check to be sure I have the latest slides and my notes and handout.
My work group will not want me on their team; they'll want someone else.	There has been a lot of visibility and pressure around this project. Other team members are also stressed and making mistakes. Nobody has asked them to leave. I've been doing my best and working hard.

I shouldn't have even tried. I'm just not good enough.	It is understandable that I feel this way, but not feeling good enough is related to my past and my parents being pretty indifferent and critical toward me, not to what is true now. I'm glad I tried. That says something about my courage and persistence, and the likelihood that I will meet my goals.
I'm a failure and will always be an outsider.	That's understandable too, I've felt lonely a lot in my life, but I have a team and relationships that are supportive. My frustration and anger at myself are part of the stress on this project.
I can just see my critical parent saying, "Who do you think you are? I told you that you weren't up to it."	I know this image really hurts me and always has, but I don't need to let it drive me now. I can think about and seek out people I trust, with whom I can take the risk to share my feelings about this, and who can give me honest and helpful feedback. I can apologize for forgetting. I've done it before. I also need to talk a bit more in our work group and do some more pleasurable activities. I've been working so hard I've been neglecting myself.
Response to transgression/mistakes	Response to transgression/mistakes
• shame, avoidance, fear	• guilt, engagement

• sinking heart, lowered mood	• sorrow, remorse
• feeling angry and aggressive toward self	• reparation

You can see from this example that whereas the criticism in the first column leads to shame, fear, and avoidance, with Sarah feeling angry and aggressive toward herself, the compassionate comments in the second column enable Sarah to feel appropriate remorse for her mistake, engage with others affected by it, and think calmly about how to do things better another time.

Having looked at this example, see if you can draw up a similar chart for an episode in your own life. Be sure to:

- acknowledge and be understanding of your feelings
- focus on your strengths and good experiences
- generate alternative self-supportive thoughts
- think about the specific behavior you would like to change with compassionate self-support

STANDING UP AND FIGHTING BACK

In addition to soothing yourself, it can also be compassionate to stand up to your internal shaming critic and fight back. Start by visualizing this internal critic. What does it look like? Is it human or nonhuman? What facial expressions do you see? What emotions are directed at you? Now imagine your wise, compassionate self, or being like someone you see as wise and compassionate. Take a few moments to get into that role. Now imagine facing up to your shaming critic and saying something like, *I'm sorry you're upset and feeling vulnerable, and want to lash out. But this is not appropriate and isn't going to work. I am taking charge now.*

It may be a good idea to write down the names of the people who have been your primary critics or have somehow helped you develop your self-criticism. Think about what they may have been thinking and feeling and whether they really had your best interests in mind. If you conclude that they didn't, complete the sentence: *I don't think you had my best interests at heart because ...* Or you may want to write a letter to the person who was most unhelpfully critical of you, telling that person why you don't think he had your best interests at heart and why you are now rejecting his criticism. You can decide later whether to send it or not. It depends on what you think the outcome might be. Even if you don't send the letter, simply putting your thoughts and feelings on paper may help you develop insight into your own internal critic.

You can also try another version of this exercise that was used in a recent research project based on compassionate mind training. Participants were told to imagine a "confident, resistant, and resilient image," an image that would stand up for them in the face of attacks or mistreatment by the inner critic. The image was to be strong, logical, persevering, and self-confident. They then wrote a letter to the inner critic to project the idea that they were strong, "unbeatable," confident in themselves as the critic was, courageous and determined to fight back, logical, resilient, and intolerant of mean and unjust treatment. Then they wrote five statements retaliating against the self-critic, and repeated them out loud three times a day for two weeks. In two weeks participants (who were acne sufferers) found that not only had their skin complaints improved, but their levels of depression and shame were lower.

MIRROR, MIRROR: CORRECTING IMAGES AS WELL AS THOUGHTS

When we feel painfully shy, we often spend a lot of time imagining how we look to others—and we distort the image of what people see in a markedly negative direction. We think about ourselves in a critical and nitpicky way, looking for any little imperfection or flaw and exaggerating it out of proportion. To help shy people come to a more realistic and less unbalanced view of their own image, I ask those who come to the groups at the shyness clinic to practice presentations and social interactions in front of a mirror—and this includes seeing themselves blushing and feeling unconfident. In fact, I think having a more realistic image of ourselves is so important that I had a mirror installed that covered a whole wall in the group room. Clients can look in the mirror when they want to check to see how they are doing, but it also helps them to be able to focus on how they are really thinking and feeling, and then compare that to what they see in the mirror. "Research has shown that mirrors prompt an awareness of our inner thoughts and feelings. It's interesting that when we disagree with the majority, we are less likely to agree aloud when looking in a mirror than we are when there is no mirror."

Often, just talking to yourself in a mirror allows you to see your whole self, rather than just the aspects of yourself, your appearance, or behavior that you're not happy with. In other words, it helps you to balance your thoughts, to correct your threat-based thoughts about yourself. One of my clients had a tremendous concern about blushing, which he felt he did in important business meetings. He believed that people who saw him blush were critical and thought less of him. He was appalled when I suggested we use the mirror. He definitely did not want to watch himself. He thought it would make him feel much worse. Still, he eventually decided to try it. He gave a brief presentation in the form of an update on the project he was managing while standing just a few feet from the mirror. When he finished the presentation and turned around to face me, he was shocked and relieved. "I don't look as bad as I thought I would," he said. "I could see myself blush, but I found that I didn't feel so critical or see the blush as so unusual. It seemed kind of ordinary." I also suggested he watch to see when others blushed in meetings. When he did, he found that, before he began to observe people, he hadn't even noticed that some people blushed just as he did. You might want to try that too.

Exercise: Using a Mirror

This exercise will help not only with developing compassion toward yourself, but also with reducing your self-consciousness and your concern that you don't look good in front of others.

Imagine yourself with all the qualities of your ideal compassionate self. Feel your gentle, genuine facial expression. As you look in the mirror, tell yourself your alternative, helpful, soothing thoughts. Express as much kind feeling while you do that as you can. See if this works for you. If not, just let it go, or wait and try it again at another time.

It can be particularly helpful to do this exercise before and after you practice a talk, or to rehearse something important you want to say to someone. In this way you can experience your ideal compassionate self with you as you practice. It can feel like having a good, gentle, supportive friend right there beforehand and afterward, so you can just feel free to concentrate on what you want to say while you are practicing your talk or your part of a conversation.

GETTING A DIALOGUE GOING

Some decades ago, a German psychoanalyst called Fritz Perls developed a school of psychotherapy that came to be known as Gestalt therapy. Perls believed that it was helpful in working to bring about change for the client to become more aware of her own thoughts and feelings, particularly through dialogue with a therapist who was committed to being open and genuine, rather than playing a role. One of the ways in which Perls suggested this could be done was to use an exercise involving having the client switch between two chairs. It's an exercise that continues to be popular in many types of psychotherapy today. The compassion-focused approach uses these ideas and the technique to help us develop a dialogue between our threat/protection system and our soothing system.

Exercise: Using Two Chairs

Begin the exercise by placing two chairs so that they are facing each other. Sit in one chair and express your worries and concerns aloud. You don't need to go deeply into your feelings because what you are interested in at this moment is the content of your thoughts. So it is best not to spend time criticizing and blaming yourself and getting deeply into those feelings. Everything we're doing is aimed at strengthening your compassion itself and your compassionate feelings.

When you have finished voicing your concerns, stand up and walk around a bit, engage your soothing breathing rhythm, and then, as you move to sit in the other chair, assume your compassion posture, that is, leaning slightly forward to indicate that you really want to hear your concerns and worries, and using your warm facial expression and kind, gentle, and accepting tone of voice.

Now, sitting in the opposite chair, the one facing the original chair, you are your compassionate self, who feels wise, assured, calm, and kind. Let that experience sink in for a moment or two. Then speak gently with a kind tone to your anxious self.

Continuing with the example we worked with in chapter 6, you might say something like:

"Hello, shy, anxious, and worried self." Try to say this warmly, with genuine care. "It's understandable that you are worried about what it means that your friend included other people during your planned time alone together. It was an unexpected thing to do and reminded you of hurtful experiences in the past. I remember those, too, but I also remember that you coped and learned from those experiences, and worked to build a better life because of them. It seems to me that you have more courage and strength than you're in touch with right now. In your heart you know that your feelings will settle down and that chances are things are okay between you and your friend; and if they're not, you can cope."

It sometimes helps to practice with another person's example to start. Here's one you might like to use.

Dan said, "I'm really afraid of walking over to a group of people at the party tonight and trying to start a conversation. When I try to do it, my palms start to sweat and I feel shaky. I also remember being made fun of in school when I tried to talk to a pretty girl. I'm afraid people will see how nervous I am and think I'm ridiculous."

If you'd like to practice by responding to Dan before you come up with a situation of your own, try to generate a compassionate response to Dan. See if you can include phrases like these:

"It's understandable that you are anxious about talking to people tonight..."

"I also remember that you coped and learned from..."

"I notice that you now..."

"I think you have more courage and strength than..."

"Chances are that..."

"If not, you can cope with..."

Perhaps the previous examples will help you get started. On your own, you'll be much more creative and accurate with the messages that will be helpful to you. Please be careful not to give yourself advice, use words like "should" and "shouldn't," or tell yourself not to feel a certain way. Doing this will invalidate your feelings, and the purpose here is to compassionately accept your feelings, to see them as understandable, and, at the same time, to compassionately generate alternative ways of thinking and dealing with situations. It is also good to spend more time in the "compassion chair" than in the "worried chair" so you can hear yourself and build on your compassionate thoughts, absorbing and feeling them as you speak. You can also use the word "we" rather than "I" to generate a feeling of connection and kinship with the compassionate part of you. Usually, you just spend a few moments in each chair, and you can go back and forth between the two as you practice and think of things you forgot to say or new things you want to tell yourself.

Now, if you are ready, try your own example, and start by saying what you are worried about.

COPING IN THE PRESENT MOMENT

It is easy to get distressed in response to the events of your day. A colleague who is having a bad day is brusque or short with you; a friend you're meeting for a quiet drink turns up with a bunch of colleagues from her office who all seem very loud and confident; your manager tells you that you must give a presentation tomorrow to a new group; an attractive person you know slightly and would like to know better suddenly turns up at a restaurant where you are having dinner, and smiles and says hello, waiting expectantly for a response, and you can't think of anything to say—any or all of these can suddenly plunge us into anxiety. However, we can use our stressed-out and socially anxious feelings as cues to make the effort to rebalance ourselves.

Exercise: Emergency Rebalancing

Imagine for a moment that something or someone has upset you.

- Move your attention to observing your thoughts, emotions, and bodily sensations. Put them into words, if you can, to give yourself a little distance.
- Slow yourself down a bit by engaging in your soothing breathing rhythm and focusing on your posture. Allow yourself a slight smile and let your muscles loosen. Imagine yourself as your compassionate ideal self, including your stance.
- Shift your attention to the soothing system. You can visualize your calm, soothing place, attending to its sensory details—breeze, light, colors, sounds, or smells—to ground you. Imagine your compassionate image, your own warm and calming voice, or a compassionate friend who understands, and is kind, supportive, and encouraging. Take the feelings into yourself.

- Using this kindness and support, focus on different perspectives using your compassionate thinking and reasoning: your coping, strengths, courage, and persistence. You can imagine what you would say or do for a friend. You might also bring to mind a memory of someone who was kind to you and helped you, or a similar time when you coped well.

What you are doing here is stepping to the side of the threat/protection system and refocusing yourself from within your positive emotional systems. Experimenting is the best way to see what will work for you, and it will probably vary from time to time. It will really help if you can practice this exercise daily. The times when you feel just a bit distressed are great ones in which to practice your skills; then, when the real crunch comes, you'll be ready for it. It's like sports practice: if you've done your drills, when the actual game starts, you are ready for the challenge.

GETTING HELP

Sometimes circumstances will be harder than we can manage by ourselves, even with good self-help advice like in this book. A really important professional or social event, a great personal upheaval like losing a loved one or discovering an affair, being bullied, having money problems or serious illness can all exacerbate our shyness and social anxiety to the point where we need not only all the resources we can muster but help from other people too. We can improve our capacity to cope with such major upheavals and stresses by balancing our thinking and being compassionate toward ourselves. And practicing compassion now will help us in the tough times, but a compassionate approach may sometimes mean reaching out for more help, including professional help. Recognizing that distress may be too intense for us to shift into different brain states on our own can be a powerful step along the road in our development of self-compassion.

COMPASSIONATE THINKING TOWARD OTHERS

In this chapter we have focused on compassionate thinking directed toward ourselves. We can use these same skills in helping us develop compassion toward others. When we feel shy and socially anxious, it is easy to withdraw into our own concerns and worries, become self-preoccupied, and forget that everyone feels shy and socially anxious sometimes, or feels sad and disappointed, or frustrated. They need our acceptance and support in just the same way that we need theirs. Using your compassion skills and the compassionate orientation you have learned toward friends, acquaintances, and people you want to get to know will help you develop good relationships. Imagine how you would feel if someone you loved were in distress. How would you talk to that person? How would you help?

Now you can focus on people in your life with the same compassionate approach you are learning to use with yourself. And this doesn't stop with your friends, family, and colleagues. All of us want happiness and none of us wants to suffer, which also means that all of us can learn to extend compassion beyond those we care for to strangers, people we don't like, and our enemies. Try to imagine yourself in the position of someone at work or in your personal life with whom you experience conflict, and see if you can think and feel as that person does. For example, if a colleague is often brusque to you, you might imagine that the person is stressed about something else, or remember how much additional work that person has had lately because someone has been away from work with the flu. It is important to remember, however, that we don't want this to become a "should" or an "ought to." That comes from the wrong emotional system. If you find it hard to be compassionate toward yourself and others, don't beat yourself up about it; it's hard because it is very hard for all of us. We are all in the same boat, just coping the best we can.

KEY POINTS

- We are continuing to build our compassionate social fitness by developing and practicing new ways of thinking and building new connections in the brain.
- The compassion-focused approach helps to balance our thoughts by purposely triggering our soothing system, which isn't threat/protection based. You have practiced shifting into the soothing system again and again by doing the exercises.
- We are using the abilities of our "new brain"—reasoning, wisdom, and logic—as opposed to the "old brain" instincts for self-protection to bring social anxiety and painfully shy thoughts back into balance. We can change beliefs about the world and ourselves that do not serve us well to those that are beneficial to us.
- A compassionate approach to shyness helps you to be more compassionate with yourself, and even more courageous as you change; and in the process, you can help change

the world by making it a more compassionate place.

CHAPTER 8

Compassionate Behavior

Compassionate behavior in humans evolved from the altruistic and caring behavior of mammals living in groups. Especially important were the different types of care a mother provided for her infants. For example, mothers in many mammals are sensitive to the distress calls of their infants and will come and help soothe or rescue them when they hear these sounds. Of course, it is not just mothers among us who are sensitive to distress in others: in fact, evolution has made it possible for us all to be sensitive to the distress in ourselves and others with a wish to relieve that stress. That, of course, is the basis of compassion.

So compassionate behavior is *taking action,* doing things that are aimed at being helpful, encouraging, and supportive, especially when we or others are confronting distress or difficulties.

Behaving compassionately means behaving toward others and ourselves in ways that will alleviate suffering and move us toward our goals. This includes behavior that aims to teach, guide, and mentor as well as to nurture, soothe, and protect. So while it may involve caring for ourselves, it may just as easily mean doing things that challenge us or scare us a bit, such as approaching new people, deepening intimacy with those we already know, expressing hurt, or being more assertive. These are behaviors that will be beneficial in the long run, but take courage and persistence in the short run. Compassionate helpfulness does not mean the kind of submissiveness, just giving in to others, that leaves us resentful and overly needy of approval. It can involve assertiveness, standing up to others, and setting limits. Sometimes people think compassionate behavior means simply being nice and hiding your anger or dissatisfaction, or always putting others first. However, that is a misunderstanding because it implies we need to accept being dishonest, to hide what we truly think and feel. On the contrary: compassionate behavior is being honest and authentic with ourselves and other people, while not deliberately trying to hurt people, and taking account of their needs and feelings too.

We also need to show ourselves compassion as we change and grow. As we develop new ways of behaving, we may also find ourselves in new dilemmas, and as we become more assertive and actively resist negative stereotypes of shyness, we may unwittingly invite dominant behavior from others. We'll explore how we can resist the impulse to do that, and also how to handle bullying.

COMPASSIONATE ACTION: MOVING TOWARD OUR GOALS

Planning New Behavior: A Step-by-Step Approach

It makes sense, when we have a goal in mind, to think about the specific things we need to do in order to move toward it. It also makes sense to begin with the easier things, taking a step-by-step approach where each step builds on the previous one. For example, if you wanted to get physically fit, you might first make a decision to join a gym, then get advice on certain exercises, and gradually develop skills in those exercises.

It is no different when working with shyness. If we are uncomfortably shy, we tend to pull back and withdraw from other people; so the skills we want to develop are those that will help us move toward other people and engage with them. The trouble is that, when we feel shy, particularly if we are also feeling a bit down, even simple things that we could do to begin chipping away at our avoidance of social contact can seem daunting. So think of some small steps that might challenge your shyness, and recognize that if you could manage just one of them, this would be a step forward. When you're trying to decide what steps to take, you might like to think of the motto we use in the shyness clinic to guide us, that is, that we look for steps that are "challenging or stretching but not overwhelming."

It helps to start small. So you might choose something as simple as saying a pleasant hello to your neighbor or the cashier at the supermarket, asking that person how he is, and making one or two comments about the weather or current events. It may be speaking up at least once during the weekly meeting at work. It may be smiling at the person you are attracted to, or to people in general. People are more likely to respond positively if you smile at them than if you keep your eyes down and look withdrawn or indifferent.

Practicing New Behavior: Beginning to Take the Initiative

So you could just practice smiling at people around you and notice their reactions. When you ask a simple question, such as, "How are you today?" take an interest in what people say in reply. Look at people rather than away from them when you're speaking to them. If you have an interest in something like computers or cars, you might try going into a shop or showroom and asking one of the staff to show you what she thinks is their best model. When the person has done this, you can thank her and walk out. If you have bought a product or piece of clothing that you don't really want, return it to the salesperson and tell him it didn't work out and you'd like to return it. When you've completed the transaction, thank the person. If you feel nervous, remember to smile. If you don't have something you'd like to return, buy something and return it so you can develop the skill. If someone at work or a friend makes what feels like an unreasonable request, such as asking you to do much more than your share on a project, say no politely and firmly with a brief explanation of why it won't work for you.

You might build up from here to asking a friend out for a drink, or even inviting her over for a meal or out to a film. These are acts where we begin to take the initiative. If someone can't make it or says no, then you have still made progress: you can think to yourself that you made an effort, that you are coping with a setback, and that you can try again until you get a yes.

You might see people you could help out; for example, an elderly neighbor might be struggling to do his garden. Offer a helping hand and take an interest in him. You can consider joining a volunteer organization where you can work together with others on your chosen activity.

Another good way to practice meeting people without challenging yourself too much all at once is to join a group of people who are doing something you're already interested in, such as painting or meditation. If sports are your passion, you could also apply to join an organized sports team; shy people often make good team players. This may be particularly helpful for those of you who are in high school or college. Coaches often don't mind if you feel shy, as long as you play as well as you can; in fact, they will sometimes help you to get more involved with other team members. If you feel socially anxious, joining a sports team can feel like a big challenge, but it is often well worth it because sports teams are great at giving us a sense of belonging. It can also really bring out the strengths of shyness. Many shy sportspeople are great team players and even team captains, very tuned in to how their players are feeling, considerate of them, thoughtful, and good at strategy. Their teammates are often devoted to them!

Whatever you decide on, the key point is that you're opening yourself up to engaging socially with other people. In this way, you're taking on your shyness and practicing social behavior. Exactly how you do this will be up to you. Just keep practicing, a step at a time, no matter how small those steps are. Remember, a journey of a thousand miles begins with a single step.

To maintain progress, it's a good idea to plan in advance what steps you're going to take. For example, in social fitness training people assign themselves three new behaviors to practice each week, such as saying hello to someone at work or talking to someone they'd like to know. Other similar actions are asking someone to go to lunch with you, making at least one comment at a meeting, and asking someone out for coffee, dinner, or a movie. It can help to brainstorm with someone else to think of warm and friendly things to say and do as part of your new way of behaving—and also what to do if things don't go as you've planned. This can include thinking about what to do when things go *really* wrong, as they do sometimes for all of us. What if, in our nervousness, we write an address down wrong or, heaven forbid, turn up at the wrong coffee shop or direct the other person to the wrong one? If you can laugh just a little at all the ordinary day-to-day screwups we all worry about and find ourselves in from time to time, that is just one more way you can be compassionate with yourself.

Exercise: A Compassionate Letter to Support Yourself

Changing our behavior is challenging to all of us, so writing a letter to yourself before you start can be very helpful. It creates a compassionate and encouraging inner orientation to begin with; and as you write, you can plan and think about what you're going to do differently. You can also put down in your letter ideas about why changing your behavior is likely to be helpful to you; and you can think about what is going to be relatively easy or more difficult, and consider how to deal with the more difficult things. As we've seen before, writing things down in this way is really helpful in clarifying your thoughts.

As you write your letter, try to get into the role of your ideal compassionate self, who is a wise, strong, deeply understanding and caring, and who believes in you, as outlined in chapter 5, in the exercise "The Compassionate Ideal Self in Action." Or, if you like, bring to mind the image of your perfect nurturer, and imagine that image communicating with you with support and encouragement, in a kind way that helps you do things you've been avoiding or find difficult.

Choose one behavior to begin. Start with: ***It is understandable that I feel socially anxious about doing this*** [asking someone for a date, going to a job interview, meeting with your boss or manager, asserting yourself with a friend or colleague] ***because ... In fact, practically everyone experiences shyness from time to time.*** Don't worry about writing the letter "correctly." You are experimenting in order to get the feel of it; you'll get more used to doing it with practice, and as you do, you'll find your letters becoming both easier to write and more helpful to you.

Next write down the things you could do that would help you cope with this situation. You might recall other times when you've coped well, even though you thought (before the event) that you might not; for example, ***I know I am feeling anxious, but I remember that two weeks ago, I was able to ...*** Now write down the steps you can take. So you might write sentences that start with ***I can ... I will be able to ...*** and ***If this happens, then I will ...*** As you write, imagine yourself coping. What you are practicing here is one of the ways of compassionate thinking we've explored earlier in this book, that is, focusing your attention on things that are helpful to you rather than just letting your mind dwell on your fears and thus stimulating your threat system.

Try to resist saying, ***I should*** or giving yourself advice. Instead, you might write something like: ***I've been feeling I could tolerate my anxiety a bit more in order to ... Now let's see, what might help me to get started?*** You can find out whether the letter is helpful by being aware of how you feel when you're writing it, and then again when you read it over in a couple of days. If it sounds kind, understanding, gentle, and warm, then you are likely to find it more helpful.

So practice writing down a few small steps you can take to move toward your particular goal, with the intention of doing them in the next week. Focus as best you can on a sense of your ideal compassionate image or perfect nurturer backing you up and supporting you in your efforts, reassuring you that your compassionate self will be waiting to applaud and nurture you after you do something socially in spite of feeling shy. Remember, this person is ideal in your mind, beyond human imperfection, because the person comes from your imagination. This person, animal, or image understands your feelings, sees them as a natural part of being human, and always cares about you, no matter how you feel. Reminding yourself of this may help you feel freer to explore: to meet people, talk to them, join clubs, or play sports and to ask for help from friends, mentors, and coaches when you need to. Asking others for help is a good way to be compassionate toward yourself and reduce your social anxiety at the same time.

Reflecting on the Steps You've Taken

It can be useful to use your memory to begin to generate a sense of confidence—even if you don't feel very confident at all to start with. For example, you could think back to the times when you took risks socially and things worked out for you, or times when you remember having felt socially anxious but then becoming comfortable in a new situation. Remember how you've coped before and come through. If you find yourself dismissing those efforts, just notice that and return your focus to your efforts. Think about how you will feel knowing you are helping yourself to grow, developing trust and confidence in yourself, regardless of any immediate outcome.

Sometimes you will find yourself thinking, *I didn't do anything today or this week.* When this happens, it can help to ask yourself, *Well, okay, is there* anything *I have done this week that I wasn't doing before?* Interestingly, you may find that this jogs your memory and you remember one or two new things that you *have* done. They may not be the steps you planned, but you did them nonetheless, and even if they're small, they're worth paying attention to. So, remember to ask yourself that question when you think you haven't done anything. You'll probably surprise yourself with what you've overlooked!

BEING ASSERTIVE

Assertiveness is the ability to express your emotions and needs without violating others' rights and without being aggressive. When we feel shy, we often try to please others in order to avoid rejection, and may violate our own rights in doing so. Assertiveness is a learned skill that involves expressing and maintaining the right to our values, beliefs, opinions, and emotions, and deciding for ourselves whether we want to justify or explain our emotions. It involves telling others how we want to be treated, expressing ourselves, and being able to say no. Sometimes it involves saying "I don't know," "I don't understand," or "I don't care." It means taking the time we need to formulate our ideas and to make mistakes, and to stand up for ourselves and what we want. It involves expecting or even demanding to be treated with respect.

Learning to be assertive can be useful, perhaps especially in the workplace. Again, this is best done in small steps so that you're not overwhelmed. Here is an exercise that gives you the chance to practice what you want to say. As you do this exercise, you will feel your social anxiety rise and then fall, and as you get used to doing it, you will feel the anxiety rising less and falling sooner. This is how you can learn to tolerate anxiety and reduce it with practice.

Exercise: Compassionate Self-Assertion

First, take a few soothing breaths. Now imagine your wise, strong, kind, and compassionate self saying one thing you really think—something that others might not want to hear, such as that your workload has become too heavy or that something can't be delivered by a certain time. Assertiveness doesn't have to involve going against what other people say or want; it still calls for assertiveness, and can be just as challenging, to give instructions to other people or to volunteer to take the lead on a project. Taking the lead on a project is a particularly valuable learning experience, and asking for help from more experienced leaders is another way to work on your assertiveness.

It helps to do this exercise in front of a mirror. When I practice with a mirror in advance of situations where I need to assert myself, I sometimes notice that I look and sound surer of myself than I think I do, or I can see a particular way of behaving that I want to change; for example, I might see the need to face another person more directly and stand up straight.

When we practice self-assertion, we can also hear the difference between straightforwardly asking for what we want, and sounding victimized or demanding. It also helps us if we remember that we are all in this situation together, and each of us is just one of the players, doing the best we can to make things work. Remember the importance of a kind, accepting, and compassionate stance toward yourself while doing this.

Compassion for Conflicting Feelings

Dilemmas can be especially challenging when we feel shy, don't want to hurt others' feelings, and find it hard to say what we think and feel. For example, you may feel angry with someone and really care about the person at the same time. Some ambivalence is part of all relationships. Maybe you haven't let the other person know what you want and how you feel, including what bothers you. Maybe you've been building up resentment without finding out what the other person thinks and feels.

Here again it can help to write a letter. Sometimes when we write down our feelings, particularly conflicting feelings, we understand them better or differently. Sometimes the feelings themselves change. Sometimes it becomes easier to act on our feelings with compassion for ourselves and others.

Exercise: Writing About a Dilemma

First engage your soothing breathing for a moment or two. Engage your compassionate, wise, strong, and understanding ideal self and feel that person's kindness and warmth toward you while you do the exercise.

Try beginning your letter with the words: ***This is hard for me to tell you because ...*** This will help get you started. Now write down all the things you're upset or angry about. It may help you to begin to assert yourself by asking for what you need, or telling the person what it is about her behavior that is triggering painful feelings in you. See if you can think of specific things the person does or says. Don't hold back—you're not hurting anyone because the letter is meant only for you. This exercise simply helps you to be more specific about what is really getting to you, so that you can decide whether you want to take action or not.

When you have completed this exercise, you may want to stretch a bit and walk around for a moment. Then try the next part of the exercise.

Smile, acknowledge your human feelings, and take some calming and soothing breaths. Now write down all the things you like and appreciate about the other person. Bring to your mind how you want that person to flourish, to be free from suffering, and to be at peace. Write about that. Even if the person in question is someone you don't like and think you never will, it can be helpful to write compassionate thoughts toward him. It may help you understand that person (and yourself) better.

This exercise is an opportunity for you to be in touch with a conflict or an intense emotion, to understand that your feelings are normal, and to work with them in a way that is helpful to you. In my work with couples, it has sometimes struck both of them and me at the same time that often the things that drive us crazy are also the things we appreciate most about someone we care for deeply.

Recognizing Unhelpful Relationships

Another dilemma involves the times when we know deep down that a friendship is not good for us, that the other person may take advantage of the fact that we like to listen and doesn't draw us out, or never asks our opinion. We know that either we need to assert ourselves in the relationship to give it another chance, or leave it.

Sometimes you know in your heart that a friend doesn't care that much about you, but you hang on to that person because you are afraid of being lonely.

It can be especially hard when we need to leave intimate relationships that are holding us back, or don't help us grow, or simply don't fit us. Many of us have struggled with leaving relationships, because the relationships have provided security and we hate to hurt the people we are leaving, knowing it is not anyone's fault that a relationship doesn't fit. Sometimes it's simply that we know what it's like to be hurt and we don't want to hurt others. Sometimes we are fearful of going out into the world alone again. It can also be very hard to change your approach to life from one of waiting to be chosen or offered things to one in which you pursue what you want yourself.

If you find yourself in a dilemma like this, remind yourself that it doesn't make you an inadequate person or a bad person, simply a human person. The good news is that we can feel compassion and understanding for our difficult feelings, soothing ourselves as we take responsibility for our behavior. You can be soothed by compassion for the natural feelings that go along with changing behavior, without avoiding the feelings or dwelling on them.

Exercise: Compassionate Withdrawal from a Relationship

Engage your soothing breathing rhythm for a few moments and bring to mind your wise, strong, understanding, compassionate self. When you can really feel the warmth and understanding, bring to mind the relationship that you know deep down is not good for you and how that person treats you. Then imagine being with a friend who really cares about you and your welfare. Think about what it would take for you to leave the relationship and look for another one. If you begin to feel overwhelmed, just return to your breathing and your compassionate self. If you feel relatively calm, just continue to consider small steps that you could take to find a better or more suitable friend or partner and leave this relationship behind. When you are ready, just be aware of the warmth and understanding of your compassionate self for a moment before you stop. If you thought of things you might do toward detaching yourself from this relationship and looking for a new friend, take a moment to write them down as manageable possible steps you can take to leave the relationship when you are ready.

Here are a couple of examples of people who realized that a relationship that had been important to them was not helpful and took steps to withdraw from it.

John and Bill had been friends since childhood. John considered Bill his only friend, but Bill, the more extroverted of the two, had lots of friends; in fact he tended to be the life of the party, nearly always the center of attention. John liked being friends with Bill because he could tag along and be with people without much effort. On the other hand, he couldn't help noticing that Bill didn't seem to be interested in what he thought or had to say; he was a good listener, and spent most of his time being an audience for Bill. When John realized that he needed to reach out to people on his own and let them get to know him as a person, as well as get to know them better, he began to take small steps to develop other friendships. His first steps were to initiate individual conversations with people at parties, rather than stay in the circle around Bill. Then he asked one person to go to a film with him and another to have lunch. He also joined a photography club and made a point of talking to at least one person at each meeting, eventually asking one of them to have coffee after class. Another he invited to go with him on a favorite hike to take pictures together.

Joan's husband was much more extroverted than she was. She felt shy among his boisterous friends and would have liked more time to herself to pursue the more solitary activities she really cared about; but her husband couldn't understand either her feelings of shyness around his friends or her need for time alone. When she tried to explain, he felt hurt and said she didn't care for him. He also frequently became angry and tried to control her behavior, telling her that she should want to be with his friends and that if she didn't, there was something wrong with her. Joan understood that he didn't mean to be hurtful, and felt they loved each other, but his constant criticism was eroding her self-esteem. She began to realize that she might need to leave the marriage.

Her first step was to tell him that she felt hurt and misunderstood. She told him that she loved him, but she preferred reading and taking walks with just him to watching football on television with a gang of his friends. They had many discussions, in which she told him about particular things he did that hurt her, and he told her more about his own frustration. She realized that they wanted different things in life. There was nothing wrong with her in being introverted, or with him in being extroverted, but they just didn't have enough left in common. After talking things through together, and making several visits to a therapist who helped them to listen to each other, they came to an agreement that though they would try to remain good friends, it was time to look for other partners.

WHEN COMPASSIONATE BEHAVIOR REQUIRES COURAGE

When we think of compassionate behavior, we usually think of small kindnesses to ourselves and others. Many of these kindnesses don't cost us much, but some compassionate behaviors do require courage. We've already talked about the courage involved in dealing with the threat/protection system, and in coping with the anxiety, fear, and anger it produces in us as we change our behavior and do the things we fear. Courage can also mean resisting your own desires, including the desire to be part of a particular group and to be admired by its leaders, when you don't really respect them or believe in what they are doing. It takes courage to leave such a group and to look for collaborative, egalitarian groups where people care for each other. In this and other situations, compassionate behavior can also require the courage to stand up to other people, including people in authority.

Resisting Our Own Desires

Our brains are equipped with desires appropriate to living in small groups of mutually dependent individuals in a world of scarce resources. Today, fewer of us live in small groups, and most of us live in a world of greater social isolation. When we feel shy, we are tempted to avoid the risks of entering into sexual intimacy, and when isolation is accompanied by severe shyness or social anxiety, the lure of sexual images on the Internet may be strong. They seem to offer an alternative, albeit lonely, way to achieve some sexual satisfaction while avoiding the anticipated awkwardness and risk of intimacy. We know in our hearts, however, that the emotional warmth and physical comfort of being close to a real person is what we need to thrive and flourish in the long run. If this applies to you, you may want to try the following exercise.

Exercise: Resisting Cybersex

Spend a few moments engaging your soothing breathing rhythm, and bring to mind your wise, strong, accepting, compassionate self, who cares deeply about your welfare. Then, when you feel calm and cared for, take out your notebook or a sheet of paper and make two columns, heading one "Advantages of Using the Internet for Solitary Sex," and the other "Disadvantages of Using the Internet for Solitary Sex." List under the headings what you see as the respective advantages and disadvantages. Try to include statements related to whether the Internet helps or hinders you reaching out for sexual partners.

After doing the exercise and taking a few more soothing breaths, if it feels right, just write down a few small steps you can take, without feeling overwhelmed, to reduce your sexual time on the Internet (maybe by just a few minutes at first) and increase your contact with potential sexual partners (perhaps starting with something as small as saying hello to people you are attracted to, having a brief conversation, beginning a friendship, or checking out an online dating service to help you start slowly).

Resisting Others

In order to practice compassion, we may need to stand up to other people as well as ourselves. These may be people in positions of authority, or they may be our own children! It can be very challenging when we are chronically shy to resist children's demands for junk food or computer games, particularly if we feel that we have been less available to them than they need us to be, either because of the time we spend at work or because we prefer to avoid taking them out to places where we'll have to mix with other parents. And then there may be the person you know you must speak to at work because her skills aren't up to the level you need to get an important job done. You know you have to do this, but you keep putting off the inevitable because you hate being the "bad person." We can see from these examples that submissive behavior isn't compassionate. Not doing the right thing when it is difficult isn't being compassionate toward ourselves or others, any more than is pursuing what we know in our hearts isn't the right thing for us.

Speaking Truth to Power

Another situation where compassionate behavior calls for courage is when we need to "speak truth to power," that is, to say what we think to someone in authority or someone who has power in a particular situation. Charismatic, strongly dominant leaders can persuade us to conform to their goals, often exaggerating threats to increase their power. Philip Zimbardo, in his course on "the psychology of mind control," helped students understand how any of us is susceptible to misguided or malevolent people in positions of power, particularly when we feel vulnerable or lonely, or are going through any of the significant transitions in life that all of us experience. For example, people are often recruited gradually into cults with offers of friendship, understanding, and care at the outset, and only gradually indoctrinated into the inner workings and beliefs of the group, which may be much less benevolent and even exploitative. When we feel shy and lonely, we may be particularly vulnerable to these situations. Or consider the autocratic and destructive leaders who so often emerge in times of uncertainty and stress, when we want confident leadership, someone who "knows what he is doing." When we are facing complex problems, it is easier to believe that someone has the answers and will protect us than to grapple with all the complexities. Power-hungry leaders exploit this desire for security and protection, and play on the fears of being inferior and ashamed that exist in all of us. This is why people will stand and watch someone be bullied, afraid of the consequences of standing up to the bullies or getting help.

When we are shy and uncertain, we may fall prey to people who are very dominant and don't have our best interests at heart. Our "better safe than sorry" strategies frequently involve hiding our thoughts and feelings, and worrying about what other people will think, rather than stepping back and asking our true selves what we really think and want to do according to our own values. Learning to speak up and to act in accordance with those values, especially in the face of pressure from powerful figures, certainly takes courage, but doing so is a life-affirming act in which we show compassion both for ourselves and for others.

COPING WITH BULLYING

Bullying has been defined as repeated behavior that is intended to harm or disturb, inflicted by a more powerful person or group on a less powerful person. The power imbalance can be physical or psychological, and the aggressive behavior may take the form of name-calling, threats, hitting, spreading rumours, or shunning and exclusion.

Bullying Among Children and Young People

A review of international research published in 2001 found that the percentage of students reporting being bullied at least once in the current term ranged from a low of 15 percent to a high of 70 percent. According to this study and others, between 9 percent and 15 percent of any student population is a victim of bullying. A British study of twenty-three schools revealed that the most common form of bullying overall was direct verbal aggression. Among boys physical aggression was most common. Indirect aggression was most common in girls, who reported name-calling, teasing, rumours, rejection, and the stealing of personal items. Those who took part in bullying in any form tended to be the less well adjusted psychologically.

If your child is shy, she may become a target for repeated bullying, which can leave lasting emotional scars.

So it's really important to know how much bullying goes on in schools that shy children attend, and what is done to keep tabs on it and stop it. Interestingly, recent research shows that gifted children are also more likely to be bullied, so a child who is both gifted *and* shy may be particularly vulnerable. Each school administration is responsible for this, but you and other parents may have to push for action and check that it is sustained—another opportunity to be assertive and to be compassionately courageous! Protecting children and young people from bullying has become a high priority in many countries, including Britain and the United States, and there are many helpful websites that offer tips for handling bullying.

Exercise: Recalling Bullying

Engage your soothing breathing rhythm and take a few moments to bring to mind your wise, understanding, kind, and compassionate self. Then, if you wish, just watch to see if any thoughts or images of bullying come to mind. They may be related to being bullied or seeing someone else be bullied. If you realize that you were bullied as a child, just feel your kind, accepting, understanding, and caring self listen to your thoughts and feelings about the bullying and its consequences for you, taking some time to really feel your compassionate self (or image) understanding your feelings.

Bullying in the Workplace

Workplace bullying has become a prominent issue in many Western countries and is now commonplace. According to one estimate, up to 37 percent of workers are repeatedly mistreated, and the percentage rises to 49 percent when witnesses are included. What's more, unless it's severe, you are unlikely to realize it's happening. According to another estimate, one in six workers is bullied at some time, and women bully as well as men. Contrary to what we usually think, however, it seems that the people who are bullied aren't necessarily those who are thin skinned or vulnerable. On the contrary, the targets appear to be personable and competent; what attracts the bullying is that they are perceived as competition in cut-throat environments that reward aggressive behavior with promotions. This includes people who want to please and don't tend to confront, but who are nevertheless seen as a threat. If you feel shy, you may underestimate your competence and fail to see yourself as a threat to an insecure boss or colleague.

A Compassionate Way to Confront a Bully

Paul Gilbert, in *The Compassionate Mind,* suggests starting to confront a workplace bully by saying something like: "I find some of your critical comments upsetting, and they stop me from performing my role well. It would be very helpful to me if you could focus on what you think I do well and build from there." This gives the bully something specific to say, in case she wants to retreat from a bullying position, and it provides the opportunity to move the dialogue to a more compassionate one. If the bully does not respond well to this approach—if he belittles or mocks it, or simply continues the bullying behavior—you may need to get help from others in the workplace, or from a union or other representative body.

If you are being bullied at work, even if you are able to get some help, you may feel ashamed of what is happening and think others are contemptuous of you. If so, to start with, it is helpful to write down your thoughts.

Exercise: Gathering Your Thoughts About Workplace Bullying

First, take a few soothing breaths, bring your compassionate self (image) into awareness, and take some moments to really feel this person's warmth, kindness, understanding, acceptance, and deep care for you.

Now make two columns on a page in your notebook or on a sheet of paper. In the first column write about what you think is going on in the minds of the people around you, and then write down your key fear in relation to that. In the second column, write down your inner experiences of shame, how you feel inside, and then write down your key fear in relation to those experiences. If you feel internal shame, you may notice that your key fears are similar to your concerns about what others think and how you exist in their minds. For example, you may fear that you aren't wanted or needed, or good enough—and that this is what other people think; or you may feel afraid as a result of feeling powerless to defend yourself against the bully, and fear that people despise you for this.

This exercise is to help you see that we are all vulnerable to misinterpreting what others think when they see someone bullied. They, like all of us, are afraid of being bullied, so they may not offer support when you need it or make their concern for you visible; that certainly doesn't mean they aren't sympathetic, let alone that they are contemptuous of you.

Resisting Bullying

Remember that psychological abuse is as powerful as physical abuse. You may need to resist apologizing for things that are not your fault, trying to avoid doing anything that could make the person angry, and blaming yourself harshly. This will be easier if you use your warm, kind voice and have compassion for your feelings while you resist doing things that are not in your or others' best interest.

You may want to start making a plan for what you want to say or do, and to start slowly putting it into practice, in small steps. If you can, get help from friends, family, or a therapist. Getting help is absolutely the compassionate thing to do for yourself in this situation. Remember, you are not alone. Bullying behavior has nothing to do with your worth as a person. It has only to do with the bully, who is trying to compensate for her own anxiety and feelings of threat.

DEALING WITH ASSERTIVENESS IN OTHERS

If we're feeling extremely shy, it can be very difficult sometimes to judge whether someone who comes across as highly assertive is dominant in an exploitative way or simply a bold individual who "goes for it" for himself but will also respond to our needs if we voice them, and who, without trying to elicit others' views, will respond positively to assertive behavior. If you've been chronically shy for a long time, you may well view such people as aggressive or predatory, and feel frustrated and angry about it. Your anger may take the form of resentment or passive aggression toward the other person, as well as self-abasement and harsh criticism of yourself. Some of you may find that you go back and forth between blaming yourself and blaming others, in the process we discussed in chapter 1 as part of the three vicious cycles of shyness. We know that these kinds of feelings and thoughts are perfectly understandable and part of the threat/protection system, but we also know that they can make it hard for us to discern the motives of others.

How Vigilance and Wariness May Be Self-Defeating

Trying to protect yourself by being vigilant and wary, while alternately blaming yourself and others, can have unintended consequences. If we're feeling wary about a business meeting that might get verbally rough and quarrelsome, we may find ourselves avoiding the meeting or arriving late. Sometimes we forget the meeting altogether, without even being aware that we are avoiding it. In our concern to keep out of the way of aggressive colleagues, we may miss the fact that others want and need us at the meeting, as a more cooperative participant, so we may be missing the opportunity to build helpful alliances with them. If we don't like a supervisor or manager, we may delay responding to that person or deliver reports late, thereby giving her reasons to be critical toward us. If we feel we can't trust anyone, we may fail to share our thoughts and feelings with anyone, thus depriving ourselves of the social support so necessary to our well-being.

Taking the Risk to Find Out Whether Someone Is Trustable

Acknowledge your courage if you decide to risk finding out whether someone who is very assertive is trustable, particularly in view of any old hurts and remaining scars you may have. It may be that the person's main concern is to express himself, not necessarily to dominate others. People in work groups where trust is strong can be pretty outspoken: they will make strong statements, and others will respond with equally strong statements either contradicting them or expressing a different point of view, and nobody has to win. Participants in groups like this tend to build on each other's ideas, once they get the definitions sorted out, and if there is enough trust, they can eventually see together which ideas make the most sense. In a less trusting and very political or hierarchical environment, people may tend to be more afraid of making such strong statements and asserting their points of view, allowing a few people to dominate.

You may want to spend a little time observing the person with whom you want to take the risk. How much does the person seem to need to win or, on the contrary, does the person just need to express himself? It may help to do the following exercise.

Exercise: Preparing to Engage with an Assertive Colleague

Take a few moments to engage your soothing breathing rhythm and your compassionate, wise, strong, and understanding self. Take the time to really feel the warmth, strength, and understanding. Then imagine yourself taking small risks to find out if the other person is trustable. These might take the form of making a strong but calm statement in a meeting to see how the person responds, making a suggestion that differs from one that person has offered, or, if interrupted in a conversation, saying, "I think this idea is important; I'd like you to hear me out," to see what the person does. After you have done this for a few minutes, just experience the warmth of your compassionate self. When you have completed the exercise, write down a few small steps you can take when you are ready. If you feel ready, decide when you will do the first one.

EXPLORING POSSIBILITIES FOR LEADERSHIP

If you always avoid taking leadership roles at your workplace, it may be helpful to see what happens if you begin to take the lead sometimes, rather than go along with others' plans and priorities. Sometimes being a follower means that we don't really need to think about what we want from work or what we want to contribute to it. If you'd like to explore this possibility, you can begin by observing carefully what is going on and keeping an eye open for opportunities to contribute in ways other than simply supporting your colleagues. It isn't usually a choice between being a superstar and part of the woodwork; there are usually lots of intermediate points. For example, you may notice a small project that nobody has offered to lead, and volunteer to take it on. (It can help to volunteer for something that matters to you or involves work you like to do.) If you notice yourself feeling fearful of making a mistake and of other people's disapproval, remember that this is natural: we all take risks to grow, and we all make mistakes—and recover from them.

You may need to push yourself to tell others what you want them to do. You can rehearse these conversations aloud at home if you like. And if people disapprove or disagree, or say they might have done something differently, this is okay. These responses will help you to learn to compassionately tolerate your fear or frustration as you try out new ways of behaving. You may find that you actually enjoy participating in this new way. The important thing is to practice with your soothing breathing rhythm and to bring your compassionate self or compassionate image into your mind frequently, each time you face a challenge. It also helps to practice at home, engaging your soothing breathing rhythm and bringing to mind your compassionate self or image as you visualize the things you want to try doing the next day, such as leading a meeting, asking questions about people's progress, or stating your understanding of the current goals.

RESISTING NEGATIVE STEREOTYPES OF SHYNESS

The negative stereotyping of shyness in Western culture came along with the rise in the media of images of highly dominant and individualistic males, and then was picked up and promoted by drug companies, who made shyness a disease they could treat for lots of money. My experience with many of you who label yourselves as shy is that you are excellent collaborators in an accepting environment, unless you have been very badly hurt and don't feel you can trust others at all. Being shy doesn't mean that you can't achieve. In fact, there are possibly more shy than nonshy people at the highest levels of education. Remember, 60 percent of college students in recent samples reported being shy. You just don't tend to want to be too much in the spotlight. You are probably also acutely aware that achievement and recognition for achievement are fickle, particularly if you are working on complex problems that defy "quick and dirty" solutions. As a result you are sometimes overlooked; and as a leader, you probably tend to lead from behind and let others take whatever glory happens to be around.

You may be overlooked in terms of visibility, but you may be sought out to work with because you tend to be conscientious. In a book called *From Good to Great,* Jim Collins notes that some of the most effective CEOs who have led businesses through times of intense change were shy. When his research team repeatedly told him that the leaders of these companies were "diffident" or "reticent," Collins did not believe them. He had to see for himself. What he found was that these individuals did not crave publicity; what they did have was an intense and dedicated commitment to achieve a certain goal, and they didn't care who got credit for it. They empowered their people and then got out of their way. The reality is that the same genuine, cooperative, collaborative tendencies that I see at the shyness clinic, when people feel accepted for themselves, are alive and well and highly valued in business, and may be an essential ingredient in developing authentic leadership. If you can reach out, communicate warmth and interest, and develop your compassionate self, who has compassion for others as well, and you work to fulfill your own potential, life will be satisfying and meaningful.

Perhaps the most overt negative stereotyping is reserved for shy men—as is evident from books like *Accidental Empires: How the Boys of Silicon Valley Make Their Millions, Battle Foreign Competition, and Still Can't Get A Date.* Women, on the other hand, tend to experience negative stereotyping most acutely in the workplace, where, ironically, shy women are valued on the assumption that they won't assert themselves with their male colleagues (and competitors).

So how are you to resist negative stereotyping, and to do it with compassion for yourself and others, for those who are shy and those who are less shy? It's often a case of quietly pursuing your own agenda in the workplace and calmly continuing to assert your beliefs about what is good for your team and your company, while maintaining a compassionate stance toward your own social anxiety, the threat/protection system responses of others, and their underlying insecurity.

DEALING WITH AMBIGUITY

Much of our behavior is ambiguous and there is a good deal of room for misinterpretation, which is why it is so important to find ways of clarifying what a person means and that person's motives. Sometimes other people are self-contained, and we mistake that for not liking us. Sometimes people may think we aren't interested in them when we are. There is also often much more room for negotiation and the swapping of leader and follower roles than we may assume when we feel very shy, and this may become more apparent when we have a better insight into how feelings and motives change from time to time. I may have taken a leadership role in a meeting yesterday on something I really cared about, yet be happy to have you take that role today when the topic is something you really care about.

Exercise: Exploring Ambiguity

Think of someone who isn't being friendly, or perhaps has sounded short with you. Spend a few moments engaging your soothing breathing rhythm and bring to mind your compassionate, wise, deeply caring self. When you are ready, in the gentlest possible way, ask yourself if anything else may be going on with that person. If you can and it feels right, wonder internally what the other person may be thinking and feeling. The important thing is just to wonder, with gentle compassion for yourself and the other person, what the other's motives might be. Could that person be stressed, preferring to focus only on her work? Perhaps the person is mulling over or worrying about something? Could he be feeling vulnerable about something and therefore protective of himself?

This is not an exercise in logic. It is simply an opportunity to wonder with an open mind and notice how you feel as you think about different possibilities.

When you are finished, you may want to think about particular ways you might behave toward that person, for example, asking the person privately whether she is okay, or just observing the person without saying anything and continuing to be friendly yourself.

Example: Clarifying Ambiguous Behavior in a Close Relationship

Paula was involved in the early stages of a relationship. Andrew was funny, upbeat, warm, and clearly fond of her. She was warm, agreeable, and dependable. Paula tended to let others take the lead, so she was glad he had pursued her. They had fun and found they had much in common. As they drew closer, however, to the point where they were deciding whether to move in together, Andrew kept referring to his disappointment in his previous relationship and seemed to be reluctant to set a date. Paula began to notice that she felt afraid as Andrew talked about his ex-girlfriend, and how that stimulated her need to be pleasing and funny and to prevent the conversation from going further.

She recognized that she was afraid, and as she experienced her fear and sadness, she understood that her motive in being with Andrew was really to build a long-term relationship and that he might not have the same desire. She recognized how easy it was to fall into the trap of seeing them both in extremes, thinking that she was unworthy and that he was callous and rejecting. (This is an example of what therapists often call "all-or-nothing thinking" or "black-and-white thinking"—one of several unhelpful thinking patterns typical of people who are anxious. For more information on these, see appendix 3 at the back of this book.) She imagined what she would say to a friend in her position. She remembered times when she was successful at speaking up about her feelings, or risked clarifying behavior when she knew she might be disappointed. She imagined risking a little more, to find out more about Andrew's intentions toward her, for the sake of her long-term happiness.

The next time they were together, rather than change the subject when Andrew mentioned his ex-girlfriend, Paula asked Andrew what he was thinking when he remembered his previous relationship and what he was thinking about moving in together. Andrew opened up about his fears and said that he thought he'd like to go more slowly, maybe just moving back to dating and perhaps seeing other people. She told him she could really understand his wanting that but that it wasn't her goal. Her goal was to find a long-term partner with whom she could be intimate. She was glad to have taken the lead in clarifying their relationship, and a little surprised when he easily followed her lead and shared his vulnerability and worry. He wasn't ready to be involved again, but he didn't want to lose her. They decided they would try to remain friends. In spite of her sadness and disappointment, Paula also put her profile back up on an online dating site and planned to have coffee with someone else the following week.

Exercise: Exploring Motives in a Relationship

If you are in a relationship where you know you need to clarify someone's motives or intentions, the following exercise may be useful. The relationship need not be a romantic one: the ambiguity is just as likely to occur in a friendship or family relationship.

Bring to mind the situation in which you want to resolve ambiguity, but feel afraid to do so. Engage your soothing breathing rhythm and, taking a few moments, bring to mind your wise, strong, kind, and gentle self, who deeply understands and is not overwhelmed by your distress. Then, when you are ready, allow yourself to feel your inner anxiety and fear, and perhaps sadness, until you really feel understood and accepted. If you wish, imagine gently supporting yourself to risk a little more to find out what the person wants for herself and from you, while remembering that your threat/protection thinking is built in biologically and thus your anxiety is perfectly natural and not cause for criticism. Imagine what you would say to a friend. Imagine yourself taking the risk of bringing up the status of your relationship; gently ask yourself what things you might say and ask, and what would be the most supportive thing you could do for yourself and the other person in the long run, even if it means a change in your relationship.

When you have finished the exercise, see if you are ready to write down one or two small steps toward clarifying the relationship, maybe as a first step just asking the other person how he sees the relationship or what he wants from relationships in general. Or you may want to start by clarifying what you each want from relationships in general, talking about the kinds of qualities you think make for good relationships and the qualities of the relationships of friends you admire.

These kinds of questions often open the door to talking about your own relationship. Because people may not have thought consciously about what they want, you may well find you need a number of conversations over a period of weeks. You don't need to pressure yourself or the other person for answers. These conversations help you clarify what is important to you and give you the chance to see whether the other person is also able to discuss things she cares about, and whether she, too, can take emotional risks to deepen the intimacy between you.

This exercise, however, may be quite challenging, and you may want to put it on hold until you have been practicing compassionately changing your behavior for a while. Sometimes these exercises are tackled after a period of weeks of doing the other exercises in this book and taking risks to meet people and to cultivate friendships. The earlier exercises help you become more aware of what you want and need in all kinds of relationships.

You will have noticed that all these exercises relating to the new ways of behaving you are learning begin with using your soothing breathing and engaging with your compassionate self or perfect nurturing image. This is to help you listen to and tolerate your fears and frustrations, sometimes also your shame and resentment, with gentleness, caring, warmth, and wisdom. Your compassionate self or image can also help you sort out your motives and behavioral choices, while being as warm, accepting, nonjudgmental, kind, and understanding of yourself and others as you can be.

KEY POINTS

- Compassionate behavior evolved from the altruistic and caring behavior of mammals living in groups.
- Compassionate behavior is *taking action,* doing things that are aimed to be helpful, encouraging, and supportive when we are confronting our social anxiety, challenges, and setbacks.
- While understanding that our threat-based responses are not our fault, we can take responsibility for

changing our behavior and pursuing our goals. You can do the right thing rather than be nice when it is hard; you can speak truth to power, according to your values; you can resist destructive relationships and groups when you feel lonely—all with your wise, kind, understanding, compassionate self as guide and companion.

• You can begin to assume leadership roles with compassion for yourself and others, and take turns in leading.

• Dilemmas and ambivalence are part of all relationships. Having compassion for, and tolerating, ambivalence while changing behavior involves courage, sometimes to leave a relationship and sometimes to take risks to build a new one. Often we must take risks to find out whether someone is exploitative or trustable; being too vigilant and wary can sabotage us and be self-defeating.

• Childhood bullying is very common, and shy children are vulnerable. Bullying in the workplace is common, but you can handle it with compassion for yourself and the bully. Knowing when to get help is important.

- Changing behavior with compassion doesn't happen overnight. Change is a lifelong process for all of us that brings increased satisfaction and joy.

CHAPTER 9

Putting It All Together

We know that shyness is a universal emotion that we all experience. We know it has many strengths, such as sensitivity, caution, thoughtfulness, conscientiousness, agreeableness, and a tendency toward collaborative behavior. We know that there have been many outstanding shy leaders throughout history, many scientific geniuses and media personalities. These are some of the role models who share your strengths and your difficulties; your preoccupations and anxieties; your feelings, motives, and thoughts; and your suffering. They achieved and do achieve their goals using these strengths and dealing with the problems of shyness.

We also know that compassion, both toward ourselves and others, can be a great help in overcoming the problems that severe shyness causes in our lives.

It's not our fault that we feel socially anxious: the brain states that produce these feelings have evolved over time to protect us. We all just find ourselves here and are doing the best we can to live the lives we want to live. What we can do is learn to foster the alternative brain state of soothing and calmness, and to learn to apply our instincts of kindness and care—which, fortunately, we have also evolved, along with other mammals—to ourselves as well as others. In pursuit of this end, we have discovered how to develop compassion, in both our thinking and our behavior, through a series of exercises involving mindful breathing and imagery.

In this final chapter we look at some suggestions for how you can continue this work to maintain the progress you have made toward overcoming the problems associated with your shyness. We'll also look at some ways in which you can protect yourself and continue to make progress when difficulties or setbacks occur.

MOVING AHEAD: WHAT TO DO NOW

Keep Writing

It's a good idea to keep using your notebook or journal as you continue to develop your mindfulness and soothing practices. Write things down as they occur to you to help you rebalance your emotions and thoughts; then you will have them on hand when you need ideas in the future.

Practice Mindfulness

See your thoughts as leaves on the surface of a river flowing quickly by. Notice how watching can help you observe your thoughts without getting caught up in them and confusing them with an unmoving, absolute reality. Try to practice this every day if you can, even just for a few minutes. If possible, work up to twenty to thirty minutes a day. You will see greater gains and experience a calmer mind the more you practice.

Focus Your Mind

Keep switching your mind to focusing on what you want and hope for, on your strengths and past good experiences. Try to do this every day at least once; several times a day is better, and you'll notice it becoming more automatic, easy, and natural as you practice. It can be pleasurable to check your watch on the hour each day to prompt yourself to remember your strengths and what you want in life.

Create Compassionate Images

Generate compassionate images in your mind, again, every day if you can. These may take the form of fleeting visual images, sounds or feelings, or a sense of a caring presence, or you may choose images from nature, such as water, trees, or animals. What counts is that the images give you a sense of feeling soothed. Remember, you are helping yourself to be open to compassion *for* yourself coming *from* yourself. You are also more likely to notice compassion from others toward you and notice your own feelings of compassion toward others. You can experiment with your perfect nurturer, your ideal compassionate self, your real compassionate self, which is already in you, just needing to be accessed. As best you can, generate images that are supportive, kind, wise, strong, understanding, and encouraging, that can tolerate painful emotion and will help you tolerate painful emotions without getting caught up in them. In the long run this will reduce your painful symptoms of anxiety. When these are severe and you are afraid of feeling overwhelmed or as though you don't deserve compassion, just release yourself from the exercise and return to your soothing breathing; you can try again later. Always release yourself when you need to.

Use Your Compassionate Reasoning

Watch your emotions as you develop alternatives to socially anxious thoughts, use supporting thoughts to balance your mind, and be compassionate toward yourself. Use your "new brain" reasoning, wisdom, and logic to bring social anxiety and painfully shy thoughts back into balance. Remember, you can change unhelpful beliefs about the world and yourself to more beneficial beliefs. Just as you train your body for sports, you are training your mind, and if you work out every day, you will notice change more quickly. This will also help you to trust and accept yourself and others.

Practice Your Compassionate Behavior

Take action; do things that are helpful to yourself and others. Volunteer for something you believe in or help an elderly neighbor. Try being a big brother or sister to a child who needs one. Develop your compassionate behavior by taking risks to do new things, learning skills like public speaking and assertive behavior, or taking an improvisational acting class. As best you can, be courageous in resisting the urge to appease the powerful or exploitative, but hear people out and listen to their concerns, and clarify ambiguous behavior and motives by asking people exactly what they would like you to do. Ask what you can do to improve your performance at work. Try to do what you believe is the right thing, even when it is hard, rather than be nice for the sake of avoiding friction. Try to say what you really think and feel, according to your values, even to those in positions of power. As best you can, resist destructive relationships and groups, even when you feel lonely, and turn instead to the wise, kind, understanding, compassionate self as guide and companion. If you are in a painful relationship and feel you can't leave, try to get help from a friend or therapist. Learn to take turns at leading. Take some small steps to assume leadership roles. Remember to take manageable steps, one at a time.

WHEN COMPASSION IS HARD

Resisting Negative Stereotyping of All Kinds, both from Others and from Yourself

Be aware of negative stereotyping of any aspect of your, your family, or your background, and use your compassionate self to help you resist its influence. Resist negative stereotypes of race, gender, religion, visible differences, and shyness itself, while staying focused on your goals and asserting yourself. Get help when you need it, from friends who understand you or from a therapist. Your family doctor can help you with referrals to qualified professionals and with medication if you need it to help you find a calmer state in which you can make fuller use of the principles outlined in this book.

Objecting to Bullying, of Children and of Yourself

Childhood bullying is very common, and shy children are vulnerable. If you have a shy child, be sure that his school does not allow bullying and will intervene to nip in the bud any that does occur, recognizing that it can cause lasting scars. If bullying is allowed or not effectively stamped out, change schools.

If you are being bullied in the workplace, remember that this is extremely common, but can be handled with compassion for yourself and the bully. If the bully does not respond positively to a compassionate approach, get help.

Practicing Compassion

You can use the exercises in this book to help yourself feel soothed and compassionate toward yourself more often, and to reduce your painful shyness and social anxiety when the world triggers it. If it is hard to find time, you can do the exercises before falling asleep, when you first wake up, in the bath or shower, or even waiting at traffic lights or in the supermarket. If you practice the exercises regularly, for just a few minutes every day or for half an hour or so several times a week, you will notice that you feel better and stronger, because you are choosing to create soothing mind states.

We have touched only in passing in this book on the third emotional system in the brain, the drive/excitement system. It's worth mentioning it again here, because it is useful to know that it comes into play when you plan a trip to the country, a bicycle ride, a museum visit, or an outing to a film or a play—anything you look forward to. If you are sad, down, lonely, or depressed, your drive/excitement system will help pick you up and give you the energy to get started; this can help pull you out of your isolation and motivate you to try a bit of your compassionate behavior, such as asking someone to go with you. If you are not ready for that, start by saying hello to neighbors, helping someone with a chore, or showing up for a local organization's volunteer event. It also helps you to reward yourself after you have made any effort like this with something you really like to do, like listening to a CD, watching a video, going to the movies, or buying yourself a new book.

Achieving and maintaining compassionate social fitness is a lifelong process. By practicing compassionate focusing, imagery, thinking and behavior toward yourself and others, you are creating the life you want to lead. You will learn to tolerate your anxiety and emotional pain, while switching your mind to a compassionate focus and activating your soothing system. You can balance your mind by generating compassionate alternative thoughts to those driven by your social anxiety and the impulse to blame and shame yourself. Focus on, plan, and execute the behavior you believe in as you accept and master the challenges life hands you. Begin to practice compassionate attention, feeling, thinking, and behavior every day, even if it is just for a few minutes. Be patient with yourself. Changing behavior with compassion doesn't happen overnight. Be compassionate about your practice and don't judge yourself.

Go in peace and kindness with your developing compassionate self by your side, and along the way, be curious and take joy.

Appendixes

These appendixes set out some additional tools and information to help you make the most of the ideas in this book.

Appendixes 1 and 2 are questionnaires that you can complete to help you measure your progress as you do the exercises and practice your compassion focus. Fill in the questionnaires before you start doing the exercises and then complete them again every eight weeks or so as you practice. How your scores change will depend on how often you do the exercises and practice new behavior.

Appendix 3 describes some unhelpful thinking patterns that are common in people who suffer from anxiety, including shyness and social anxiety. If you are aware of these patterns, it will help you to identify more helpful alternatives and rebalance your thinking.

Appendixes 4, 5, and 6 are blank copies of the worksheets that appear in the text for you to use as you continue to work with developing your compassionate approach. You can make additional copies of the worksheets and carry them with you so you will have them on hand to use as challenging situations arise. Choose the ones that suit you best, and feel free to modify them if you feel confident that you understand the intent of the exercise and want to vary it a little.

APPENDIX 1

The Estimations of Others Scale

To what extent do you relate to each of these statements? Please make a rating on a seven-point scale from 1 (not at all) to 4 (moderately) to 7 (very much).

1 If I let people know too much about me, they will say hurtful things to me or talk about me behind my back to others. ______

2 People will make fun of me and ridicule me. ______

3 People are indifferent to my feelings and don't want to know about me. ______

4 If people see my discomfort, they will feel contempt for me. ______

5 People are more powerful than I am and will take advantage of me. ______

6 I must not let people know too much about me, because they will misuse the information. ______

7 If I'm not watchful and careful, people will take advantage of me. ______

8 People do not relate to my problems. ______

9 People will be rejecting and hurtful if I let them close to me. ______

10 People do not identify with me when I am uncomfortable. _____

11 When people see my discomfort, they feel superior. _____

12 People do not care about me. _____

To obtain your average score, add up your responses to the twelve items, and divide by 12. If your average score is 3.6 or above, you are in the top 15 percent, which suggests you may struggle more with trusting others than the average person. The average score for shyness clinic clients is around 4.4, and the average score for college students is 2.3. About 70 percent of people score between 1 and 3.5.

Source: L. Henderson and L.M. Horowitz, *The Estimations of Others Scale (EOS)* (Shyness Institute, 1998). Reprinted with kind permission of the Shyness Institute.

APPENDIX 2

The Henderson/Zimbardo Shyness Questionnaire

Please indicate, for each of the statements below, how characteristic the statement is of you, that is, how much it reflects what you typically think, feel, and do, on a scale from 1 to 5, where 1=not at all characteristic, 2=somewhat characteristic, 3=moderately characteristic, 4=very characteristic, and 5=extremely characteristic.

1 I am afraid of looking foolish in social situations. _____

2 I often feel insecure in social situations. _____

3 Other people appear to have more fun in social situations than I do. _____

4 If someone rejects me, I assume that I have done something wrong. _____

5 It is hard for me to approach people who are having conversation. _____

6 I feel lonely a good deal of the time. _____

7 I tend to be more critical of other people than I appear to be. _____

8 It is hard for me to say no to unreasonable requests. ______

9 I do more than my share on projects because I can't say ______

10 I find it easy to ask for what I want from other people. ______

11 I do not let others know I am frustrated or angry. ______

12 I find it hard to ask someone for a date. ______

13 It is hard for me to express my real feelings to others. ______

14 I tend to be suspicious of other people's intentions toward me. ______

15 I am bothered when others make demands of me. ______

16 It is easy for me to sit back in a group discussion and observe rather than participate. ______

17 I find myself unable to enter new social situations without fearing rejection or going unnoticed. ______

18 I worry about being a burden on others. ______

19 Personal questions from others make me feel anxious. ______

20 I let others take advantage of me. ______

21 I judge myself negatively when I think others have negative reactions to me. ______

22 I try to figure out what is expected in a given situation and then act that way. ______

23 I feel embarrassed when I look or seem different from other people. ______

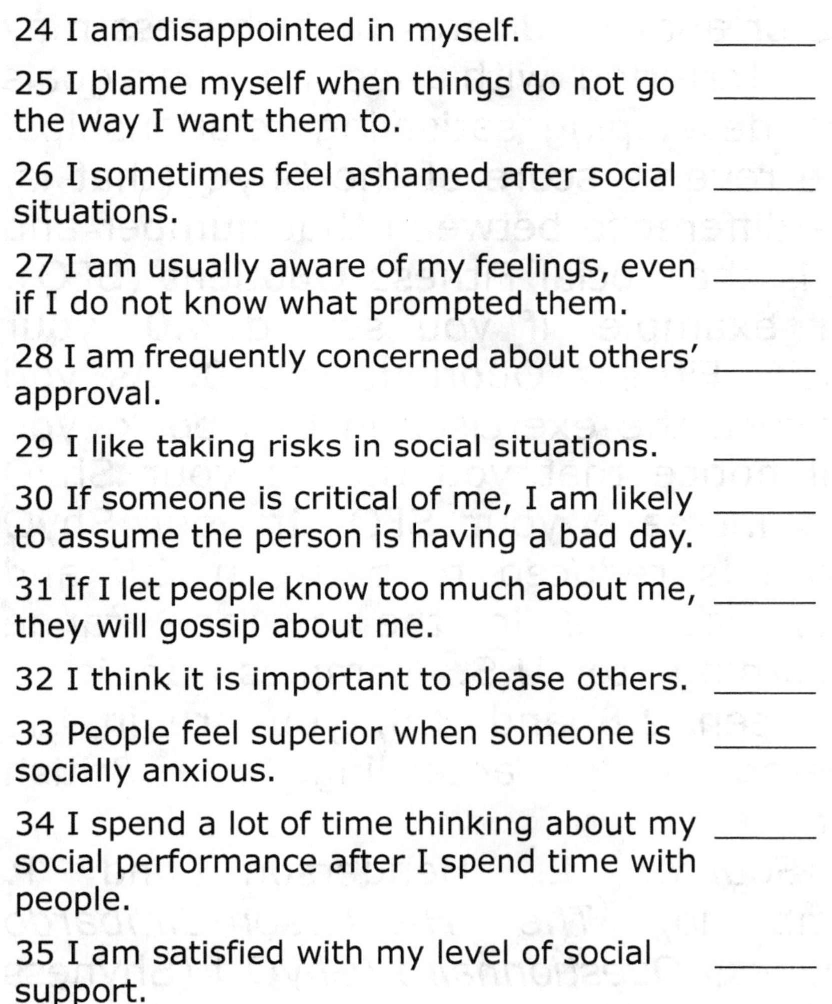
24 I am disappointed in myself. ______

25 I blame myself when things do not go the way I want them to. ______

26 I sometimes feel ashamed after social situations. ______

27 I am usually aware of my feelings, even if I do not know what prompted them. ______

28 I am frequently concerned about others' approval. ______

29 I like taking risks in social situations. ______

30 If someone is critical of me, I am likely to assume the person is having a bad day. ______

31 If I let people know too much about me, they will gossip about me. ______

32 I think it is important to please others. ______

33 People feel superior when someone is socially anxious. ______

34 I spend a lot of time thinking about my social performance after I spend time with people. ______

35 I am satisfied with my level of social support. ______

Items 10, 29, 30, and 35 are reverse scored so that 1=5, 2=4, 3=3, 4=2, and 5=1. Change those scores; then take the mean of the items by adding them all up and dividing by 35 to get your average score, that is, your Shyness Quotient, or ShyQ. A score of

3.2 or above indicates that shyness may be interfering with meeting your goals and developing satisfying relationships. The reverse score of the ShyQ (that is, the difference between that number and 5) is the Social Fitness Quotient (SFQ). For example, if you scored 4.0, your Social Fitness Quotient is 1.0. As you practice the exercises in this book, you will notice that you reduce your ShyQ and increase your SFQ. If your ShyQ score is reduced to between 2.5 and 3.1, you are in the average range according to U.S. samples. If it is between 2.8 and 3.8, you are in the average range according to a British sample.

Source: L. Henderson and P. Zimbardo, *The Henderson/Zimbardo Shyness Questionnaire (ShyQ.)* (Shyness Institute, 2002). Reprinted with kind permission of the Shyness Institute.

APPENDIX 3

Thinking Patterns in Painful Shyness

The following sections set out some types of thinking that we all engage in sometimes, but are especially common in people who are painfully shy. When we are very shy, we also tend to believe these thoughts as if they were facts. Try to notice any thoughts like this as soon as they occur; and when they do, step back and bring balance to your thinking by asking yourself questions in a gentle and caring way. You might like to look back at the exercises in chapters 6 and 7 for some guidance on how to do this with compassion. Remember to look for alternatives to these thoughts and to really consider the evidence for and against them. Test them out whenever you can. For example, if you think *Alex doesn't like me,* you could test out this thought by smiling at Alex, initiating a brief conversation, asking about the past weekend, or suggesting having coffee or lunch together, and then noting how Alex responds (and remembering to balance any new unhelpful thinking patterns that arise when considering the response!).

ALL-OR-NOTHING THINKING OR BLACK-AND-WHITE THINKING

You see things in extremes, as either absolutely good or absolutely bad. For example, if your performance falls short of perfection, you see yourself as a total failure.

OVERGENERALIZATION

You think that one instance is typical; for example, you may see a single negative event as bound to be repeated indefinitely in a never-ending pattern.

MENTAL FILTER

You pick out a single negative detail and dwell on it exclusively, so that it colors your entire vision of reality in the way that a single drop of ink darkens a whole jar of water.

DISQUALIFYING THE POSITIVE

You reject positive experiences by insisting they "don't count" for some reason or other. In this way you maintain a negative belief that is contradicted by your everyday experiences.

JUMPING TO CONCLUSIONS

You make a negative interpretation of an event or experience even though there are no definite facts that convincingly support your conclusion.

MIND READING

You arbitrarily conclude that someone is reacting negatively to you, without actually checking whether this is true or not.

FORTUNE-TELLING

You anticipate that things will turn out badly, and you feel convinced that your prediction is an already established fact.

CATASTROPHIZING

If you think you have committed some social error, you expect extreme and horrible consequences for yourself. If someone turns you down for a date, you take this as meaning you'll be on your own forever. If you make a mistake at work, this means that you will be fired and will never get another job.

MAGNIFICATION OR MINIMIZATION

You exaggerate the importance of things (such as your tiny slipup or someone else's achievement), or you inappropriately shrink things until they appear tiny (your own desirable qualities or someone else's imperfections). This is also called *the binocular trick.*

EMOTIONAL REASONING

You assume that your negative emotions necessarily reflect the way things really are: *I feel it; therefore it must be true.*

"SHOULD" STATEMENTS

You try to motivate yourself with "shoulds" and "shouldn'ts," as if you have to be whipped and punished before you can be expected to do anything. "Musts" and "oughts" are also offenders. The emotional consequence is guilt. When you direct "should" statements toward others, you feel anger, frustration, and resentment.

LABELING AND MISLABELING

This is an extreme form of overgeneralization. Instead of describing your error, you attach a negative label to yourself, such as *I'm a loser.* When someone else's behavior rubs you the wrong way, you attach a negative label to that person: *He's a stupid jerk, She's just ignorant.* Mislabeling involves describing a person with language that is highly colored and emotionally loaded.

PERSONALIZATION

You see yourself as the cause of some negative external event for which, in fact, you were not primarily responsible.

UNHELPFUL THOUGHTS

Unhelpful thoughts are any thoughts that are not useful to you in a given situation and do not help you reach your goal.

COMPENSATORY MISCONCEPTION

You believe that you need to inflate your achievements or impress others to be socially successful, rather than believe that people will accept you for yourself.

APPENDIX 4

Self-Critical Thoughts and Fears

This exercise helps you to stand back from your habitual thoughts and recognize what you are thinking. Engage your soothing breathing rhythm before you begin. When you have filled in both columns of the chart, refocus your attention and try to balance your thoughts with some questions, making sure to keep your tone kind and gentle. See table 6.1 in chapter 6.

External shame thoughts: How I think others feel about me and view me	Internal shame thoughts: What I feel and think about myself
My key fear is:	My key fear is:

Kind and gentle questions:

1. ______
2. ______
3. ______

4. ______
5. ______

APPENDIX 5

Compassionate Alternative Thoughts

This exercise gives you a chance to think of and write down some compassionate alternatives to shy thoughts. See example in chapter 7.

Shy thoughts	Compassionate alternatives

Shy thoughts	Compassionate alternatives

APPENDIX 6

Compassionate Self-Correction

This exercise helps you to substitute compassionate self-correction for shame-based, self-attacking criticism.

Remember the key differences. When you have made a mistake or done something wrong, self-attacking criticism leads to shame, avoidance, and fear, and you feel angry and aggressive toward yourself. Compassionate self-correction, on the other hand, kindly and calmly engages with guilt; you feel sorrow and remorse, and then make appropriate reparation.

Be sure to acknowledge and be understanding of your feelings, focus on your strengths and good experiences, generate alternative self- supportive thoughts, and think about the specific behavior you would like to change with compassionate support from yourself, for yourself. See example in chapter 7.

Shame-based, self-attacking criticism	Compassionate self-correction

Useful Books and CDs

ON SHYNESS AND RELATED TOPICS

Antony, M.M. (2004). *10 simple solutions to shyness: how to overcome shyness, social anxiety, and fear of public speaking.* Oakland, CA: New Harbinger Publications.

Antony, M.M., and R.P. Swinson. (2008). *The shyness and social anxiety workbook: proven, step-by-step techniques for overcoming your fear.* Oakland, CA: New Harbinger Publications. Includes helpful cognitive behavioral exercises.

Aron, E.N. (1996). *The highly sensitive person: how to thrive when the world overwhelms you.* New York: Broadway Books. Good discussion of sensitivity and how it differs from problematic shyness.

Butler, G. (1999). *Overcoming social anxiety and shyness: a self-help guide using cognitive behavioral techniques.* London: Constable and Robinson. Very readable and helpful.

Carducci, B.J. (1999). *Shyness: a bold new approach.* New York: HarperCollins Publishers.

Cheek, J.M., and B. Cheek. (1989). *Conquering shyness: the battle anyone can win.* With L. Rothstein. New York: G.P. Putnam's Sons. One of the early books on shyness that is based on research and is still very relevant.

Dayhoff, S.A. (2000). *Diagonally parked in a parallel universe: working through social anxiety.* Placitas, NM: Effectiveness-Plus Publications.

Flowers, S. (2009). *The mindful path through shyness: how mindfulness and compassion can help free you from social anxiety, fear, and avoidance.* Oakland, CA: New Harbinger Publications. Helpful mindfulness exercises and good discussion of shyness, with many examples of shyness from Flowers' firsthand experience.

Forsyth, J.P., and G.H. Eifert. (2007). *The mindfulness and acceptance workbook for anxiety: a guide to breaking free from anxiety, phobias, and worry using acceptance and commitment therapy.* Oakland, CA: New Harbinger Publications. Very helpful book based on acceptance and commitment therapy.

Gilbert, P. (2007). *Overcoming depression: talks with your therapist.* London: Constable and Robinson. Calming and helpful CD for depression, which often accompanies chronic and painful shyness.

______. (2009). *Overcoming depression: a self-help guide using cognitive behavioral techniques.* Rev. ed. London: Constable and Robinson. Very helpful book for depression.

Henderson, L. (1992). Shyness groups. In *Focal group psychotherapy,* ed. M. McKay and K. Paleg, 29-66. Oakland,

CA: New Harbinger Publications. Description of working with shyness in groups. Helpful to therapists who want to work with shyness in groups.

_____. (2006). Gifted and shy. *Duke Gifted Letter* 6(2):10.

_____. (2007). *Social fitness training: a cognitive behavioral protocol for the treatment of shyness and social anxiety disorder.* Palo Alto, CA: Shyness Institute.

_____. (2008). *The social fitness client manual.* Palo Alto, CA: Shyness Institute.

Henderson, L., P. Zimbardo, and E. Rodino, eds. (2002). *Painful shyness in children and adults* (brochure). Washington, DC: Psychologists in Independent Practice, a Division of the American Psychological Association (APA) and the Shyness Institute. Useful introduction that helps parents decide if a child's shyness is a problem. A pdf of the brochure may be found at www .apa.org/helpcenter/shyness.pdf.

Huber, C. (2001). *There is nothing wrong with you: going beyond self-hate.* Murphys, CA: Keep it Simple Books. Very helpful book by a well-known Zen teacher in dealing with shame.

Johnson, D.W. (2008). *Reaching out: interpersonal effectiveness and self-actualization.* 10th ed. Needham Heights, MA: Allyn and Bacon. A useful, general, research-based book on effective communication that we use at the Shyness Clinic.

Laney, M.O. (2002). *The introvert advantage: how to thrive in an extrovert world.* New York: Workman Publishing Company. Interesting and useful book on the advantages of introversion.

Layard, R.(2005). *Happiness: lessons from a new science.* New York: Penguin Press.

Leahy, R.L. (2006). *The worry cure: stop worrying and start living.* New York: Piatkus. Helpful in tackling rumination and agitation that can go along with shyness. Comes with a CD.

Lyubomirsky, S. (2008). *The how of happiness: a new approach to getting the life you want.* New York: Penguin Press. Written by a social psychologist, this is a very helpful, positive psychology book.

Ricard, M. (2003). *Happiness: a guide to developing life's most important skill.* New York: Little, Brown, and Company. An adaptation of this book on CD is available from www.soundstrue.com.

Sapolsky, R.M. (1994). *Why zebras don't get ulcers: an updated guide to stress, stress-related disease, and coping.* New York: W.H. Freeman.

_____. (1997). *'The trouble with testosterone and other essays on the biology of the human predicament.* New York: Scribner. Sapolsky writes with great humor and compassion about our all-too-human nature.

Tompkins, M.A., and K. Martinez. (2009). *My anxious mind: a teen's guide to managing anxiety and panic.* Illustrated by M. Sloan. Washington, DC: Magination Press. Offers helpful strategies for teenagers, written in a very accessible writing style.

Zimbardo, P.G. (1977). *Shyness: what it is, what to do about it.* Reading, MA: Addison-Wesley. Based on his groundbreaking research and reprinted many times, this book is still a classic and one of the bestselling self-help books of all.

Zimbardo, P.G., and S.L. Radl. (1981). *The shy child: a parents guide to preventing and overcoming shyness from infancy to adulthood.* New York: McGraw-Hill. Another older book that is still very relevant.

ON THE NEGATIVE STEREOTYPING OF SHYNESS

Lane, C. (2007). *Shyness: how normal behavior became a sickness.* New Haven, CT, and London: Yale University Press.

Scott, S. (2007). *Shyness and society: the illusion of competence:* Basingstoke, UK: Palgrave Macmillan.

ON HANDLING BULLYING IN THE WORKPLACE

Namie, G., and R. Namie. (2009). *The bully at work: what you can do to stop the hurt and reclaim your dignity on the job.* 2nd ed. Naperville, IL: Sourcebooks.

ON MEDITATION

Chödrön, P. (2007). *How to meditate: a practical guide to making friends with your mind.* Boulder, CO: Sounds True. CD.

Kornfield, J. (2004). *Meditation for beginners.* New York: Bantam Books. Book and CD.

Thich Nhat Hanh. (2004). *Taming the tiger within: meditations on transforming difficult emotions.* New York: Riverhead Books. This book is helpful for tackling anger and resentful feelings as well as social anxiety and fearfulness.

ON MINDFULNESS AND COMPASSION

Begley, S. (2009). *The plastic mind: new science reveals our extraordinary potential to transform ourselves.* London: Constable and Robinson. A great introduction to the science of mindfulness.

Brantley, J. (2003). *Calming your anxious mind: how mindfulness and compassion can free you from anxiety, fear and panic.* Oakland, CA: New Harbinger Publications.

Chödrön, P. (2009). *Taking the leap: freeing ourselves from old habits and fears.* Boston, MA: Shambhala Publications.

Dalai Lama (1995). *The power of compassion: a collection of lectures by his holiness the XIV Dalai Lama.* London: Thorsons Publishers.

Germer, C.K. (2009). *The mindful path to self-compassion: freeing yourself from destructive thoughts and emotions.* New York: The Guilford Press.

Gilbert, P. (2010). *The Compassionate Mind.* Oakland, CA: New Harbinger Publications.

Kabat-Zinn, J. (2005). *Coming to our senses: healing ourselves and the world through mindfulness.* New York: Piatkus.

Stahl, R., and E. Goldstein. (2010). *A mindfulness-based stress reduction workbook.* Oakland, CA: New Harbinger Publications. This book includes a CD with twenty-one guided meditations. Robert Stahl is a former Buddhist monk with many years of experience in teaching mindfulness-based stress reduction classes and training MBSR practitioners.

Helpful Organizations and Websites

FOR SHYNESS AND SOCIAL ANXIETY

American Psychological Association
750 First Street NE
Washington, DC 20002-4242
Tel.: 800-374-2721 or 202-336-5500
Web: www.apa.org
Helpful website with articles on mental health, and shyness and social anxiety.

Anxiety Disorders Association of America
8730 Georgia Avenue
Silver Spring, MD 20910
Tel.: 240-485-1001
Web: www.adaa.org
Includes help in finding a therapist.

Association for Behavioral and Cognitive Therapies
305 7th Avenue, 16th Floor
New York, NY 10001-6008
Tel.: 212-647-1890
Web: www.abct.org

Behavior Therapy of New York
51 East 42nd Street, Suite 1400
New York, NY 10017
Tel.: 646-522-7795
Web: www.behaviortherapyny.com

The American Institute for Cognitive Therapy 136 East 57th Street, Suite 1101
New York, NY 10022
Tel.: 212-308-2440
Web: www.cognitivetherapynyc.com

The Shyness Home Page,
sponsored by The Shyness Institute
Palo Alto, CA 94306
E-mail: clinic@shyness.com
Web: www.shyness.com

FOR COMPASSION-FOCUSED WORK

The Compassionate Mind Foundation
www.compassionatemind.co.uk

This is a charity set up in 2007 by Paul Gilbert and colleagues. On this site you can find essays and references to other sites studying compassion, as well as material you can use for meditation.
Mind and Life Institute
www.mindandlife.org

The Dalai Lama and Western scientists have come together in this project to study and to explore the possibilities of a more compassionate lifestyle.
Self-Compassion
www.self-compassion.org

This is the website of Dr. Kristin Neff, one of the early and leading researchers on self-compassion.

Notes

The following notes provide academic references and other additional information relating to the research and ideas discussed in this book.

CHAPTER 1 UNDERSTANDING SHYNESS

On shyness as "a blend of fear and interest":

Izard, C.E., and M.C. Hyson. 1986. Shyness as a discrete emotion. In *Shyness: perspectives on research and treatment,* ed. W.H. Jones, J.M. Cheek and S.R. Briggs, 147–60. New York: Plenum Press.

On brain design and difficulties associated with shyness:

P. Gilbert.2009. *The Compassionate Mind.* London: Constable and Robinson.

D. Keltner. 2009. *Born to be good: the science of a meaningful life.* New York: Norton.

On stereotypes about shyness.

Steele, C.M. 1997. A threat in the air: how stereotypes shape intellectual identity and performance. *American Psychologist* 52(6):613–29.

Steele, C.M., S.J. Spencer, and M. Lynch. 1993. Self-image resilience and dissonance: the role of affirmational resources. *Journal of Personality and Social Psychology* 64(6):885-96.

On statistics about student shyness:

Carducci, B.J., Q.A. Stubbins, and M. Bryant. 2007. *Still shy after all these (30) years.* Boston: American Psychological Association.

On fear of becoming intimate with people:

Henderson, L. 2003. Social fitness: facilitating self-expression in the socially inhibited. *Society for Interpersonal Research and Theory (SITAR) Newsletter* 3 (29):2–3.

Pilkonis, P.A. 1977. Shyness, public and private, and its relationship to other measures of social behavior. *Journal of Personality* 45(4):585–95.

Pilkonis, P.A., and P.G. Zimbardo. 1979. The personal and social dynamics of shyness. In *Emotions in personality and psychopathology,* ed. C.E. Izard, 131–60. New York: Plenum Press.

St. Lorant, T., L. Henderson, and P. Zimbardo. 2000. Comorbidity in chronic shyness. *Depression and Anxiety* 12(4):232–7.

Zimbardo, P.G. 1986. The Stanford shyness project. In *Shyness: perspectives on research and treatment,* ed. W.H. Jones, J.M. Cheek, and S.R. Briggs, 17–25. New York: Plenum Press.

On signs and symptoms of social anxiety/social phobia:

Diagnostic and statistical manual of mental disorders (DSM-IV-TR). 2000. 4th ed. Arlington, VA: American Psychiatric Association.

On the prevalence of social anxiety disorder:

Kessler, R.C., W.T. Chiu, O. Demler, K.R. Meridangas, and E.E. Walters. 2005. Prevalence, severity, and comorbidity of 12-month DSM-IV disorders in the national comorbidity survey replication. *Archives of General Psychiatry* 62(6):617–27.

On stereotype threat:

Steele, C.M. 1997. A threat in the air: how stereotypes shape intellectual identity and performance. *American Psychologist* 52(6):613–29.

On bad experiences and normal shyness:

Aron, E. 1996. The highly sensitive person: how to thrive when the world overwhelms you. New York: Broadway Books.

Aron, E.N., and A. Aron. 1997. Sensory-processing sensitivity and its relation to introversion and emotionality. *Journal of Personality and Social Psychology* 73(2):345–68.

Kagan, J. 1994. *Galen's prophecy: temperament in human nature.* 1st ed. New York: Basic Books.

Kagan, J., J.S. Reznick, and N. Snidman. 1988. Biological bases of childhood shyness. *Science* 240(4849):167–71.

On behavior of shy adolescents and inward focus:

Davis, M.H., and S.L. Franzoi. 1991. Stability and change in adolescent self-consciousness and empathy. *Journal of Research in Personality* 25(1):70-87.

On health in shy and non-shy children:

Bell, I.R., M.L. Jasnoski, J. Kagan, and D.S. King. 1990. Is allergic rhinitis more frequent in young adults with extreme shyness? A preliminary survey. *Psychosomatic Medicine* 52(5):517–25.

On how pursuing safety can interfere with interacting with others:

Alden, L., and P. Bieling. 1998. Interpersonal consequences of the pursuit of safety. *Behavior Research and Therapy* 36(1):53-64.

On complementary behavior:

Kiesler, D.J. 1996. *Contemporary interpersonal theory and research: personality, psychopathology, and psychotherapy.* New York: John Wiley and Sons.

On famous shy people:

The list is endless. Phil Zimbardo named several in his 1977 book *Shyness: what it is, what to do about it.* Reading, MA: Addison-Wesley. A particularly useful website in this area is Renee Gilbert's, which I found by searching for "famous shy people" online: www.shakeyourshyness.com/shypeople.htm.

On Lincoln:

Goodwin, D.K. 2005. *Team of rivals: the political genius of Abraham Lincoln.* New York: Simon and Schuster.

On Poitier:

Milloy, M. 2008. Sidney Poitier. *AARP: The Magazine* 50–52 (Sept.–Oct.): 114.

On prevention focus and promotion focus:

Mischel, W., and Y. Shoda. 1995. A cognitive-affective system theory of personality: reconceptualizing situations, dispositions, dynamics, and invariance in personality structures. *Psychological Review* 102(2), 246–68.

Mischel, W., Y. Shoda, and R.E. Smith. 2004. *Introduction to personality.* 7th ed. Hoboken, NJ: Wiley.

Gray, J.A. 1972. The psychophysiological basis of introversion-extraversion: a modification of Eysenck's theory. In *The biological basis of individual behaviour* ed. V.D. Nebylitsyn and J.A. Gray 182–205. San Diego, CA: Academic Press.

Gray, J.A. 1987. Perspectives of anxiety and impulsivity: a commentary. *Journal of Research in Personality* 21(4):493–509.

Carver, C.S., and T.L. White. 1994. Behavioral inhibition, behavioral activation, and affective responses to impending reward and punishment: the BIS/BAS scales. *Journal of Personality and Social Psychology* 67(2):319–33.

On the difficulties of shy extroverts:

Pilkonis, P.A. 1977. Shyness, public and private, and its relationship to other measures of social behavior. *Journal of Personality* 45(4):585–95.

Pilkonis, P.A., and P.G. Zimbardo. 1979. The personal and social dynamics of shyness. In *Emotions in personality and psychopathology,* ed. C.E. Izard, 131–60. New York: Plenum Press.

On trustworthiness in shy graduate students:

Kagan, J. 1994. *Galen's prophecy: temperament in human nature.* New York: Basic Books.

On bullying:

Nansel, T.R., M. Overpeck, R.S. Pilla, W.J. Ruan, B. Simons-Morton, and P. Scheidt. 2001. Bullying behaviors among US youth. *Journal of the American Medical Association* 285:2094–100.

On behaviorally inhibited children:

Henig, R.M. 2009. Understanding the anxious mind. *New York Times,* Oct. 4.

Kagan, J. 1994. *Galen's prophecy: temperament in human nature.* New York: Basic Books.

On sensitivity:

Aron, E. 1996. *The highly sensitive person: how to thrive when the world overwhelms you.* New York: Broadway Books.

Aron, E.N., and A. Aron. 1997. Sensory-processing sensitivity and its relation to introversion and emotionality. *Journal of Personality and Social Psychology* 73(2):345–68.

On attribution style and self-blaming:

Anderson, C.A., and L.H. Arnoult. 1985. Attributional style and everyday problems in living: depression, loneliness, and shyness. *Social Cognition* 3 (10):16–35.

Girodo, M., S.E. Dotzenroth, and S.J. Stein. 1981. Causal attribution bias in shy males: implications for self-esteem and self-confidence. *Cognitive Therapy and Research* 5(4):325–38.

Henderson, L. 2002. Fearfulness predicts self-blame and shame in shyness. *Personality and Individual Differences* 32(1):79–93.

Henderson, L., and P. Zimbardo. 1993. Self-blame attributions in shys vs. nonshys in a high-school sample. Paper presented at the annual conference of the Anxiety Disorders Association of America, Charleston, SC.

Minsky, S. 1985. Social anxiety and causal attribution for social acceptance and rejection. *Abstracts International* 46:2632A.

Trower, P., G. Sherling, J. Beech, C. Harrop, and P. Gilbert. 1998. The socially anxious perspective in face-to-face interaction: an experimental comparison. *Clinical Psychology and Psychotherapy* 5(3):155–66.

On shame as a self-conscious emotion:

Lewis, H.B.1971. *Shame and guilt in neurosis.* New York: International Universities Press.

On shame as an activator of stress responses:

Dickerson, S.S., and M.E. Kemeny. 2004. Acute stressors and cortisol response: a theoretical integration and synthesis of laboratory research. *Psychological Bulletin* 130(3):335–91.

Gilbert, P. 2009. *The Compassionate Mind.* London: Constable and Robinson.

On how people assign responsibility for what happens:

Anderson, C.A., and L.H. Arnoult. 1985. Attributional style and everyday problems in living: depression, loneliness, and shyness. *Social Cognition* 3 (10):16–35.

Girodo, M., S.E. Dotzenroth, and S.J. Stein. 1981. Causal attribution bias in shy males: implications for self-esteem and self-confidence. *Cognitive Therapy and Research* 5(4):325–38.

Minsky, S. 1985. Social anxiety and causal attribution for social acceptance and rejection. *Abstracts International* 46:2632A.

On how shy people see others in relation to shyness:

Henderson, L., and L.M. Horowitz. 1998. *The Estimations of Others Scale (EOS).* Palo Alto, CA: Shyness Institute.

On social fitness training:

Henderson, L. 2007. *Social fitness training: a cognitive behavioral protocol for the treatment of shyness and social anxiety disorder.* Palo Alto, CA: Shyness Institute.

Henderson, L. 2008. *Social fitness client manual.* Palo Alto, CA: Shyness Institute.

CHAPTER 2 THE WAY WE ARE: SHYNESS AND HOW WE'VE EVOLVED

On social rank theory:

Gilbert, P. 2000. The relationship of shame, social anxiety and depression: the role of the evaluation of social rank. *Clinical Psychology and Psychotherapy* 7:174–89.

Gilbert, P. 2001. Evolution and social anxiety: the role of attraction, social competition, and social hierarchies. *Psychiatric Clinics of North America* 24 (4):723–51.

Gilbert, P. and P. Trower. 1990. The evolution and manifestation of social anxiety. In *Shyness and embarrassment: perspectives from social psychology,* ed. R. Crozier, 144–77. Cambridge: Cambridge University Press.

On more collaborative social styles:

Taylor, S.T. 2006. Tend and befriend: biobehavioral bases of affiliation under strain. *Current Directions in Psychological Science* 15(6):273–77.

Taylor, S.E., J.S. Lerner, D.K. Sherman, R.M. Sage, and N.K. McDowell. 2003. Are self-enhancing cognitions associated with healthy or unhealthy biological profiles? *Journal of Personality and Social Psychology* 85(4):605–15.

On shy men and traditional ideas about masculinity:

Bruch, M.A. 2002. Shyness and toughness: unique and moderated relations with men's emotional inexpression. *Journal of Counseling Psychology* 49 (1):28–34.

Bem, S., and S.A. Lewis. 1975. Sex role adaptability: one consequence of psychological androgyny. *Journal of*

Personality and Social Psychology 31:634–43.

On what people look for in a partner:

Buss, D.M., and M. Barnes. 1986. Preferences in human mate selection. *Journal of Personality and Social Psychology* 50(3):559–70.

On the effect of social exclusion on the brain:

Baumeister, R.F., C.N. DeWall, N.J. Ciarocco, and J.M. Twenge. 2005. Social exclusion impairs self-regulation. *Journal of Personality and Social Psychology* 88(4):589–604.

On the importance of accepting things as they are and finding our core values:

Hayes, S.C. 2005. *Get out of your mind and into your life.* With Spencer Smith. Oakland, CA: New Harbinger Publications.

On self-compassion:

Neff, K. 2003. Self-compassion: an alternative conceptualization of a healthy attitude toward oneself. *Self and Identity* 2:86–101.

Neff, K. 2004. Self-compassion and psychological well-being. *Constructivism in the Human Sciences* 9(2):27–37. Kristin Neff, one of the early researchers to study self-compassion, has a helpful website at www.self-compassion.org. There is a questionnaire on the site to measure how self-compassionate you are, and there are suggestions for increasing your self-compassion.

On good news:

You can find the online magazine at www.goodnewsnetwork.org. Greater Good, the website on the evolution of human goodness was started by Dacher Keltner at Berkeley, and you can find it at http://greatergood.berkeley.edu. All these ventures are about where we focus our attention and what we want to build together. See Keltner, D., 2009. *Born to be good: the science of a meaningful life.* New York: W.W. Norton and Company.

CHAPTER 3 DEVELOPING YOUR COMPASSIONATE MIND

On the beneficial effects of compassion on the brain:

You can read more about the evidence for this in Sharon Begley's important 2009 book *The plastic mind: new science reveals our extraordinary potential to transform ourselves.* London: Constable and Robinson. See also Gilbert, P. 2009, *The Compassionate Mind.* London: Constable and Robinson.

CHAPTER 4 SWITCHING OUR MINDS TO KINDNESS AND COMPASSION

On mindfulness-based stress reduction (MBSR):

Kabat Zinn, J. 1990. *Full catastrophe living: using the wisdom of your body and mind to face stress, pain, and illness.* New York: Delacorte Press.

Kabat-Zinn, J. 2005. *Coming to our senses: healing ourselves and the world through mindfulness.* New York: Piatkus.

These are two excellent books by the founder and disseminator of the Mindfulness-Based Stress Reduction program at the University of

Massachusetts Medical Center. See also Flowers, S. 2009. *The mindful path through shyness.* Oakland, CA: New Harbinger Publications. This book was written by an experienced teacher of MBSR.

On equipment for meditation:

You can see examples of meditation cushions and benches at websites such as www.dharmacrafts.com or www.bluebanyan.co.uk.

On Pema Chödrön:

Chödrön, P. 2009. *Taking the leap: freeing ourselves from old habits and fears.* Boston: Shambhala Publications.

On CDs of sounds that facilitate meditation:

Karma Moffett titles one such CD *Golden bowls of compassion.* His Tibet Shop is in San Francisco, and his website is w ww.karmamoffett.com.

On the image of a sturdy oak tree in meditation:

I learned this image in mindfulness-based stress reduction practical training with Robert Stahl in Mountain View, California.

On the role of oxytocin in sexual arousal:

Keltner, D. 2009. *Born to be good: the science of a meaningful life.* New York: W.W. Norton and Company.

CHAPTER 5 COMPASSIONATE MIND TRAINING USING IMAGERY

On studies showing how MBSR can help to reduce

negative thoughts about the self in social anxiety:

Goldin, P., W. Ramel, and J. Gross. 2009. Mindfulness meditation training and self-referential processing in social anxiety disorder: Behavioral and neural effects. *Journal of Cognitive Psychotherapy* 23(3):242–57.

For the poem by Mary Oliver:

Oliver, M. 1992. *New and selected poems.* Boston: Beacon Press. Reproduced with kind permission of the publisher.

On Edna Foa's post-traumatic stress disorder treatment center,

see www.med.upenn.edu/ctsa.

Foa, E.B., and M.J. Kozak. 1986. Emotional processing of fear: exposure to corrective information. *Psychological Bulletin* 99(1):20-35.

Foa, E.B., and M.J. Kozak.1986. Clinical applications of bioinformational theory: understanding anxiety and its treatment. *Behavior Therapy* 29(4):675–90.

On the "perfect nurturer" model:

Lear, D.H. 2005. The perfect nurturer: a model to develop a compassionate mind within the context of cognitive therapy. 2005. In *Compassion: conceptualizations, research, and use in psychotherapy,* ed. P. Gilbert, 326–351. New York: Routledge.

CHAPTER 6 DEVELOPING COMPASSIONATE WAYS OF THINKING

On the human tendency to develop theories about others and the world based on experience and social relationships:

Kelly, G. 1963. *A theory of personality: the psychology of personal constructs.* New York: W.W. Norton and Company.

On Cheri Huber and the things children are told:

Huber, C. 2001. *There is nothing wrong with you: going beyond self-hate.* Murphys, CA: Keep it Simple, 2-3. You can find information about Cheri Huber's workshops, retreats, and peace projects at her website, www.livingcom passion.org.

On Beck's work with depression:

Beck, A.T.1991. Cognitive therapy: a30-year retrospective. *American Psychologist* 46(4):368–75.

Beck, A.T., A.J. Rush, B.F. Shaw, and G. Emery. 1979. *Cognitive therapy of depression.* New York: The Guilford Press.

On Albert Ellis's work about "shoulds" and "oughts":

Ellis, A. 1961. *A guide to rational living.* Englewood Cliffs, NJ: Prentice-Hall.

Ellis, A. 1998. *How to control your anxiety before it controls you.* New York: Citadel Press.

On cognitive behavioral therapy in treating shyness and social anxiety:

In social fitness training the first thirteen weeks of treatment are CBT, based on the learning model used by Philip Zimbardo in early shyness groups and on controlled studies of social anxiety disorder. See Henderson, L. 1992. Shyness groups. In *Focal group psychotherapy,* ed. M. McKay and K. Paleg, 29–66. Oakland, CA: New Harbinger Publications.

Henderson, L. 2007. *Social fitness training: a cognitive behavioral protocol for the treatment of shyness and social anxiety disorder.* Palo Alto, CA: Shyness Institute.

Henderson, L. 2008. *Social fitness client manual.* Palo Alto, CA: Shyness Institute.

Heimberg, R.G., C.S. Dodge, D.A. Hope, C.R. Kennedy, L.J. Zollo, and R.E. Becker. 1990. Cognitive behavioral group treatment for social phobia: comparison with a credible placebo control. *Cognitive Therapy and Research* 14 (1):1–23.

An excellent self-help book in this area is Gillian Butler's 2008 title *Overcoming social anxiety and shyness: A self-help guide using cognitive behavioral techniques.* London: Constable and Robinson. Another very good book that uses a learning model and has lots of helpful exercises is Signe Dayhoff 's 2000 title *Diagonally-parked in a parallel universe.* Placitas, NM: Effectiveness-Plus Publications.

Zimbardo, P.G. 1986. The Stanford shyness project. In *Shyness: perspectives on research and treatment* ed. W.H. Jones, J.M. Cheek, and S.R. Briggs, 17–25. New York: Plenum Press.

On approaches that combine insights from East and West:

Several psychologists have developed treatments based on a combination of Western treatments, such as CBT, and principles, techniques, and exercises based on Eastern thought, particularly Buddhism. Marsha Linehan published a book in 1993 called *Dialectical behavior therapy* (New York: The Guilford Press), integrating radical behavior therapy (based on the principles of learning theory) which stressed that changing behavior would change our thoughts and feelings, and that we could not learn to face things we were afraid of until we "desensitized" (our fear was reduced) and drew on the tenets of Zen Buddhism. We work with behavior change in social fitness training through activities like practicing approaching and talking to people in situations that trigger uncomfortable shyness and social anxiety. The dialectical part involves accepting and tolerating difficult emotions rather than trying to change them, as a compassionate approach suggests. A psychologist named Steven Hayes developed acceptance and commitment therapy on the basis of the same combination of principles. He believes that difficulties occur when we don't accept our painful emotions, and try to avoid certain feelings and emotions, a process he calls experiential avoidance. Hayes worked with people who suffered trauma, such as Vietnam veterans, helping them accept what happened to them, in order to develop, or rediscover, goals and values that make their lives meaningful and worth living. These principles can also apply to painful events and experiences that led to chronic shyness. His 2005 self-help book, *Get out of your mind and into your life: the new acceptance and commitment therapy.* Oakland, CA, New Harbinger Publications, with Spencer Smith, is a good overview and contains many acceptance-based exercises.

On using an alarm to help with self-monitoring thoughts and feelings:

The Washington Mindfulness Community website offers a free mindful clock for PC users that you can download at www.mindfulnessdc.org/mindful-clock.html.

CHAPTER 7 TAKING COMPASSIONATE THINKING FURTHER

On social fitness training, and viewing thoughts and emotions as theories to be tested:

Henderson, L. 2007. *Social fitness training: a cognitive behavioral protocol for the treatment of shyness and social anxiety disorder.* Palo Alto, CA: Shyness Institute.

Henderson, L. 2008. *Social fitness client manual.* Palo Alto, CA: Shyness Institute.

On Albert Ellis's principles:

Ellis, A. 1998. *How to control your anxiety before it controls you.* New York: Citadel Press.

On compassionate mind training and resisting the inner critic:

Kelly, A.C., D.C. Zuroff, and L.B. Shapira. 2009. Soothing oneself and resisting self-attacks: the treatment of two intrapersonal deficits in depression vulnerability. *Cognitive Therapy and Research* 33(3):301–13.

On mirrors and fidelity to our inner thoughts:

Scheier, M.F., C.S. Carver, and F.X. Gibbons. 1979. Self-directed attention, awareness of bodily states, and suggestibility. *Journal of Personality and Social Psychology* 37(9):1576–88.

On Gestalt therapy:

Perls, F. 1973. *The Gestalt approach and eye witness to therapy.* Ben Lomand, CA: Science and Behavior Books.

CHAPTER 8 COMPASSIONATE BEHAVIOUR

On being assertive:

Johnson, D. 2008. *Reaching out: interpersonal effectiveness and self-actualization.* 10th ed. Needham Heights, MA: Allyn and Bacon.

On Zimbardo and "the psychology of mind control":

Zimbardo, P. 2008. *The Lucifer effect: understanding how good people turn evil.* New York: Random House.

Review of international research on bullying:

Nansel, T.R., M. Overpeck, R.S. Pilla, W.J. Ruan, B. Simons-Morton, and P. Scheidt. 2001. Bullying behaviors among US youth: prevalence and association with psychological adjustment. *Journal of the American Medical Association* 285(16):2094–100.

On bullying in the workplace:

Van Dusen, A. 2009. Ten signs you are being bullied at work. www.forbes.com .

Namie, G., and R. Namie. 2009. *The bully at work: what you can do to stop the hurt and reclaim your dignity on the job.* Naperville, IL: Sourcebooks.

On a compassionate way to confront a bully:

Gilbert, P. 2009. *The Compassionate Mind.* London: Constable and Robinson, 395.

On shy leaders:

Collins, J. 2001. *From good to great: why some companies make the leap ... and other don't.* New York: Harper Business.

On authentic leadership:

Gardner, W.L., B.J. Avolio, F. Luthans, D.R. May, and F. Walumbwa. 2005. "Can you see the real me?" A self-based model of authentic leader and follower development. *Leadership Quarterly* 16(3):343-72.

On negative stereotyping of shy men:

Cringely, R.X. 1992. *Accidental empires: how the boys of Silicon Valley make their millions, battle foreign competition, and still can't get a date.* New York: HarperCollins Publishers.

Horowitz, L.M., K. Wilson, B. Turan, P. Zolotsev, M. Constantino, and L. Henderson. 2006. How interpersonal motives help clarify the meaning of an interpersonal behavior: a revised circumplex model. *Personality and Social Psychology Review* 10(1):67–86.

Lynne Henderson, PhD, is a clinical psychologist, founder of the Social Fitness Center, and founder and codirector, with Phillip Zimbardo, of the Shyness Institute in Berkeley, CA. She has been a visiting scholar in the psychology department at Stanford University, and is a faculty member in Stanford's Continuing Studies program. She has directed the Shyness Clinic for over twenty-five years and is an adjunct research faculty member at the Institute for Transpersonal Psychology. Her research interests include translating the results of social psychology and personality theory into treatment methods for shyness, the influence of personality variables and cultural influences on interpersonal perception, cultural influences on self-conceptualizations, interpersonal motivation, leadership styles, distance collaboration, and mindful social fitness.

Foreword writer **Paul Gilbert, PhD,** is a professor at the University of Derby in the United Kingdom, director of the mental health research unit at Derbyshire Mental Health Trust, and author of *The Compassionate Mind.*

www.ingramcontent.com/pod-product-compliance
Lightning Source LLC
Chambersburg PA
CBHW071823270326
41929CB00013B/1886

* 9 7 8 0 3 6 9 3 2 3 6 9 9 *